SAVING **HISTORY**

Parsippany-Troy Hills Library
Main Library
449 Halsey RD
Parsippany NJ 07054
973-887-5150

WHERE RELIGION LIVES

Kristy Nabhan-Warren, editor

Where Religion Lives publishes ethnographies of religious life. The series features the methods of religious studies along with anthropological approaches to lived religion. The religious studies perspective encompasses attention to historical contingency, theory, religious doctrine and texts, and religious practitioners' intimate, personal narratives. The series also highlights the critical realities of migration and transnationalism.

SAVING **HISTORY**

HOW WHITE EVANGELICALS TOUR

THE NATION'S CAPITAL AND REDEEM

A CHRISTIAN AMERICA

LAUREN R. KERBY

The University of North Carolina Press

Chapel Hill

This book was published with the
assistance of the Anniversary Fund of
the University of North Carolina Press.

Cover illustrations by PlusONE, Hunter Bliss Images,
Steve Heap, and Byjeng, all courtesy Shutterstock

Library of Congress Cataloging-in-Publication Data
Names: Kerby, Lauren R., author.
Title: Saving history : how white evangelicals tour the nation's capital and redeem
a Christian America / Lauren R. Kerby.
Description: Chapel Hill : The University of North Carolina Press, 2020. |
Series: Where religion lives | Includes bibliographical references and index.
Identifiers: LCCN 2019041170 | ISBN 9781469655895 (cloth) |
ISBN 9781469658773 (paperback) | ISBN 9781469655901 (ebook)
Subjects: LCSH: Tourism—Washington (D.C.)—Religious aspects—Christianity. | Heritage
tourism—Washington (D.C.) | Evangelicalism—United States—History—21st century.
Classification: LCC G156.5.R44 K47 2020 | DDC 910.9753—dc23
LC record available at https://lccn.loc.gov/2019041170

For my students,

who, despite everything,

make me an optimist

Contents

....

Illustrations

Acknowledgments

No book is a solo endeavor, but this is doubly true of ethnography. This project would not have been possible without the kindness and cooperation of the tourists and guides I encountered during my research. While in the field, I met many people who amazed me with their interest in me as a person and their enthusiasm about my research, even if they were skeptical at first. They are, of course, anonymous here, but their experiences are at the heart of this project. I am thankful to them for sharing their lives and vacations with me.

This project has also benefited from the thoughtful input and occasional provocation of many colleagues at both Boston University and Harvard Divinity School. Stephen Prothero asked incisive questions that have shaped critical elements of the book. I am also grateful for the support and generous feedback of Nancy Ammerman, Anthony Petro, and Christopher Evans on early drafts. At the Religious Literacy Project, I have benefited from the insight and encouragement of Diane L. Moore, Judy Beals, Reem Atassi, Kris Rhude, John Camardella, and Mario Cader-Frech. My thanks go especially to Sarabinh Levy-Brightman and Anna Mudd for their friendship and their willingness to think through new ideas with me.

At UNC Press, I am grateful to Elaine Maisner and Kristy Nabhan-Warren for their enthusiasm for this project and their guidance as I completed it. My anonymous readers also offered truly transformative commentary on the manuscript, showing me new directions and connections that I might never have realized on my own. I am thankful for the time and care they devoted to this project.

Every stage of this project has been made possible by the support and encouragement of my friends and family. Laura Heath has been a sympathetic listener and co-conspirator against the kyriarchy. Claire Sadar has never failed to remind me that she can't wait to read this book. Kathleen Cooney has helped me see things more clearly with her sage advice and endless compassion. Georgia Frank introduced me to the study of religion many years ago, and her wisdom continues to help me find my way. Marie and John Langlois have welcomed me into their family and believed in me like one of their own. Sejal Patel has taught me how to tell better stories and to expect more of myself and others. Jo Anna Nevada has believed in me all along and always been on my side. Jack Daly has explored the world with me and helped me discover where I fit in it. These friends were some of the first readers for this project, and their interest and excitement bolstered my own.

My parents, Ron and Cheryl, have never doubted I would succeed in my academic endeavors. Their faith in me is humbling, and I will always be grateful for their love and acceptance. My partner, Adrienne Langlois, makes each day brighter. Her love gives me courage to reach beyond my limits. This would have been a different book without her, and I would have been a different writer.

For me, the best parts of academic life will always be found in the classroom. This project has spanned many years, but one constant has been the students who have challenged me and inspired me. Conversations with them are what kept me going, even through the worst points of writer's block and American politics. They are determined to make the world a better place, and I believe that, someday, they will.

SAVING **HISTORY**

Christian heritage tours start early. The streets of Washington, D.C., are mostly empty when tourists board their buses for the first time, clutching Styrofoam cups of coffee and pastries from the hotel's breakfast buffet. They settle into their seats two by two. This group is a mixture of older couples and families with young children or teenagers. All are white. The adults sip their coffee and talk quietly about the itinerary for the day. As far as I can tell, I am the only solo traveler on the bus. I spot an empty seat next to an older woman and am relieved when she invites me to sit down. She introduces herself as Gladys, from Oregon, and explains that she's traveling with her friends, the two women seated in the next row. She'd be so glad to have me as "bus buddy" for the trip, she says, someone to sit with every day. We make small talk until our tour guide boards the bus and picks up the microphone.

Mark is a white man in his sixties, dressed in jeans, a polo shirt, and a baseball cap. He has been leading Christian heritage tours of D.C. for decades and is something of a celebrity in this world. He speaks with the confidence of someone used to people hanging on his every word, and he quotes the Bible and the Founding Fathers with equal ease. In his spare time he writes books, gives lectures, appears on radio programs, and consults on films. Just last night I overheard two tourists at check-in talking about how excited they were to meet him. He had been featured on their local Christian radio station, and they were impressed by how knowledgeable he seemed.

We fall silent as Mark welcomes us. He says he'd like to start the day off by reading a prayer that our second president, John Adams, offered at the first meeting of the U.S. Congress in Washington, D.C.: "It would be unbecoming the Representatives of this nation to as-

The U.S. Marine Corps War Memorial, better known as the
Iwo Jima Memorial, August 2014. Photo by the author.

semble, for the first time, in this solemn temple, without looking up to the
Supreme Ruler of the Universe and imploring his blessing. May this territory be the residence of virtue and happiness! In this city may that piety and
virtue, that wisdom and magnanimity, that constancy and self-government
which adorned the great character whose name it bears, be forever held in
veneration! Here, and throughout our country, may simple manners, pure
morals, and true religion flourish forever!"[1] "Amen," Mark concludes, and
a few tourists add their own amens, including my buddy Gladys. With that,
the bus pulls out of the hotel parking lot, headed to the first stop of the day.
It is just after 8 A.M. and few buildings are open, but there is still plenty to
see. Christian heritage tours pack every minute of the day with sites. During
the morning and evening hours when museums and government buildings
are closed, they visit outdoor monuments such as this morning's destination, the Marine Corps War Memorial, better known as the Iwo Jima Memorial. It's a short ride from the hotel, and the guide keeps up a steady stream
of chatter as we go.

The bus pulls into the driveway that circles the memorial, and tourists
lunge for their cameras. The driver tells us to watch the flag as he continues
around the statue. All around me, tourists *ooooh* and *aaaah* at the optical

illusion the bus's motion creates—the flag appears to be being raised as we drive around. On the opposite side of the memorial, the driver parks and we disembark. Only half of the tour group was on our bus; the other half is just arriving in the next bus. When we are all assembled at the base of the monument, Mark and Dan, another guide, take their position at the top of the stairs. Dan spots me on the edge of the crowd and gestures at me to join them. He welcomes the group again and introduces me.

"This is Lauren. She's from Boston. She's not a terrorist." The crowd chuckles awkwardly while I try to look amused instead of uncomfortable. This is the third tour in which I've been introduced as "not a terrorist." He continues, "She's doing some research on Christian tours, so that's why she's joining us." For a brief moment, 110 pairs of eyes seem to be on me as the tourists process my role. Then Mark draws their attention to the monument, and I step back into the crowd.

The site before us is a monument to the Marine Corps, he tells us. Does anybody know their song? Someone starts it up, and we stumble together through the first two lines: "From the halls of Montezuma, to the shores of Tripoli. . . ." With the practiced wave of a conductor, Mark silences us. "Tripoli!" he exclaims. "What's Tripoli?"

When no one rushes to answer, he tells us that the base of the monument before us is inscribed all around with the names of battles in Marine Corps history, including Tripoli. It was part of one of our first wars as a new nation, fought against the Barbary pirates between 1801 and 1805.

"Who were the Barbary pirates?" Mark asks, pausing for effect. "Muslim terrorists." He goes on, talking over the gasps and mutters of the crowd. "You see, our current war is not a new war. We've been at war with Islam since the very beginning." The Barbary pirates, he tells us, would demand tribute from ships, and Britain and other European nations simply paid it. When American ships began sailing under the new American flag, however, they were no longer protected by Britain's tribute, and the pirates attacked. But the new United States was not so easily intimidated. When Thomas Jefferson became president, he sent the new U.S. Navy to fight the Barbary pirates, and they won, prompting the pope at the time to remark that America had done more to defeat the Barbary pirates than all the European nations combined. "Even then," Mark concludes, "we were fighting for others."[2]

With that the crowd disperses, snapping photographs of the monument and the view of the National Mall. I offer to take family photos, which usually helps break the ice with new tourists. Sure enough, I have several short, friendly conversations about my research as cameras change hands.

Just as the photo shoots are winding down and people are turning to look for the bus, we hear someone singing.

"Amaaaaaaazing Grace, how sweeeet the sound . . ." Our bus driver has come to lead us in song at the base of the monument. We gradually join in, all 111 of us, singing the first verse together in the hazy morning sun.

Amazing grace, how sweet the sound
That saved a wretch like me!
I once was lost, but now I'm found
Was blind, but now I see.

CHRISTIAN HERITAGE AND LIVED HISTORY

In the late 1980s a new subset of the D.C. tourism industry emerged, one that catered to white evangelical Christians seeking proof of the United States' Christian heritage.[3] These tours were part of a broader trend sparked by the nascent Christian Right, whose leaders had called for renewed attention to the role of Christianity in American history.[4] As they saw it, the United States had been founded as a Christian nation, and Christianity (specifically, white conservative Protestantism) was integral to American institutions, laws, and social norms. In the second half of the twentieth century, however, Americans had forgotten the Christian foundations of the nation, leading to moral decay at home and political impotence abroad. Only by reclaiming America's Christian heritage could the nation be saved.

The notion of Christian heritage quickly became an essential rhetorical tool for the Christian Right, providing a warrant for white conservative Christians' political activism. It featured prominently in the sermons of Jerry Falwell, the writings of Francis Schaeffer, the TV broadcasts of D. James Kennedy, and the textbooks of Peter Marshall and David Manuel, to name a few. Nor has its appeal or utility diminished with time. Over the last four decades the Christian heritage story has become a staple of Republican political discourse, particularly in presidential elections. It has also become ubiquitous in white evangelical popular culture, appearing in films, art, fiction, textbooks, music, Bible studies, prayer journals, and America-themed Bibles.[5] Today Christian heritage is its own industry, capitalizing on white evangelicals' hunger for a national myth of origin in which they play a starring role.

Christian heritage tours of D.C. are an extension of this industry. They offer more than media to consume—they offer tourists a chance to experience America's Christian heritage for themselves. Tourists see the evidence of the nation's Christian past, written in the very stones of D.C., and they walk in the footsteps of their Christian forefathers. Since the tours' inception, they have found a ready market. Several thousand tourists now flock to D.C. every year for specialized Christian heritage tours.[6] In some ways, the tours I observed were quite ordinary. They saw all the major sights, including Capitol Hill, the war memorials, Arlington National Cemetery, Mount Vernon, and a variety of museums. Tourists took endless pictures, bought T-shirts, and crammed extra shopping and sightseeing into their free time. But the tours' stories and themes were straight out of the Christian Right's playbook. At each stop tour guides talked about the role of white Christians and their God in American history and pointed to the Christian features of the memorial or building to corroborate their claims. At the same time, they warned tourists that these stories will soon be forgotten, and this evidence will soon be erased as the nation strays ever further from its Christian origins. The tours struck an odd chord, but one that resonated with white evangelical tourists. This dissonant relationship to the nation and its history was familiar to them. Their visit to D.C. merely confirmed what they already knew about their place in the United States.

Christian heritage tours of D.C. are a window into how white American evangelicals use American history to make sense of who they are and how they ought to behave vis-à-vis the nation. This history is not the history of scholars, the kind that is documented, footnoted, and peer reviewed. Rather, it is lived history, the messy, partial, and often contradictory narratives that people tell about the past in their everyday lives.[7] As they saw the sights of D.C., white evangelical tourists told stories about the past shaped by a variety of sources, including the tour guides' talks, the literature and signage available at the sites, their embodied experiences, and the material features of the sites themselves. But they also drew on fragments of stories they had once heard in church or school, stories they had heard from friends, and stories they had seen on the news and social media. This lively and sometimes haphazard process produced a dynamic set of stories that signaled a range of options for how white evangelicals fit into American politics and culture.

At certain moments, white evangelical tourists and guides appealed to the Christian Right's myth of origin, casting themselves as the nation's founders. At other moments, however, they described looming threats to American Christians and their heritage, casting themselves in alternate roles as exiles from powerful institutions and victims of secularizing forces. And throughout the tours, they cast themselves as the nation's would-be saviors. These roles derive from white evangelicals' complex and shifting relationship to the nation since its founding, a relationship in which they have been both insiders and outsiders. We can observe white evangelicals playing all four roles far beyond the context of Christian heritage tours. Each role entails a distinct kind of rhetoric and behavior. For instance, when they speak as founders, white evangelicals argue that their Christian values are normative in American society and should be reflected in American laws. As victims, in contrast, they deplore their mistreatment by those in power and demand equal protection. White evangelicals move fluidly among these roles, as each offers a different position from which to claim moral authority. They are political shape-shifters, playing whichever part grants them the most power in a given situation.

This book argues that to understand white evangelicals' political activity, we must pay attention to how they imagine and reimagine the American past and their place in it. Christian heritage tours offer an opportunity to observe this process in action. In recent years white evangelicals have confounded both scholars of religion and the American public with their political behavior, including their overwhelming support for Donald Trump and many of his policies.[8] This confusion exists at least in part because we expect white evangelicals make their political decisions based on decontextualized theological principles and the rigid morality of the culture wars. In reality, white evangelicals exist in the same complex cultural matrix as any other American religious group, and their political choices are informed by a multitude of factors in addition to theology and morality, including race, gender, class—and history.

White evangelicals see history as the key to America's salvation. In their view, the past provides a blueprint for how things ought to be: Christians running a Christian nation. But they also see history itself as endangered by liberal academics and other secularists who wish to erase Christianity from normative accounts of the American past. If they hope to save the nation, they must first save its history.

WHITE EVANGELICALS AND D.C. TOURISM

Christian heritage tours draw an audience composed primarily of white evangelicals whose views have been shaped by the legacy of the Christian Right. For many, the fusion of conservative Christianity and Republican politics is all they have ever known. The tour guides, too, are products of this tradition. In some cases the tours are even organized by the flagship institutions of the Christian Right and feature their best-known personalities. Christian heritage tours thus provide a glimpse into multiple levels of white evangelical discourse about American history, from the leadership to the laity.

In 2014 and 2015 I conducted participant observation of nine multiday Christian heritage tours in D.C. Gaining access to these tours was surprisingly easy. After identifying relevant tour companies with a simple Google search, a few e-mails and phone calls granted me permission to join the tours for the purposes of my research.[9] In every case, I explained that I was conducting an academic study of Christian tourism in D.C. and that I was interested in Christianity and politics. I gave similar explanations to each tour group I observed. One company wanted me to meet their tour guide, Jonathan, in advance; I learned at the end of that tour that his job was to vet me. "You never know when you'll get a terrorist on your bus," the owner told me, laughing. The fact that I was a young white woman and a graduate student worked in my favor, as I seemed in no position to pose a threat. I had the added advantage of having grown up in white evangelical churches, giving me some familiarity with the norms of the tour groups.

Participant observation meant that I accompanied tourists throughout the experience, from their arrival to their departure. I rode with them on the bus between sites, and I stood in line with them to pass through the security checkpoints that guard most major buildings. We ate all our meals together, sang together, and sometimes prayed together. It was important, of course, to pay attention to what the tour guides said and how tourists responded, and I took copious notes during every guide talk, usually in the Notes app on my iPhone. But interstitial moments were equally valuable in terms of the insights they yielded. Any group tour involves a surprising amount of time spent waiting around, and the informal conversations we used to fill that time helped me understand how tourists were responding to what they saw and heard. At the same time, those conversations let me get to know them and learn about the values, anxieties, knowledge, and ideas they brought with them to D.C.

I include many excerpts from those conversations in this book, in an effort to let my subjects speak for themselves when possible. In some cases I was able to write down what someone said in their exact words. This was often easier with guides than with tourists, since guides usually spoke one at a time and at length in situations where note-taking was easy, such as on the bus. I was sometimes able to capture tourists' exact words, but it was more difficult to take notes on a conversation when I was an active participant in it. In such cases, I took notes as I was able, writing down keywords and phrases, and I reconstructed the conversations in my notes at the next opportunity, often on the next bus ride or in the next security line. In addition, I conducted semi-structured qualitative interviews with twenty-nine tourists and guides after their tours ended, which let me ask more probing questions about their experience and how they felt about it after the fact. I recorded these interviews with permission, allowing me to quote interviewees accurately. When I draw on these sources in this book, I use quotation marks to indicate when I am quoting someone verbatim, either because the conversation was recorded or because I indicated in my notes that it was exactly what they said. When direct quotation is not possible, I paraphrase or summarize conversations based on my notes, without using quotation marks. To protect the privacy of my sources, I use pseudonyms throughout the book for all participants in the tours I observed, including tourists, guides, and guest speakers.

The tours I observed varied in some respects, including size and duration. The two largest tours each included 110 tourists and required two full-size buses (and extra time for everyone to make it through security at most sites). The smallest tour included only fifteen people and a hotel shuttle bus. In terms of duration, the tours ranged from a day and a half to seven days. Most lasted four days, which turned out to be just enough time to visit the major sites and still give tourists a free afternoon or evening to explore on their own. The tours were also operated by six different organizations. Of these, two were for-profit tourism companies that target a broadly Christian audience with the majority of their offerings as part of the Christian leisure industry. They offer tours to D.C. in response to demand from their customers. Two others were small for-profit companies (fewer than five full-time employees) founded by leaders who felt called to tell what they understand to be the truth of American history in D.C. The last two were well-known national nonprofits. For these organizations, tourism is only one small part of their work. Their broader focus is on media and political activism on behalf of conservative Christians. However, they see Christian heritage tours of D.C. as aligned with their mission because the tours promote their core message about the nation's foundational Christian values to their target audience.

With few exceptions, Christian tourists traveled in families or couples. Parents brought their children, or grandparents brought their grandchildren. In some cases three generations of one family traveled together. The couples who came on the trips tended to be older and retired, though one couple I met were newlyweds. On one of the largest tours, I met a group of three retired women traveling together after one was widowed, as well as a single man traveling alone. And one tour I observed was arranged for a private Christian school. Along with middle school students, it included teachers, students' mothers, and a handful of students' fathers as chaperones. As the only solo traveler on nearly every tour, I stood out, even without being introduced as a researcher. In some ways, however, I benefited from the oddity of being a young woman on my own. Curious tourists easily struck up conversations with me, and there were always at least one or two older women watching out for me. My age and gender limited me in only one respect: married male tourists were reluctant to be interviewed on their own, leading me to interview married couples together.

The tourists I met came from all over the United States, from the Deep South to the Oregon coast. With rare exception, however, they shared a common racial, political, and religious identity as white conservative evangelical Protestants. Of the more than four hundred total tourists on the tours I observed, only five were African American, and one family of six was Hispanic. The rest were white, including all the guides. Their politics were by all appearances equally homogeneous, as every tour guide and most tourists I spoke with expressed conservative social values and unwavering allegiance to the Republican Party. The vast majority also expressed religious identities that fit David Bebbington's classic four-part definition of evangelicalism: biblicism, conversionism, crucicentrism, and activism.[10] They regarded the Bible as the ultimate moral authority, or, in evangelical terms, they "took the Bible seriously" (biblicism).[11] They believed that one must be "born again" in order to be saved (conversionism), and they believed salvation was made possible by the atoning death of Jesus on the cross (crucicentrism). Finally, their faith informed all other aspects of their life, and they saw it as their Christian duty to live out their faith so as to convert others and reform society (activism). In addition to individual expressions of evangelical faith, evangelical language dominated group practices, including the prayers, devotions, and songs that took place on the bus.

In referring to my subjects as white evangelicals, however, I am not referring only to their theological commitments. Bebbington's definition has rightly been critiqued as normative theological claims masquerading as dispassionate analysis.[12] As Kristin Kobes Du Mez has observed, "evangelicalism" can mean many things, including a "theological category," a "consumer culture," a "white religious brand," and "a diverse global movement."[13] While I do employ the term *evangelical* to signal my subjects' theological positions, I also employ it because it operates as a recognizable political category in American public discourse and a recognizable consumer culture in the American marketplace. In this book, I argue that the white people who inhabit this particular theological, political, and cultural nexus tend to share a way of thinking about American history that informs their political behavior. I call these people *white evangelicals*, not in an attempt to be definitive but in an effort to draw legible boundaries around my subject of inquiry.

In addition, the overwhelming whiteness of the tourists I encountered is just as important as their shared religious beliefs and practices. Their racial homogeneity would be notable in any study, but the 2016 presidential election drew renewed attention to the racial divide in American evangelicalism. White evangelicals voted for Republican Donald Trump by a margin of 81 percent. Evangelicals of other races, however, were much less likely to support him. Among self-identified "born-again" Latinx and Asian American voters, Trump received 31 percent and 37 percent of the vote, respectively, and among self-identified "born-again" black voters, he received only 7 percent of the vote.[14] As these trends have come to light, scholars and journalists have begun to use more specific language to identify the groups in question.[15] Whereas before 2016 *evangelicals* typically meant only the white people in that tradition, it is becoming the norm (at least for specialists) to name race as well as religion.[16]

I specifically identify this group as *white evangelicals* to avoid erasing the many people of color who are equally a part of the evangelical tradition yet differ on many political issues. But I also draw attention to their race because it is an inextricable part of their experience of the United States. This study focuses on white evangelicals' relationship to the nation, which cannot be separated from the legacy of white supremacy. Even when white evangelicals have been relative outsiders in American culture, they have not been subjected to enslavement, genocide, or the countless other forms of violence that nonwhite communities have experienced at the hands of white Americans. Any discussion of white evangelicals' power in the United States would be incomplete without acknowledging how their race grants them a significant degree of privilege and safety, even when they experience marginality.

However, in the language of the tours, the racial, political, and religious identities of their participants were subsumed in one word: *Christian*. In this context *Christian* was not a broad umbrella term that encompassed all the internal diversity of American Christianity.[17] Rather, participants in Christian heritage tours used *Christian* to denote a specific brand of white conservative evangelical Protestantism that matched the demographics of this audience. This was a strategic choice. Rather than acknowledging other forms of Christianity as different ways of being Christian, this use of *Christian* implies that conservative white evangelicalism constitutes the whole of Christianity. Mainline Protestants, Catholics, progressive evangelicals, non-white evangelicals, and myriad other expressions of Christianity are written out of the story. In some cases, tourists and guides went so far as to self-identify as "real Christians" as opposed to "nominal Christians." When they told stories about the past, they identified historical figures, events, and the nation itself as "Christian" in this sense. When I quote, paraphrase, or summarize their stories and conversations in this book, I use *Christian* as they do in order to accurately represent how they speak. I also refer to them collectively as "Christian tourists," both for economy of language and because it is how they identified themselves. In the context of my own analysis, however, I draw attention to their specific identity as white evangelicals. In doing so, I hope to capture the subtle way that tours use the broad term *Christian* to stand for a narrow subset of white conservative evangelicals and, in doing so, elide all the other Christians who do not fit that description.

It is important to note one other thing that every tourist I met had in common: they could all afford to make the trip. A typical four-day (three-night) trip to D.C. ran about $900 per person, with some discounts available for shared rooms and additional family members. That price included lodging and most meals, but not airfare or ground transportation to D.C. Most groups stayed in two- or three-star hotels in the suburbs, and they tended to eat at low-end chain restaurants and food courts, in part because it was the only way to quickly feed so many people. For some this experience was luxurious, while others found it lacking. One woman confided that she and her husband were "spoiled" and used to much nicer hotels and restaurants. However, despite the range in their income and expectations, everyone there had the discretionary income to participate in this trip.[18] This is, after all, part of what it means to be a tourist. As one classic study defines it, a tourist is "a temporarily leisured person who travels away from home for the purpose of experiencing a change."[19] To be such a person requires three things: leisure time, discretionary income, and social validation of the choice to spend that time and money on travel.[20] All three things are tied to class, and being a tourist requires a certain amount of class privilege. The tours I observed catered primarily to middle-class sensibilities, erring on the side of efficiency rather than luxury. I heard one phrase repeated over and over, as we all dragged ourselves out of bed and onto the bus at 7:30 A.M. each day, yawning into our coffee: "At least we're getting our money's worth."

THE CHRISTIAN RIGHT'S SEARCH
FOR CHRISTIAN AMERICA

The idea of Christian America was not invented by Christian heritage tours, or even by the Christian Right. After all, for much of American history it was not an inaccurate descriptor. If ever there were a time that the United States could be called a Christian nation, it was the nineteenth century. In the wake of the American Revolution, evangelical revivals swept across the country, nearly doubling church membership between 1776 and 1850.[21] Despite the fact that religion had been formally disestablished, a de facto white Protestant establishment emerged.[22] A white "evangelical hodge-podge" dominated not only religious life but also the major institutions of the new nation, including the government and the public schools.[23] White evangelicals worked to reform society and train moral citizens, and they did so with the tacit blessing and financial support of state and federal governments.[24] And throughout the nineteenth century a broadly Protestant morality continued to inform laws, norms, and public discourse.[25] This unofficial Protestant establishment did not go unchallenged. Catholics battled Protestant hegemony in public schools during the midcentury Bible wars, for instance, while Mormons resisted Protestant social norms in the name of religious freedom in the contest over polygamy.[26] In these and other cases, however, white Protestants held their ground and maintained their dominance. They were at this point the quintessential American insiders.

By the early twentieth century, however, this insider status had weakened. In the decades following the Civil War white American Protestants split into two camps: liberal or mainline Protestants, on the one hand, and evangelicals and fundamentalists, on the other. Liberal or mainline Protestants would remain dominant for a time, but conservative Protestants found themselves in a new position as outsiders after their humiliation in the 1925 Scopes trial.[27] Attorney Clarence Darrow may have failed to defend the teaching of evolution in Tennessee public schools, but he and journalist H. L. Mencken persuaded a national audience that creationists were a bunch of backward bumpkins. In the decades that followed, white conservative Protestants tended to stay out of the national political spotlight. They did not fully retreat from the public square, as some historians have argued.[28] On the contrary, they remained engaged in American public life, actively participating in debates about civil rights, feminism, poverty, and Vietnam.[29] Perhaps most importantly, they formed alliances with business leaders that offered a new vantage point from which to influence American culture: the marketplace.[30] And they continued to build a robust subcultural infrastructure, including institutions of higher education and grassroots organizing networks that would later be crucial to the success of the new Christian Right.[31] Nevertheless, their absence from the most powerful institutions in American politics suggested that they no longer possessed the overwhelming political and cultural power they had once taken for granted. For the first time, they came to understand themselves as outsiders.

This period of relative exile left its mark on white conservative Protestants. As outsiders, they were excluded from certain kinds of power and institutions, but they gained a unique sort of moral authority. In the mid-twentieth century, Americans fell in love with the idea of being an outsider. Being on the margins was widely seen as more authentic and meaningful than being in the mainstream. Difference itself became a source of power.[32] As this shift occurred, white conservative Protestants were well positioned to benefit from being different.[33] In the 1970s they began to engage in politics on a new scale, driven by deep anxieties about the tectonic shifts occurring in American culture. It is not possible to pinpoint a single cause for the emergence of the Christian Right, but three intersecting factors were critical: school prayer, abortion, and desegregation. In 1962 and 1963 the Supreme Court ruled against teacher-led prayer and devotional Bible reading in American public schools, while in 1973 *Roe v. Wade* legalized abortion within certain restrictions.[34] These changes horrified many white evangelicals, and leaders of the Christian Right often pointed to them as the reason conservative Christians should get back into politics.[35] Desegregation, however, was just as important, if not more so. In 1978, the Internal Revenue Service threatened the tax-exempt status of all-white Christian private schools on the grounds that they were racially discriminatory. The Christian Right characterized this move as an attack on religious freedom and mobilized both white evangelicals and Catholics in massive protests that were ultimately successful.[36] But it was only the beginning. As the culture wars escalated, white conservative Protestants found themselves engaged in a political battle for the soul of the nation.

At the heart of that battle was American history.[37] Leaders of the Christian Right crafted a new version of American history that played up white evangelicals' movement from the center to the margins of American society. This history had two main narrative arcs, which I refer to in this book as the *insider* and *outsider narratives*. The insider narrative tells the story of an America founded by devout white Christian men and blessed by their God. It is imperative to note the narrow and anachronistic meaning of *Christian* in this context: it designates a kind of conservative evangelicalism more familiar to twentieth-century culture warriors than to the Founding Fathers. According to this narrative, however, the American founders intended that the nation's leaders and citizens would be Christian in this narrow sense. As long as this was the case, the nation prospered. In this story, Christians— specifically white evangelicals—are the rightful insiders in the United States, and the nation's well-being depends upon their cultural and political dominance. The outsider narrative tells the contrasting story of what happens when the founders' intentions are disregarded. In this story, Christians have been exiled from American politics and culture and victimized by a hostile, secular establishment. As a result, the nation has declined and faces divine judgment. Only if Christians retake their rightful position as insiders can the decline be reversed. Neither of these narratives is pure fiction; both are rooted in the real experience of white American Protestants since the colonial era. But the Christian Right simplified and combined them into a jeremiad that maximized their political utility.

This jeremiad capitalized on white conservative Christians' experience as outsiders since the Scopes trial, even as it also drew on their legacy as undisputed insiders prior to the Civil War. The combination proved politically powerful, offering two different positions from which the Christian Right could claim authority. As insiders, they could justify their policies and activism by appealing to history and the original intent of the founders as they understood it. Their successes reinforced their feelings of belonging and responsibility toward the nation. As outsiders, in contrast, they could interpret opposition and failure as a sign that they were a righteous remnant in a sinful world. In a nation that reveres tradition yet cheers for underdogs, the Christian Right managed to have it both ways.

The leaders of the Christian Right also succeeded in establishing white evangelicals an essential base for the Republican Party. The election of Ronald Reagan demonstrated the power white evangelicals could wield when they showed up at the polls, as did the success of their grassroots efforts on behalf of Republicans in the 1994 midterm elections. As a result, it became de rigueur for Republican candidates to speak the language of conservative Christian values. But influence is a two-way street, and Republican values and priorities came to take on new religious significance among white evangelicals. Not all white evangelicals embraced this alliance. Particularly after the failed attempt to remove Bill Clinton from office, a number of prominent white evangelicals publicly washed their hands of the dirty business of politics, Republican or otherwise.[38] But many more remained involved, seeing in politics their best opportunity to reclaim the nation. In 2000 their efforts paid off with the election of one of their own, George W. Bush. And by the beginning of the twenty-first century, most Americans took it for granted that white evangelicals would vote Republican.[39]

After the election of Barack Obama in 2008, however, some observers wondered if the Christian Right had finally lost its sway.[40] Democrats controlled both houses of Congress and the White House, and liberals appeared to be making gains in the culture wars, particularly on issues of gender and sexuality. The percentage of Americans who self-identified as Christians was declining, while the number who identified as spiritual but not religious (SBNR) or nonaffiliated ("nones") was on the rise.[41] White evangelicals appeared more embattled than ever, with little chance of victory. But their doubters underestimated the extent to which white evangelicals had learned to use marginality as an asset. They had not given up their fight to save the nation, but it would take a fellow outsider to mobilize their full potential.

That unlikely outsider was Donald Trump, a twice-divorced gambler who used profanity, bragged about sexually assaulting women, separated children from their families, and claimed never to have needed to repent from sin. Despite his moral shortcomings, 81 percent of white evangelical voters voted for Trump in the 2016 presidential election.[42] During his administration, they continued to support his policies at far higher rates than other religious groups.[43] To many observers, their support appeared at odds with their stated commitment to family values. After all, there was no shortage of 2016 Republican candidates with less checkered pasts who would have enacted white evangelicals' policies on abortion, same-sex marriage, and other social issues. But white evangelicals' support for Trump was not only about morality or policy. Trump spoke their language and told their stories. He, too, was an outsider who wanted to reclaim the nation. His campaign slogan, "Make America Great Again," resonated with them. Like their own narratives, it implied that the nation was in decline from an idealized past but recovery remained possible. It was a jeremiad for the twenty-first century.

NARRATIVES AND IDENTITY

When white evangelicals arrived in D.C. for Christian heritage tours, they already knew how the stories would go. Perhaps they did not know the historical details—names, dates, and other minutiae—but they knew the major arcs of the insider and outsider narratives, in part because these narratives have dominated elite white evangelicals' political discourse and writing of history since the 1970s. Moreover, both narratives have come to permeate white evangelicals' popular culture in the United States today, echoing in sermons, films, novels, art, and even Bibles. Christian tourists traveled to D.C. to hear them retold and to see corroborating evidence in the nation's capital. In the tours I observed, white evangelicals from across the country revealed a preexisting shared understanding of how American history has played out, directed by the Christian God and featuring Christian leaders in starring roles. They also shared a sense of exile and victimization. Regardless of where they lived, they felt that they had been personally disrespected by the mainstream culture, as had Christians in general. The insider and outsider narratives shaped how they understood themselves vis-à-vis the nation, both at home and in D.C.

During conversations at sites, on the bus, in security lines, and around the dinner table, I heard Christian tourists and their guides telling one another stories that were fragmented versions of the insider and outsider narratives. Tour guides told stories about God's divine intervention at critical moments, such as George Washington's miraculous victory in the French and Indian War. They talked about the deep faith of the Founding Fathers, expressed in their prayers at the Constitutional Convention. At the same time, they warned that Christians were in danger in the United States. They called on tourists to be brave like Queen Esther, proclaiming their faith in a hostile culture even if it may cost their lives.[44] In many cases their stories were prompted by features of the city around them. Biblical inscriptions on building or monuments offered a convenient starting point, as did statues of American leaders who professed Christianity. Tourists also reiterated the insider and outsider narratives, both in casual conversations and in follow-up interviews, using them to explain why they came on the tour, what they liked or disliked about the experience, and what they planned to do with their new knowledge of the nation's Christian heritage. Finally, tour companies deployed these narratives in advertisements to encourage their potential consumers to purchase a tour. Their marketing resonated with white evangelicals because these narratives were already so deeply embedded in how they think about the nation.

The insider and outsider narratives are more than stories that are consumed as entertainment in D.C. or other contexts. Narratives are how we make sense of who we are and how we relate to other individuals, institutions, and communities—in other words, our identities. Identity is not fixed or static.[45] Rather, it is something we continually produce as subjects. In discussing identity, this book employs a sociological model first developed by Margaret R. Somers and later adapted by Nancy T. Ammerman to better fit the study of religious identities.[46] From this perspective, identity itself can be understood as a story that is constantly being retold by subjects, who draw on previous life experiences, social expectations, cultural meta-narratives, and material culture in understanding at any given moment who they are. These narratives provide a plot into which the subject can situate new information or experiences. That plot in turn gives direction for the next action. Yet an identity narrative is not fixed: it will shift as another event occurs, as the subject meets a new audience, or simply as time passes. Understanding identity in narrative terms captures the dynamic processes by which identities are produced.

All of us draw on different types of narratives in producing identity. One type is the public narrative, which is collectively composed and recognizable to other individuals in the same social milieu. According to Ammerman, public narratives "are attached to groups and categories, cultures and institutions. Whether it is the court system or shopping malls, ethnic group or gender, these social institutions and categories provide recognized 'accounts' one can give of one's behavior, accounts that identify where one belongs, what one is doing, and why."[47] Public narratives provide a plot that makes an individual's actions intelligible to both her and her community. At any given moment the individual may choose from a range of public narratives, selecting the one that best fits the situation. She has agency in making this choice, though she is constrained by which narratives are available and intelligible to her audience.[48] Even so, old narratives can be deployed in new and creative ways, shifting their meaning in the process.

Among white American evangelicals, the insider and outsider narratives are public narratives, in that they are the result of collective effort over time by families, churches, parachurch organizations, businesses, and the state.[49] Each one provides a ready-made plot that can be used to link events to one another in order to explain what is happening and why. They are not specific to a particular series of events; rather, they are interpretive grids that can be superimposed on a wide range of events to make them meaningful. For instance, Starbucks Coffee famously produced a blank red holiday cup in 2015, rather than printing the cups with snowflakes, trees, or other festive patterns as they had in years past. On its own, this event has no immediate significance. However, when it is plotted into one of the great dramas of the outsider narrative, the War on Christmas, it becomes one more instance of Christianity being erased from the public square.[50] The outsider narrative provides an interpretive framework that links something as simple as a Starbucks cup to the persecution of the Puritans in England and the elimination of state-sponsored prayer in American public schools. In doing so, it also suggests how evangelicals should respond: by protesting.

In addition to public narratives, subjects can also draw on metanarratives in producing identity. Like public narratives, metanarratives are collective, but they tend to be far broader in their scope, encompassing whole societies rather than individual subjects or groups. Somers calls them "the epic dramas of our time: Capitalism vs. Communism, the Individual vs. Society."[51] These stories are often so taken for granted that they go unseen. They shape action without appearing to do so. Individuals may resist them, but they are difficult to discard completely. Metanarratives intersect with other types of narratives, forming a tangle of connected options from which a person may choose in producing her identity.[52]

Three metanarratives are salient to the experience of Christian tourists in D.C. and to white evangelicals more broadly. The first is the metanarrative of Christian salvation history: Eden, the Fall, the Incarnation, the Crucifixion, the Resurrection, and Christ's eventual return. American history has long been understood by white evangelicals in the context of this redemptive story, and this metanarrative underlies every other story they tell. Equally significant is a second metanarrative, that of American exceptionalism. In this story, the United States is a "shining city on a hill," singled out by God to be a light to the nations.[53] The nation is thus in covenant with God, promising righteousness in exchange for liberty and divine protection. This metanarrative is the dominant interpretive framework for American history among white American evangelicals today. The third metanarrative relevant here is secularization. Social scientists may have largely discarded the myth of secularization, or the idea that religion will disappear as society modernizes, but it lives on in white evangelicals' imagination.[54] To them, it is a story of religion being eradicated by hostile secularists, and it casts white evangelicals as the righteous remnant fighting to maintain Christianity's

God-given place at the center of the public square. These three metanarratives work together to shape the other stories white evangelicals tell about themselves, their communities, and their nation.

These narratives are not discrete: they overlap, intersect, and blur, both in D.C. and beyond. Their messiness is generative, allowing white evangelicals to move fluidly among them and to combine them strategically for their own political purposes. This book argues that white evangelicals have created four roles for themselves vis-à-vis the nation: they are founders, exiles, victims, and saviors. They produce these roles by drawing on the public narratives and metanarratives I have discussed in different combinations. The insider narrative casts them as the nation's founders, tasked by God to create and maintain a righteous society. This role is reinforced by the metanarratives of Christian salvation history and American exceptionalism. At the same time, the outsider narrative casts them as exiles and victims in a hostile nation. This claim depends on both the metanarrative of secularization, which provides an antagonist in the form of modernity, and the insider narrative, which depicts the nostalgic past that has been lost. Finally, all of these narratives work together to cast evangelicals as the nation's saviors. The nation may be on the brink of disaster caused by secularization and moral decline, or so the story goes, but if white evangelicals can reclaim power and return the nation to righteousness, the crisis might yet be averted. White evangelicals move easily among these four roles—founders, exiles, victims, and saviors—and this flexibility is in turn a source of political power. They can be victors in one moment and victims in the next. All they require to recreate themselves is a good story.

EMBODIED EXPERIENCE

If D.C. has an *axis mundi*, or sacred center, it is the Washington Monument. Once the tallest structure in the world, it remains the tallest structure in D.C. Its stark form erupts from the grass of the National Mall, stretching up as if to bridge heaven and earth. Other monuments orient themselves around it—one side of the black wall of names at the Vietnam Veterans Memorial is angled to point to it, while the World War II Memorial is recessed six feet below street level so as to avoid interrupting the view to the Lincoln Memorial.[55] Opportunities to ascend the monument are few and far between these days, but for those lucky enough to get a ticket, the observation deck offers a god's eye view of the capital.

The first time I ascended the monument was on Clay's tour. This was one of the more expensive tours, and it showed in the bus, which was much

Visitors to the National Mall seeking shelter from the summer sun in the shadow of the Washington Monument, July 2016. Photo by the author.

nicer than average. Each seat had a power outlet where we could charge our phones and cameras, and the air conditioning was more than a match for D.C. in late summer. I was not the only one reluctant to leave this portable haven behind. But we were here to see the sights, and not just through the bus windows, so we dutifully disembarked and set off across the lawn. The grass underfoot was a pleasant change from sidewalks and marble halls, even when the ground changed to a slight incline. But as we straggled onto the plaza at the base of the monument, nearly everyone collapsed onto the granite benches that curved around its edge. Clay went to the booth to collect our tickets, while the rest of us stared upward.

From this vantage point, it was impossible to see the pyramid-shaped peak of the monument. All we could see were sheer white walls rising straight up into the deep blue sky. Closer to the ground, fifty American flags flew from poles that circled the plaza. On the southeast side, the dark shadow of the obelisk cut through the vivid grass. Other tourists huddled in that narrow bit of shade, the only available respite from the summer sun. I hoped it would be a short wait to go inside the monument.

When Clay returned, he told us it would just be another fifteen minutes before it was our turn to take the elevator to the observation deck. Most of the group stayed put. It was hot on the plaza, but at least we had seats. A few people stood and spread out to take more pictures. I watched one man, Gary, pace around the monument with his hands in his pockets, as if inspecting the structure from different angles. His path brought him inward, until he stood only an arm's length from the east wall. Slowly, almost furtively—we'd spent all week being told not to touch things by security guards—he reached out and placed his palm flat against the marble. Almost immediately he recoiled, shaking his hand. He stared at the wall, then turned and walked back to the group. "It's warm," he told us, with something like awe in his voice.

Given that the marble blocks of the obelisk had been baking in the sun all day, it should perhaps come as no surprise that they would retain heat even when the sun had moved to the west. But Gary, like the rest of us, was primed to experience the extraordinary in this place, not the ordinary. We were at the sacred center of the city and the nation. Is it so surprising, then, that he would touch warm marble and experience it as presence or even transcendence?

For Christian tourists, D.C. acted as more than a scenic stage for their stories about the American past. As a growing body of scholarship demonstrates, narratives of identity are inseparable from embodied experience.[56] One is not prior to the other. Rather, the relationship between the two is recursive, each affecting the other.[57] In other words, tourists' identity narratives shaped how they experienced the city, determining to some extent what they observed or ignored, where they went, and how they behaved. At the same time, their experiences in turn fed back into those identity narratives to reinforce, disrupt, or otherwise reshape them in light of the new information gathered in the experience. Thus, their sensations and gestures mattered. They craned their necks to look up at the monumental architecture and squinted to read distant inscriptions. They crouched low to the ground and waited impatiently for crowds to part so they could take the perfect photo. They shifted their weight from side to side trying to bring relief to their aching feet. They fanned themselves with extra brochures and itineraries. They cupped their hands to their ears to hear the guide talking at crowded sites. They gaped at the ornate decor inside historic buildings. They rolled their eyes at overzealous security guards. They experienced the city in their bodies, and that experience was just an important as any tour guide's monologue.

Some of their experiences made them feel welcome, as if they belonged here at the center of the nation. Many tourists reported feeling a thrill of recognition at being in places they had only seen on TV, walking in George Washington's footsteps at Mount Vernon, and seeing the original copies of the nation's founding documents. They were moved and uplifted by being in the proverbial room where it happened. In addition, the private tours of the Capitol, the "secrets" that guides imparted, the group reservations that let them (sometimes) bypass the long lines of less fortunate tourists—they felt special as a result, the privileged few granted access and knowledge. Perhaps more importantly, the sites and objects they came to see corroborated their claims about the central place of Christians and Christianity in the United States. The city is chock full of Christian iconography, biblical inscriptions, and statues of Christian leaders. Seeing this evidence of America's Christian heritage is tours' raison d'être, and it had the desired effect. Tourists felt a sense of ownership for the city and, by extension, the nation.

At the same time, other aspects of the tour were deeply alienating. The security ritual of emptying their pockets, placing their bags in the scanner, and walking through a metal detector reminded them several times a day that they were suspect until proven otherwise. They did not belong here. The heat was oppressive, and there were never enough opportunities to sit down. Guards yelled at them to be quiet. Guides begged them to hurry up. They were all far from home, and their every movement around the city seemed to remind them of it. Moreover, many conservative Americans have an ambivalent attitude toward D.C., the seat of the federal government, and the tourists I encountered were no exception. They were appalled by the massive government buildings that occupy whole city blocks in D.C. Though "big government" was a familiar concept to them, they were taken aback by just how big it was. Tourists in several groups even remarked on the size of the White House lawn, wondering how much money it cost the taxpayers to keep it mowed. The monumental scale of D.C.'s architecture did not help matters, either. The federal buildings that line the National Mall are designed to make mere mortals feel small and insignificant. No matter how many biblical inscriptions decorated their facades, they represented the opposite of most Christian tourists' values around government.

These alternating experiences of belonging and displacement were an important feature of Christian tourists' time in D.C. Like the stories they heard and told, these experiences suggested to them an ambivalent relationship to the nation. But these experiences were deeply felt in the body. Their interactions with the city—its architecture, stairs, lines, crowds, smells, noise—validated their understanding of themselves as simultaneously insiders and outsiders in the United States.

In addition, D.C.'s material culture played an important role in revealing how Christian tourists moved between the insider and outsider narratives. Buildings, objects, and spaces tell their own stories, which sometimes jibed with the stories Christian tourists want to tell at any given point. As multiple tourists noted, the city's very "stones cry out" in praise of the Christian God, in that many buildings and monuments are inscribed with biblical quotations or imagery.[58] In Matthew Engelke's terms, Christianity is "ambient" in D.C., meaning it is ubiquitous but operates largely in the background.[59] Most people entering Union Station, for instance, pay little attention to the Bible verses inscribed on the front facade. Christianity is everywhere in D.C.'s landscape, yet it remains invisible to most passersby. One key task of Christian heritage tours is to activate ambient religious objects, making them visible to Christian tourists.[60] Sometimes guides did the work of activation, drawing tourists' attention to a statue honoring a Christian leader from American history or to a historical artifact related to Christian practices. However, some objects did not need guides to activate them: powerful symbols or phrases captured Christian tourists' attention on their own.[61] Once activated, these objects asserted that Christianity was the founding faith of the nation and ought to play an outsize role in American politics and the public square. Understood this way, D.C.'s material culture stabilized the insider narrative.

However, the insider narrative was not the only story being told during Christian heritage tours. When tourists spoke of how American Christians had been exiled from power and persecuted for their faith, they did so in front of these same Christian objects. In such moments, material culture was not stabilizing but disruptive. These objects raised an inconvenient question: if Christians are so marginalized today, how is it that these prominent symbols of Christianity persist in the nation's capital? Tourists and guides had to reckon with that question, and as they did so, they demonstrated one strategy for shifting between insider and outsider narratives. In almost every case, they would identify a threat to the object, positioning it as the next victim of anti-Christian forces. Either the object was subject to misinterpretation, or it was moments away from being removed or destroyed. This imminent threat caused the object to recede into the background, fading into the ambient Christianity of the city where it could not disrupt the outsider narrative. In fact, this move invited tourists to identify with the object in question insofar as they, too, felt threatened. Of course, if tourists wanted to move back to the insider position, all they had to do was appeal to the authority of history and tradition.

These moves between narratives are significant for two reasons. First, they demonstrate the multiple ways in which religious objects can participate in identity formation. Studies of religion and material culture have often examined how objects can stabilize religious identity.[62] Less frequently discussed is the disruptive potential of objects, or how a religious object by virtue of its existence, appearance, placement, or other characteristic can challenge a dominant identity narrative. Christian heritage tours were an opportunity to observe how tourists interacted with disruptive objects and how they adjusted or stabilized their identity narratives in response.

Second, in responding to disruptive objects, Christian tourists demonstrated how white evangelicals maneuver between the insider and outsider narratives beyond the context of Christian heritage tours. The same patterns can be observed on a larger scale in white evangelicals' political discourse. In some situations they can benefit from being insiders, so they appeal to history. They turn to the past to legitimize the power or privilege they seek to claim. In other situations, though, they benefit more from being outsiders, a persecuted minority seeking equal protection under the law. To take this position, they identify a threat either to a white evangelical individual or community, or to the legacy of Christianity in the United States. Some threats are plausible, while others are hyperbole. Regardless, white evangelicals can use the threat to claim an outsider position and the moral authority that comes with it. They can strategically move from the center to the margins and back again. On a political level, white evangelicals benefit from this ability to continually redefine who they are vis-à-vis the nation. In a nation that loves a rebel but cherishes tradition, their dynamic identity ensures that they can always claim whichever position will give them the upper hand.

SAVING HISTORY

This book explores how white evangelicals imagine and reimagine the American past and how their dynamic relationship to the nation informs their political behavior. In the chapters that follow, I trace the historical development of the insider and outsider narratives and examine how they manifest on the ground during Christian heritage tours of D.C. Like studies of lived religion, this study of lived history is necessarily interdisciplinary, drawing on ethnography, intellectual history, and the study of material culture in order to capture the dynamic ways in which people understand themselves in relation to the world around them.[63] Stories about the past—written, verbal, and material—are essential to identity production, as individuals plot themselves into larger narrative arcs about their families or communities. Each subsequent chapter focuses on one of the roles that white evangelicals create for themselves by combining these narratives in different ways: founders, exiles, victims, and saviors. But those roles are themselves partial, multiple, and shifting. In short, what follows is an attempt to impose order on complex lived experience. Few clean lines can be drawn without risking distortion; few distinct beginnings, middles, and ends can be found in these stories.

There is, however, an underlying theme that connects these stories, no matter how partial. In the biblical terms favored by Christian tourists, this theme is best expressed by 2 Chronicles 7:14: "If my people, who are called by my name, will humble themselves and pray and seek my face and turn from their wicked ways, then I will hear from heaven, and I will forgive their sin and will heal their land." As white evangelicals see it, if they can persuade Americans to repent and return to the righteous ways of the past, the nation may yet be saved. When they tell stories about the faith of the Founding Fathers or prayer and Bible reading in nineteenth-century schools, they are not just waxing nostalgic for their glory days. Rather, they are offering a solution to the problems the nation faces today. The Christian heritage industry thrives on this perception, holding out hope that a return is possible if only more Americans knew about the nation's true history. Whether through books, films, or tours of D.C., representations of "Christian America" promise white evangelicals that the nation can repent and be saved.

However, white evangelicals also believe that Christianity is in danger in the United States in large part because of Americans' collective ignorance of the nation's past. In their view, liberals and secularists in the academy and the media have done their best to erase Christianity from the normative accounts of American history. As stewards of the nation, white evangelicals are charged with restoring Christianity to its rightful place in the history books. They are also responsible for protecting the evidence of the nation's Christian past; they must preserve it from secularists' efforts to destroy or distort it. Christian heritage tours of D.C. are one way they learn about this responsibility to protect "true" Christian history of the United States. They must first save history in order to save the nation.

Chapter 1 **Founders**

....

Just south of Constitution Avenue on the western edge of the National Mall sits a memorial that is often overlooked. Signers Island occupies the middle of Constitution Pond, a free-form body of water that meanders between the memorials to World War II and Vietnam veterans. The island is linked to the mainland with a simple wooden bridge. On its mainland end, the bridge is inscribed with a dedication from the 1976 American Revolution Bicentennial Administration, the organization that paid for the memorial. On the other end, the bridge features the final lines of the Declaration of Independence: "And for the support of this Declaration, with a firm reliance on the protection of Divine Providence, we mutually pledge to each other our Lives, our Fortunes, and our sacred Honor."

As a group of tourists crosses the bridge, many of them pause to take a picture of this second inscription, momentarily halting traffic. Eventually, all twenty-five of them make it onto the island, urged gently onward by their guide, Jonathan. A few steps from the bridge, they find themselves in the middle of a semicircle of short stone pillars that opens onto the pond, with views of the Washington Monument across the water. Each of the fifty-six pillars bears the signature of one of the signers of the Declaration of Independence, accompanied by his printed name, occupation, and county. Some of the names are easily recognized: John Hancock, Thomas Jefferson, Benjamin Franklin. Others are less familiar: Edward Rutledge, Button Gwinnett, Charles Carroll of Carrollton. If there is any ambient Christianity here, it remains quiet in the background. Tourists browse the pillars casually, photographing the names they know. Soon their eyes (and cameras) drift

Square stone pillars honoring the signers of the Declaration of Independence on Signers Island, July 2016. Photo by the author.

View of the Washington Monument from Signers Island, July 2016. Photo by the author.

away from this memorial to the Washington Monument and its picturesque reflection in the pond. There is little shade and nowhere to sit, so they are reluctant to linger.

As if their restlessness is his cue, Jonathan begins to tell stories about the men this memorial honors, the fifty-six signers of the Declaration of Independence. He starts with Samuel Adams of Massachusetts, who reportedly asked for a prayer to open the Constitutional Convention. In Jonathan's telling, the delegates initially could not agree on a prayer, largely due to objections from the Quaker contingent. They settled on a reading of Psalm 35: "Plead my cause, O Lord, with them that strive with me: fight against them that fight against me." As some tourists murmur appreciatively, he moves on to talk about Benjamin Rush, the founder of the Sunday School movement and another signer of the Declaration who was "a strong believer." Jonathan also draws his tourists' attention to John Witherspoon, who was the president of the College of New Jersey (now Princeton University), a Presbyterian minister. He was the "grandfather of the nation," Jonathan says, because he taught so many of the future leaders of the new United States. He continues through the list, identifying the many signers who were ordained as ministers and in some cases reciting key lines from their writings about their faith. By doing so, he activates these pillars as Christian objects with significance for Christian heritage seekers. As he speaks, tourists who had wandered to the water's edge come back to take a second look at the pillars, examining the professions of the signers more carefully. Jonathan wraps up his talk by exhorting his audience to remember that these men were "strong Christians" willing to sacrifice everything—"their lives, their fortunes, and their sacred honor"—for the cause of liberty.

Signers Island is not one of D.C.'s marquee attractions, but it nevertheless played an important role in the Christian heritage tours I observed. Tourists visited it only if time permitted—for those on a tight schedule, the modest memorial could not compete with the allure of Capitol Hill, the war memorials, and Arlington National Cemetery. But even if a group did not have time to stop, the guides still pointed it out from the bus, and tourists dutifully took photos as the bus crawled past in the heavy traffic on Constitution Avenue. The island itself was significant in these tours only insofar as it prompted a discussion of the signers of the Declaration of Independence and their "strong Christian faith."

These visits and drive-bys to Signers Island offer a snapshot of the kind of stories featured on Christian heritage tours. These stories echo the Christian Right's revisionist history of the United States, in which the founders were proto-evangelicals who intended Christianity to occupy a privileged place in the nation, and white evangelicals today are responsible for ensuring that the nation fulfills their intentions. This history is, in a sense, not history at all. Rather, it is heritage. According to historian David Lowenthal, "While it borrows from an enlivens historical study, heritage is not an inquiry into the past but a celebration of it, not an effort to know what actually happened but a profession of faith in a past tailored to present-day purposes."[1] Like other heritage makers, the Christian Right's purpose was to use a particular narrative of the past to build a communal identity around an inheritance, in this case, of the nation.[2] This narrative has some flexibility, particularly in the choice of heroes to feature and evidence to marshal. It does not, however, leave room for error.[3] Its characters cannot be doubters, and its evidence cannot be ambiguous. This story must be uncompromising, for any compromise would leave it vulnerable to its many detractors. If this history is to be the blueprint for saving the nation, it must not waver in its claims about the Christianity of the founders and their prescriptions for American public and political life.

Academic historians greet Christian heritage history with skepticism (and often derision), largely because it rests on two claims that are antithetical to the academy. First, Christian heritage history uncritically accepts that the founders and other American heroes are utterly sincere in any word or action that references Christianity.[4] Actions that academic historians might understand as expressions of civil religion, political expediency, or social control are understood by Christian heritage proponents to be sincere acts of devotion. This approach flattens the complexity of human behavior and ignores historical context. Second, Christian heritage history views the Christian God as a historical actor. Past events can be explained in terms of divine intervention. Academic historians reject this approach as part of their broader rejection of supernaturalism. Academic explanations of the American Revolution or the Great Depression can begin with politics or economics, but not divine providence. As a result of these two fundamental points of disagreement, Christian heritage proponents routinely clash with academic historians in a battle for the "real" history of the United States.

Christian heritage tours intervened in this debate by promising material evidence for their side of the story. D.C.'s many Christian statues, objects, and inscriptions can act as proof that, at some point in the past, Christians did occupy the privileged place that Christian heritage proponents say they did. Christian tourists understood these material objects, like the words and actions of the founders, to be sincere expressions of faith. In their view, the materiality of the objects made them incontrovertible proof of the Christian heritage story. Here, too, an academic perspective would be more critical in considering the intent of an object's creators and its shift in meaning over time. But Christian heritage tours presented D.C. as their trump card in the debate over the historical relationship between Christianity and the nation. At least in this regard, Christian tourists' experience in D.C. confirmed their belief that the founders were Christian and that they are the heirs to the founders.

FOUNDING FAITH

D.C. is full of memorials to great white men. Christian heritage tour guides took full advantage of these memorials as backdrops for the stories they wanted to tell, and they pointed out the features of the memorials that corroborated those stories. Three men dominated the tours' stories just as their memorials dominate the landscape: George Washington, Thomas Jefferson, and Abraham Lincoln. At the Washington Monument and Mount Vernon, the Jefferson Memorial, and the Lincoln Memorial, as well as at other stops and on the bus, tour guides told stories about the "strong Christian faith" of these men. They were particularly concerned with defending each great American from accusations of deism or "lukewarm" Christianity and with showing that each man participated in public displays of religion that would be criticized today for blurring the line between church and state. In these stories, Washington, Jefferson, and Lincoln were exemplars of the kind of Christian leadership that the Christian Right seeks to promote today.

When Christian heritage guides talked about George Washington, they turned him into something of a saint. In addition to being a "strong Christian," he is also said to have been specially chosen by God to lead the nation.[5] At the Washington Monument, guides had two starting points for these stories. One was the inscription at the apex of the monument: *Laus Deo*, or "Praise Be to God." Guides emphasized that this inscription is in recognition of Washington's "strong Christian faith," as are the Christian inscriptions on the interior of the monument.[6] As they made these claims, guides acknowledged that tourists may have heard conflicting stories: as one guide put it, Washington was "a Christian man, despite what secular historians say today." Another guide complained about the "denigration" of Washington, meaning historians' arguments that he was a deist or nominal Christian at best, based on his irregular church attendance and abstract language for the divine.[7] Christian heritage guides assured their tourists that these stories are secularist lies. As proof, they quote Washington's Farewell Address and his Thanksgiving Proclamation. In the former, he calls "religion and morality . . . indispensable supports" to "political prosperity." In the latter, he declares that it is "the duty of all Nations to acknowledge the providence of Almighty God, to obey his will, to be grateful for his bene- fits, and humbly to implore his protection and favor." He then declares a day of prayer and thanksgiving for the entire nation.[8] To many academic historians, these are instances of "civil religion," intended more to sacral- ize the political process rather than to express personal piety.[9] In the hands of Christian tour guides, these quotations are proof that Washington was a devout Christian and that he saw Christianity and government as naturally intertwined.

Christian guides also found evidence of Washington's Christianity in ac- counts of his life in which he seemed to be divinely protected. At Mount Vernon every guide told the story of the Battle of Monongahela, which is also featured in a film at the visitors' center.[10] According to Mount Ver- non's interpretation, a young George Washington was serving as an aide- de-camp to the British general Edward Braddock during the French and Indian War in 1755. When Braddock was injured in the battle, Washington took command, coordinating the retreat of the few remaining British troops and earning a reputation as a war hero. However, Christian heritage guides tell this story very differently. To them, it was a miracle that Washington sur- vived the battle. According to Mark, "Four bullets passed through his coat, and two horses were shot out from under him, but God preserved him. . . . God had a plan for him not to be killed in battle." Stacy, a longtime guide for a large for-profit tour company, said much the same thing. But she also added to it, saying, "That was just one of many times when God's hand was miraculously upon this man and caused him to be spared." She told her group of forty people that God's protection and plan went all the way back to when Washington contracted smallpox as a young man in Barbados. As a result, when the disease swept through the American army during the Revolution, Washington was immune. From a Christian heritage perspec- tive, God orchestrated these events in Washington's life so that he would survive to lead the nation first as general and then as president. He was divinely chosen and protected, which implied both that he was himself a Christian and that God had a hand in the creation of the new nation.

Like Washington, Jefferson also received outsize attention on Christian heritage tours, but for a different reason. Jefferson's faith has long been called into question: he was called an atheist by his opponents in the election of 1800, and that accusation has followed him into the twenty-first century.[11] However, the insider narrative demands that the founders be devout Christians, so tour guides summarily dismissed the idea that Jefferson was an atheist. As evidence, they pointed to his famous line in the Declaration of Independence: "The Laws of Nature and Nature's God." No atheist would write such a phrase, they concluded, since it grounds the whole project of American independence in an appeal to the divine. Even if he was a skeptic at one point, some guides added, struggling with faith does not make anyone less of a Christian, especially if they overcome their doubts. At the Jefferson Memorial, Mark admitted to one group that, yes, Jefferson did "question the deity of Christ." Some of his tourists sighed, disappointed. But, he went on, the only reason Jefferson doubted was because of the rise of Unitarianism.[12] At the time, he said, "Unitarians just wanted to get back to first-century Christianity." His audience was relieved to hear this. They were mostly Protestants, and the desire for reformation was an impulse they could forgive, no matter how misguided.

For further proof of Jefferson's Christian credentials, Christian guides pointed to Jefferson's support of taxpayer-funded displays of religion during his presidency. During his monologue at Signers Island, Jonathan told us that church services were held in the Capitol during Jefferson's presidency. "It was the first megachurch in the country," he said. Jefferson attended services there, Jonathan said, but that was not all. He pretended to be scandalized as he confided that Jefferson *used tax money* to pay the Marine Corps Band to play during services.[13] And, can you believe it, he even used tax money to send missionaries to the Indians. "I guess he wasn't such a believer in separation of church and state!" Jonathan quipped. Most of his tourists laughed out loud. Other Christian guides made a similar argument. From their point of view, Jefferson's own actions contravene the way his iconic phrase, "separation of church and state," has been interpreted by those who would use it to exclude religion from public life altogether.

Christian guides also took time to explain the famous "Jefferson Bible," which came up on every tour. In the last decade of his life, Jefferson extracted the teachings of Jesus from the New Testament, leaving out any references to miracles and the supernatural, and pasted them into a new volume he titled "The Life and Morals of Jesus of Nazareth."[14] Secularists and atheists like to hold up this text as an example of Jefferson's atheism, and many tourists had heard about it in this context. Christian guides, however, argued that it was proof of Jefferson's desire to distill the essence of Christianity. And where better to focus than on the words of Jesus? Jefferson was only doing what generations of Protestants have done in trying to extricate the truth from the accretions of tradition. In Mark's view, the Jefferson Bible was merely "a red-letter edition before its time." In other words, Jefferson was not really an atheist or even a skeptic; he was a proto-evangelical Christian who has been willfully misunderstood by historians. This rendering maintains the narrative that the founders were uniformly sincere Christians whose faith galvanized their work to build the nation.

Though he is not a Founding Father, Abraham Lincoln is also the subject of much discussion on Christian heritage tours. From an academic perspective, Lincoln's faith is ambiguous at best. Despite his frequent and compelling use of the Bible in his speeches and writings, he never joined a church or clearly professed anything resembling orthodox Christian beliefs.[15] But Christian guides defended Lincoln's faith against academic historians who would question it. When Christian tourists visited the Lincoln Memorial, they heard stories about Lincoln's deep Christian faith, sometimes to the exclusion of anything else. Mark had one group sit on the steps for nearly half an hour while he told them about Lincoln's spiritual journey as a Christian. According to this story, Lincoln told a pastor in New York City that he wanted to make a public profession of faith but felt compelled to wait until he finished his term as president lest it be construed as a political move. Had he not been assassinated while in office, Mark assured us, Lincoln would have publicly declared his position and put to rest any doubts about his faith. During the whole talk, Mark never mentioned the Civil War or slavery once. Other guides drew their tourists' attention to Lincoln's biblical allusions in his Second Inaugural Address, inscribed on the north wall of the memorial. They argue that Christianity shaped how Lincoln saw the war and how he led the country through it; they also point out how explicitly Lincoln invoked God's judgment and aid in this very public moment. Like Washington and Jefferson, Lincoln was depicted as a Christian who brought his faith with him into public office.

In depicting the founders and other leaders as evangelical in all but name, Christian tour guides made an important claim about not only evangelicalism but also mainline Protestantism in the United States. Washington, Jefferson, and many of the framers of the U.S. Constitution were at various points members of the Anglican church, which became the Episcopalian church after the American Revolution. Many of the other framers were Presbyterians. By virtue of statistics alone, mainline Protestants could plausibly claim to be the direct descendants of the founders in terms of both theology and extant religious institutions. Such a claim, however, would disrupt the narrative arc that makes the Christian Right's jeremiad coherent. White evangelicals' authority to reform the nation derives from their claim to an unbroken line of descent between them and the founders. To draw that line, they omit mainline Protestants from the story. Christian heritage tours' narrow use of *Christian* to mean only conservative white evangelicals assists in this elision. Mainline Protestantism is implicitly categorized as one of many less legitimate forms of Christianity, forms that are excluded from the genealogies of the American founders.

In follow-up interviews, Christian tourists echoed their guides' claims about the founders, albeit more in broad strokes than in details. Constance was an eighty-one-year-old retired nurse who traveled to D.C. with her daughter for one of Mark's tours. When asked what she had learned about Washington or other founders, what stuck out most for her was the hospitality of Mount Vernon. "What a job for Martha!" she exclaimed, laughing. Thinking about Martha Custis Washington's workload reminded her of other things she had not heard before this tour, including that George Washington owned slaves and freed them.[16] And, she added, "He was quite religious, I didn't know that. Didn't he, oh, I can't remember now, but didn't he read the Bible every day, and didn't he preach some?" She went on, not waiting for an answer: "You know, one thing I did learn about, you know, most all of the presidents in those early years were very good church-abiding, church-going people. . . . They all spoke about God and Christianity and all of that." Faith was at the front of their mind, she said, because it was everywhere in D.C. "But it's not anymore," she added sadly. Like many other tourists I met, Constance saw the founding era as a poignant counterpoint to the present. She was not sure of the details, but she was certain that Christianity had once been much more important to America's leaders.

AMERICAN SCRIPTURES

While stories about great individuals were a significant component of Christian heritage tours' lived history, stories about the sacred texts of the nation were just as important. Many of these documents were on display in D.C., and like the faith and actions of Washington, Jefferson, and Lincoln, they were understood to corroborate the tours' claims about the proper place of Christianity in the United States. Both form and content mattered: the grand displays of the founding documents and historic Bibles augmented the tour guides' close readings of the texts themselves. Together, they convinced tourists that Christianity was always intended to be entwined with American government.

The most significant shrine to sacred texts in D.C. is the National Archives Museum, which houses the original copies of the Declaration of Independence, the U.S. Constitution, and the Bill of Rights. Most Christian guides dedicated time to a close reading of these documents, aiming to prove to their audience that these documents are indisputably Christian. In the Declaration of Independence, they focused on the mention of a "Creator" who is the source of "inalienable rights," and its closing reference to the signers' "firm reliance on divine providence." At Signers Island, Jonathan called the document "a sacred covenant," arguing that it is both a declaration to the world and a promise to God. Guides had to work harder to find Christianity in the U.S. Constitution, but they point to two phrases as proof. The first is "In the Year of Our Lord," which appears as part of the date in Article VII, just above the list of signers. Christian guides took this line as indicating deep devotion rather than mere convention.[17] The second is in Article I, Section VII, in which the president is given ten days to sign a law, "Sundays excepted." In the guides' arguments, this line demonstrated that the authors of the Constitution took for granted that Sundays ought to be a day of rest and worship, including for the president. At one point in his explanation, an exasperated Jonathan quipped, "People say that God's not in the Constitution, but you wouldn't have that in Iran!" These critical phrases are almost impossible to see on the original document, thanks to dim lighting and faded cursive script. But with guides' advance prompting, tourists knew what they should see, even if it was not truly visible to the naked eye.[18]

The aura of sacredness around the nation's founding texts was amplified by the space in which they are housed. The National Archives Museum displays many documents and exhibits, but its core is a shrine to the original copies of the founding documents. Officially known as the Rotunda for the Charters of Freedom, the high-ceilinged, windowless room showcases a semicircle of display cases holding key documents from American history. At the apex is the Constitution, flanked by the Declaration of Independence on the left and the Bill of Rights on the right. The arrangement of the space gives the impression of an altar housing sacred relics.[19] Between the area with the documents and the outer vestibule where the line forms is a gilded fence and gate that resembles the rood screen in a western medieval church. Guards ask visitors to speak quietly, but hushed voices still echo reverently off the marble walls. The giant bronze doors that open onto Constitution Avenue are the second largest in D.C., adding to the outsized scale of the space.[20] On the floor in the outer vestibule is a depiction of the Ten Commandments, inlaid in marble, which every Christian guide made sure to point out. I heard from many tourists that the atmosphere at the National Archives felt nothing short of "sacred." One tourist compared it to seeing an exhibit of the Dead Sea Scrolls on another trip: "It was so old and had so much meaning behind it. It's just neat to see, you know, something so well preserved and something people have such respect for, I just loved that." Guides used this emotional experience of the space to reinforce their over-all message about the sacredness of the nation, merging their stories about the documents with tourists' awed reactions to the Archives.

However, these legal documents were not the only founding texts of the nation, according to Christian guides. The Bible was equally important, if not more so. Christian guides' stories almost always included biblical allusions or quotations, and they never missed an opportunity to remind tourists that the founders had studied the Bible extensively. Their most memorable stage for discussing the Bible was the Great Hall of the Library of Congress, which houses a Gutenberg Bible in an alcove near the Main Reading Room. This 1455 edition, printed on vellum, was purchased by an act of Congress in 1930. In a matching case on the opposite side of the alcove is the Giant Bible of Mainz, an illuminated handwritten Bible that dates from the same de-cade. Neither display is showy, and many visitors to the Library of Congress barely glance at them. Once Christian tourists noticed them, however, the presence of these Bibles told a powerful story about not only the place of Christianity in America but also the place of America in Christianity.[21]

During one visit, Mark waved his group over to a gathering spot near the stairs. A few of them hurried to claim a spot at the front of the crowd, the better to hear Mark's talk, but most of them were more interested in staring upward at the ornate marble columns, gold accents, and mosaic ceiling. When they were loosely congregated, Mark took a few steps up the grand staircase and began his talk on the acquisition of the nearby Gutenberg Bible. "That's the most valuable book America owns," he began. To know its true value, we needed to go back to the fourteenth century, to a man named John Wycliffe who first translated the Bible into vernacular English but lacked the technology of the printing press to disseminate it. But, Mark as-sured his audience, "God had a plan." Over a century later, a German monk named Martin Luther—some tourists murmured at the familiar name—translated the Bible into vernacular German, and Johannes Gutenberg's printing press made that translation available to the masses who could not afford an elaborate hand-copied manuscript.[22] "And guess what happens when you read the Bible? People are changed, and they have a standard by which to judge the conduct of both priest and king," Mark said. The people who read and applied the Bible this way, he added as an aside, "were called 'Protestants.' And hopefully we, too, are protesting against civil and religious tyranny today." One tourist shouted "Amen."

Returning to history, Mark told us that access to the Bible was what led to the founding of the United States, a nation in which the Bible was the ultimate standard by which the government is judged. He concluded, paraphrasing Andrew Jackson, "The Bible is the bedrock upon which this nation rests." This story stuck with his tourists, several of whom mentioned the Gutenberg Bible later as a highlight in their follow-up interviews. Charlene from Texas exclaimed, "I never learned about that, that was actually the first Bible that was printed on the printing press. That's pretty remarkable, and that is like the beginning of where America came from." Almost as an afterthought, she added, "And it's kind of sad we've moved away from that, in a sense. But I loved the Library of Congress." Most of her fellow tourists felt the same. Though Mark's account of this history was the most detailed, other guides told similar versions that followed the same narrative arc. They situated the United States within the broader history of Christianity, using the presence of the Gutenberg Bible as both inspiration and evidence.

Other elements of the Library of Congress reinforced this message about Christianity's place in the nation. The Jefferson Building's ornate decoration showcases the knowledge of Western civilization, primarily from the classical and Christian traditions. Guides highlighted the statues of biblical figures Moses and Paul in the Main Reading Room, where they represent religion as a field of knowledge. Above them is inscribed the King James translation of Micah 6:8: "What doth the Lord require of thee, but to do justly, and to love mercy, and to walk humbly with thy God?" Guides also pointed out Christian leaders who represent other fields as well. These included Francis Bacon (philosophy), Christopher Columbus (commerce), and Isaac Newton (science). "Newton might be known for calculus," Mark said, "but he wrote far more about God than he did about physics or astronomy." He wrapped up with a quotation from Tennyson's "In Memoriam" that is inscribed in the Main Reading Room: "One God, one law, one element, and one far-off divine event to which the whole creation moves." His tourists responded with a chorus of resounding amens that drew stares from other visitors. As they spread out to take their pictures and explore the exhibits, they did so with certainty that this magnificent building was *theirs*—it was a celebration of Christian knowledge and achievement and further proof that Christianity was an integral part of American history.

View of the statue representing History by Daniel Chester French in the Main Reading Room of the Jefferson Building at the Library of Congress, April 2009. Above the statue is a quotation from Tennyson: "One God, one law, one element, and one far-off divine event to which the whole creation moves." Carol Highsmith Collection, Library of Congress.

THE CHRISTIAN HERITAGE MARKET

Christian heritage tours' version of American history drew on the revisionist history of the Christian Right, whose leaders have rewritten the past to legitimize their agenda in the present.[23] What I am calling the insider narrative was not entirely new in the 1970s, but it was during the 1970s and especially the 1980s that it settled and spread in its present form. Fragments of it were present in the colonial period, including in John Winthrop's claim that the Puritans were building "a city on a hill."[24] Later, in the early republic, the idea of America as a Christian nation gained strength as missionaries to the frontier spread both the gospel and nationalism.[25] This link between Christianity and national identity grew stronger in the early twentieth century with the conservative alliance of Christianity and capitalism.[26] The Christian Right's version builds on these past forms, and in some ways it goes further by using revisionist history to make its case. It baptizes the whole of North American history, from the landing of Columbus to the present day, rewriting the story to place white Christians at the center.

This new story of Christian America was disseminated through a variety of media beginning in the 1970s. What started in books and sermons by leaders of the Christian Right grew into a whole genre that includes films, art, Bibles and devotional literature, and textbooks. This genre is characterized by a shared set of claims: America is a divinely chosen nation; the founders (and any other historical characters of significance) were devout Christians of the evangelical variety; the Declaration of Independence, Constitution, and Bill of Rights are all derived from biblical tradition; and Christianity was always intended by the founders (and God) to occupy a central place in American politics and culture.[27] Authors and artists may choose to focus on a particular historical moment, or on an individual character's biography, or on a single social issue, but these claims recur across the genre, allowing audiences to consume them in whatever form they choose.

One of the first and most enduring examples of the Christian heritage genre is Peter Marshall and David Manuel's 1977 bestseller *The Light and the Glory*, which has sold nearly one million copies and remains a favorite textbook for private Christian schools and Christian homeschoolers.[28] Beginning with Columbus, Marshall and Manuel narrate American history from "what might have been God's perspective," covering the colonial period up through the American Revolution.[29] The United States, they argue, was called to be in covenant with God and an example to the world:

"In the virgin wilderness of America, God was making His most significant attempt since ancient Israel to create a new Israel of people living in obedience to the laws of God, through faith in Jesus Christ."[30] When Americans upheld their end of the covenant, God blessed the nation as he did ancient Israel, but when Americans strayed they faced God's judgment. Like the many Christian heritage authors who would come after them, Marshall and Manuel are writing a jeremiad: the purpose of their historical account is to demonstrate how far contemporary America has declined from its early years and to call Americans back to the covenant with God. They continue this call in two subsequent books, *From Sea to Shining Sea* in 1985 and *Sounding Forth the Trumpet* in 1997, which together cover American history from the early republic through the Civil War. In all three of their books, they "search for the hand of God in the different periods of our nation's beginnings," believing that the study of history will allow Americans to "rediscover [their] spiritual moorings" and regain God's blessings.[31]

As the Christian Right gained momentum in the 1980s, so did this Christian heritage approach to history. Leaders of the movement, including Jerry Falwell, Francis Schaeffer, Tim LaHaye, D. James Kennedy, and Gary DeMar, advanced the cause of America's Christian heritage through a variety of publications and speeches. In doing so, they embedded this narrative in the political strategy of the Christian Right. As they saw it, if they could reveal the lost or hidden Christian heritage of the nation, their audience would be inspired to revive it.[32]

The most prominent evangelist for Christian heritage has been David Barton, who remains a prolific author and conservative political activist. He is perhaps best known as the author of the controversial 2012 bestseller *The Jefferson Lies*, which was withdrawn from print by its publisher due to its inaccuracy.[33] Barton's books scrupulously follow the Christian Right's jeremiad, in that he idealizes the nineteenth century's white Protestant moral establishment, and he predicts severe consequences if the nation fails to repent. If Americans can rediscover the "real" meaning of the Constitution and the "real" history of the nation, however, they can avert the "potential downfall of the republic."[34] As his books gained a large popular audience, Barton turned Christian heritage history into a full-time job, touring churches across the country to share his findings.[35] He also began leading Christian heritage tours of D.C., and in 2000 he published a popular guidebook, *A Spiritual Heritage Tour of the United States Capitol*. Barton has led trainings for other Christian heritage guides in D.C., and according to several professional Christian heritage guides I interviewed, he regularly leads private tours of the U.S. Capitol for incoming members of Congress to introduce them to the Christian features of their new workplace. He also founded WallBuilders, a conservative Christian organization that publishes books, pamphlets, curricula, films, audio recordings, and other resources for Christian churches and schools.[36] Barton has many critics, both evangelical and secular, but no one has done more to shape and advance the Christian heritage approach to American history.

One reason the Christian heritage argument has been so widely disseminated is that Barton and his fellow heritage makers have not limited themselves to books and sermons. They have actively sought out other forms of media that can tell the story of America's Christian heritage in far more compelling ways than a historical monograph. Specialty Bibles, for instance, are nothing new; white evangelicals are consumers just like other Americans.[37] But today's Christian history buffs can purchase the *Founders' Bible*, edited by David Barton himself; the *Holy Bible: Patriot's Edition*, subtitled *The Word of God and the Shaping of America*; the *1599 Geneva Bible*, marketed as "the Bible of the Pilgrims and the Reformers"; or the *American Patriot's Pocket Bible*, complete with a camouflage-print cover. These special editions include articles by leading Christian heritage proponents, who sometimes also serve as editors or consultants. Each specialty Bible features articles on American history alongside the text of the Bible. The *Founders' Bible*, for instance, includes an article on creationism alongside Genesis 1 that quotes the "creationist" positions of founders Thomas Paine, Daniel Webster, Benjamin Franklin, and Thomas Jefferson. An article titled "God's Deliverance: The Birth of a Nation" accompanies Exodus 1–14, drawing parallels between ancient Israel and early America and again quoting several founders. Between the Old and New Testaments is a timeline of American history, a list of American presidents, and maps of early America and the world. These specialty Bibles offer a way for Christian heritage makers to literally write the United States into the Bible. There are also American-themed devotional books, such as *Devotions for Patriots* and *In God We Still Trust: A 365 Day Devotional*. Tea Party politician Sarah Palin released her own patriotic devotional, *Sweet Freedom*, in 2015. Through such publications, the Christian heritage narrative is inserted into the heart of the daily religious practices of white evangelicals, making America and the Bible virtually inseparable.

The Christian heritage story also shows up in documentary films, which are screened by churches, private Christian schools, and homeschool groups, though they rarely gain a wider audience.[38] The closest thing to a blockbuster in this genre is actor Kirk Cameron's *Monumental: In Search of America's National Treasure*, released in 2012. Christian heritage tours frequently referred to this film, and one tour group watched it on the bus on the drive to D.C. The film follows Cameron as he searches for "the real treasure" of America, meaning "the people, places, and principles that made America the freest, most prosperous and generous nation the world has ever known."[39] He finds the key in the National Monument to the Forefathers at Plymouth, Massachusetts: "This is the trail of freedom that leads us all the way back to the ancient Hebrews under Moses where he first delivered those laws of liberty—when he told them to elect leaders, men of character that you willingly submit yourself to, to self-govern rather than have a king."[40] Like the books discussed above, this story is framed by Cameron's desire to find a solution to the problems plaguing American society in the twenty-first century. The website for *Monumental* includes a Bible study guide that links the film, the Bible, and contemporary American life. That Cameron follows the Christian heritage narrative so closely is unsurprising, given that Christian heritage advocate Marshall Foster produced it and David Barton contributed interviews. For audiences disinclined to read history books, films like *Monumental* offer an easy alternative that communicates the same message in an entertaining package.

Another significant means of disseminating the Christian heritage argument is textbooks from both Christian and secular publishers. Christian educational publishers such as Abeka, Bob Jones University Press, Sonlight, and Alpha Omega Publications produce American history textbooks for all grade levels, including the homeschooling market.[41] These textbooks tell an extended version of the Christian America narrative, starting with the assertion that America was founded by Christians to be a Christian nation. They emphasize God's role in virtually every moment of American history, and they highlight the idea that America, like ancient Israel, has made a covenant with God.[42] Less explicit versions of the Christian heritage argument have also made their way into history textbooks from secular publishers. In 2010, Texas revised its state social studies standards to require students to learn Christian heritage cornerstones, such as that the "Judeo-Christian (especially biblical law)" tradition influenced the nation's founding, and to identify Moses as an influence on the nation's founding documents.[43] Such revisions are hardly surprising given that both David Barton and Peter Marshall served on the board of expert advisers in the curriculum overhaul.[44] But these changes had an impact on textbooks nationwide, since Texas is one of the largest buyers of textbooks and thus wields disproportionate influence over their content.[45] As a result of this strategic intervention in Texas, Christian heritage arguments entered into mainstream history textbooks, to be presented as uncontested facts to children across the country.[46]

These efforts to insert Christian heritage into history curricula remain part of the broader political strategy of the Christian Right, which relies on a particular understanding of the past to legitimize its actions in the present and goals for the future. Project Blitz is a campaign led by the Congressional Prayer Caucus Foundation and WallBuilders to encourage legislation and policies that, in the campaign's terms, "fully protect religious liberty and the free exercise of our faith in the public square by eliminating paths for legal retribution or government interference." In practice, this means protecting conservative Christian individuals and organizations that refuse to recognize same-sex marriage or transgender identities, including churches, wedding vendors, and adoption agencies.[47] Significantly, the campaign also seeks to "reclaim and properly frame the narrative and the language of religious liberty issues."[48] Judging from Project Blitz's templates for legislation and proclamations, the proper framing is the Christian heritage of America, and the proper language is respect for history and tradition. Religion has always held a privileged position in American politics and society, the argument goes, so it follows that broad exemptions should be made to protect religious freedom, and "traditional" religious values may be rightfully codified in law. The templates support this argument with lists of decontextualized anecdotes about the role of Christianity in American history, all of which routinely appear in other Christian heritage books and media.[49] This approach aims to make opposition to the Christian Right's narrow definition of religious freedom appear to be opposition to religion itself—and it paints all such opponents as inherently un-American. The results of this strategy have been mixed so far, but if nothing else, Project Blitz has made clear how central Christian heritage is to the political maneuvering of the Christian Right.

RESISTING CHRISTIAN AMERICA

The Christian heritage genre has attracted a great deal of criticism from both scholars and activists. Rebuttals of the "Christian nation myth," as critics call it, are themselves a cottage industry. For every book purporting to prove the Christian foundations of the United States, there is another book arguing—often in equally absolutist terms—for the secularist vision of the founders.[50] As historian John Fea points out, however, these arguments "generate more heat than light."[51] The discussion of Christianity's role in the nation's origins is too enmeshed in today's culture wars to be useful. Both sides are more interested in gaining political capital than in writing careful history.

More robust critiques of the Christian heritage genre focus on the lack of rigor in its methodology rather than advancing an alternative interpretation of the founders' intentions.[52] Many conservative Christians take a "proof-texting" approach to the Bible in the culture wars and in their own devotional practices, emphasizing passages that support them and ignoring those that do not. Christian heritage writers expand this approach to the writings of the founders, choosing excerpts from the writings of Washington, Jefferson, and others as proof-texts for the Christian heritage argument. The Christian heritage genre's credibility is built on its deference to primary sources, and books often include long lists of quotations drawn from the writings of early Americans in support of each point. Christian heritage makers see this approach as the surest way of discovering the truth of the founders' beliefs. In some cases, however, these proof-texts are badly distorted or even fabricated, as was the case with Barton's *The Jefferson Lies*.[53] Even with accurate texts, academic historians still reject this approach for failing to take into account the larger context of a given quotation.[54] As Stephen P. Miller points out, writers who rely on proof-texting also tend to take the founders' words at face value rather than critically interrogating them as they would any contemporary politician's statements.[55] This is, of course, one of the key features of that distinguishes the writing of history from the making of heritage.[56] Despite their occasional protests to the contrary, the purveyors of Christian heritage are not out to write history that will withstand peer review. Their goal is to create a past that, if reclaimed, will give them power.

Some prominent white evangelical historians have also offered theological critiques of the Christian heritage argument. In 1983 evangelical historians Mark A. Noll, Nathan O. Hatch, and George M. Marsden wrote *The Search for Christian America* largely in response to the Christian Right's growing interest in history.[57] They brought their considerable combined historical expertise to bear on this problem, making their case with a degree of nuance that is often absent from this debate.[58] But the key thrust of their argument is theological.[59] Baptizing the past, they argue, risks overlooking our predecessors' moral failings and even perpetuating them. Doing so, they argue, is to "do the cause of Christ a disservice."[60] Other white evangelical historians, including John Fea, John Wilsey, and Greg Frazer, have made similar arguments against the search for America's Christian heritage.

The white evangelical community is thus divided on the issue. As Fea ironically notes, both David Barton and Mark Noll appeared on *Time*'s 2005 list of "Most Influential Evangelicals in America."[61]

At the same time, there is no doubt that the works of Barton and other defenders of Christian heritage influence the lived history of a far broader audience than those of their academic counterparts, in part because they have a huge range of media at their command. Moreover, academic critiques do little to damage their reputation with their target audience. Barton, for instance, remains the favored historian of conservative Christian political circles even after *The Jefferson Lies* was voted the "least credible book in print."[62] His credibility with the Christian heritage audience is not damaged by opposition from accredited academics and the media. Rather, such opposition only reinforces his central message: that the secularist mainstream will do anything to eliminate Christianity from discussions of American history. The vast cultural marketplace for Christian heritage insulates its proponents from academic criticism. They are, however, well aware of their critics, and they use their popular platforms to provide what they see as incontrovertible evidence for their position. Christian heritage tours are one such platform.

EXPERIENCING CHRISTIAN AMERICA

Christian heritage tours build on the many dimensions of the Christian heritage genre, but they also offer something that books, films, and Bibles cannot: experience. American Protestants have given primacy to religious experience at least since the Second Great Awakening. In the face of criticism from academic historians and ridicule from secularists, some white evangelicals turn to the experience of D.C. to corroborate their claims about the past. Christian heritage tours invite their audience to experience this history for themselves. A sample tour advertisement highlights this element:

> Those who have been to the Holy Land know there is nothing like
> being in the actual places where Jesus and the great heroes of the faith
> walked. The same is true with America's Christian origin[;] being in the
> actual places where history was made, soaking in the sights, sounds,
> and smells on location creates a powerful and potentially life-changing
> experience. These great heroes from the pages of history will almost
> come to life. We will get to know them and be inspired by them. It is
> simply impossible to duplicate this rich experience in a church class-
> room.

What do the Founders' own writings (not the writings of a 20th century author) tell us about their beliefs? When you see their words engraved in stone, and hear what else they had to say, it becomes clear their intent was to forge a nation built on Christian principles. But it is not limited to just the Founding Fathers. Architects, presidents, builders and stone masons from the 20th Century left the same Christian messages in the memorials and monuments they built in the Nation's Capital.

Don't miss this opportunity to see the memorials, monuments and statues throughout the District that will give you a better understanding of what the Founders, and those that came after them, really believed. Hear their own words, and see the monuments that were built to honor them, and the God they believed in.[63]

This advertisement points to the key selling points of Christian heritage tours, all of which relate to the theme of individual experience. It promises that tourists will walk in the footsteps of the founders and in some sense re-live the history of the nation. It promises that they will see for themselves the legacy of Christianity in D.C.'s landscape, proof that Christianity once held a privileged place in American government and public life. And it promises that they will hear the unadulterated words of the founders and other great Americans of the past that further validate their claim.

Other advertisements make similar promises. One website invites potential tourists to "experience a tour that will bring life to the founding of our great nation." Tourists will "explore together our rich heritage, etched in marble and stone and woven into the very word of America's culture through the architectural, artistic, and historical themes inherent within and without her national landmarks, monuments, and memorials." They are promised a view of the "indelible mark" stamped by God on the nation and its capital. As another company puts it, "A tour of our historic sites reveals that America was a nation birthed by men who had a firm reliance upon Almighty God and His Son Jesus Christ." D.C.'s sites are said to do what mere words cannot: they offer concrete, physical, seemingly irrefutable proof of Christianity's central role in American history. The founders' words can be taken out of context and twisted, the argument goes, but Christianity is literally written in stone across the nation's capital where tourists can see it for themselves. From this point of view, critics can assail books, films, and so on with ease, but they cannot attack the authority of individual experience.

Christian tourists' visits to the U.S. Capitol demonstrated this use of experience to override criticism. The Capitol building abounds with statues, images, and inscriptions that prompted and corroborated stories about the dominant role of Christians and Christianity in American history. On the bus ride to the Capitol, Jonathan told one of his groups that, of the one hundred statues contributed by the states to the National Statuary Hall Collection, at least twenty are of "ordained ministers." Marcus Whitman of Washington State, for instance, was a missionary to the Northwest Territories with his wife Narcissa, and Peter Muhlenberg of Pennsylvania was a minister, a brigadier general in the American Revolution, and a member of the first Congress. Jonathan also mentioned Peter's brother Frederick Muhlenberg, who was both a minister and the first Speaker of the House of Representatives: "Clearly the founders had no problem working with ministers!" Several people chuckled. As with many of Jonathan's stories, the truth appeared so obvious it was funny. Other guides also highlighted the same statues to make the same point, as proof of the presence of Christians in American government from the beginning.

Other features of the Capitol lent themselves to a related argument about the central place of Christians and Christian rituals in American history. In the Capitol Rotunda, Christian guides drew attention to the eight paintings that ring the walls, depicting key scenes from the colonial period and the American Revolution.[64] As numerous guides pointed out, the scenes include "two prayer meetings and a baptism." Robert W. Weir's *Embarkation of the Pilgrims* depicts the Pilgrims praying just prior to departing for North America. At the center of the image, William Brewster holds open a Geneva Bible, while the figures around him kneel or bow their heads in prayer. Across the Rotunda, William Henry Powell's *Discovery of the Mississippi by De Soto* features a shadowy foreground scene in which a kneeling monk prays as soldiers plant a crucifix in the ground. De Soto himself looks on from horseback, flanked by his own soldiers and wary Native Americans, while the Mississippi glitters in the background. A third painting draws every visitor's eye with its dramatic portrayal of the baptism of Pocahontas: in John Gadsby Chapman's rendering, Pocahontas kneels before a baptismal font, wearing a white dress with a long train that often leads visitors to think they are viewing a wedding scene. Standing over her is Reverend Alexander Whitaker, whose white robes match her dress, giving the effect of a spotlight in the center of the painting. Other colonists and Native Americans look on, some with disapproval; the painting's caption and other Capitol literature, however, indicate that Pocahontas's conversion to Christianity and subsequent marriage to John Rolfe were essential in making peace between the colonists and the local Native American tribes.

It may seem odd that Christian heritage guides focused on these paintings rather than depictions of George Washington's military victories or the signing of the Declaration of Independence. After all, much of their storytelling featured Washington and the signers. These three paintings, however, capture something not illustrated elsewhere in D.C. The "two prayer meetings and a baptism" feature public displays of Christianity at key moments in American history. The prayer meeting scenes in particular imply that their subjects asked for and received divine blessings on their seemingly secular endeavors. Christian tourists took these paintings as accurate representations of historical events, not works of art that reflect the nineteenth-century context of their creation. From tourists' perspective, they offered straightforward evidence for the Christian America argument, which is further validated by the fact that they are displayed at the very center of the nation's government.[65]

Beyond the Rotunda paintings, guides also drew on the Christian iconography in the Capitol to make explicit claims about the proper relationship of Christianity to American law and government. Biblical quotations and references to the Christian God abound in commemorative plaques and decorative inscriptions throughout the building, such as the large "In God We Trust" inscribed over the speaker's rostrum in the House of Representatives Chamber. Joining these texts are key images from Jewish and Christian traditions. The House Chamber, for instance, is ringed by twenty-three engraved relief portraits of famous lawgivers, including Hammurabi, Justinian I, and Jefferson. Mark and other Christian guides claimed that seventeen of the twenty-three were Christian lawgivers. They paid special attention to the relief portrait of Moses: while the other portraits are in profile, Moses is depicted in full face over the central doors to the chamber. Guides interpreted this position as proving the centrality of Mosaic law to the American legal system. Jonathan told his tourists that Moses is there as a reminder to the Speaker of the House, who faces the portrait and must conduct House business with Moses "watching him." The broad implication of this iconography, at least as Christian heritage guides present it, is that not only were the founders Christian but so was the system they founded. Most visitors might not have noticed these instances of ambient Christianity, but Christian guides activated them, bringing the images into focus for their audience. They did so to reveal the political irony that, despite the

The House of Representatives Chamber during George W. Bush's State of the Union address to Congress, February 2005. "In God We Trust" is engraved below the clock above the speaker's rostrum. Architect of the Capitol.

principle of separation of church and state, Christianity was everywhere in D.C. Once seen, it was impossible to unsee.

The Christian tourists I spoke with on these visits found their guides' arguments persuasive. To them, it seemed that Christian heritage was everywhere they looked in the Capitol. As they walked through the crowded public hallways, they dutifully snapped pictures of the Christian statues and images. One woman, Olivia, told me she was grateful to Mark for drawing her attention to things she would not have noticed otherwise. "I don't think on a regular tour that you would know that there's Bible verses going up the side of the Washington Monument," she said. "I think it was in the Senate [*sic*] how Moses was full face and that Moses was there—I just don't think other tours are going to point that out, you know, that the Bible and God and faithfulness is just embedded through, the whole city is set up around that." Other tourists, including Constance, took these claims further, attributing D.C.'s Christian iconography to the founders themselves rather than later artists and architects. She had been to all the sites many times, Constance said, but her guide Jonathan opened her eyes to the countless biblical inscriptions at the Capitol and elsewhere in D.C. "He brought out all the engraving that was done and how important that was," she explained, "that

MOSES

Marble bas-relief portrait of Moses above the central door of the House of Representatives Chamber, directly opposite the speaker's rostrum, August 2010. Architect of the Capitol.

the fathers of our nation wanted to make sure that we never forgot that. And that's why they engraved that all over, and how, you know, they wanted us to be able to relate that to the Bible." To Olivia, Constance, and many other Christian tourists, these statues, images, and inscriptions were proof of what their guides had been saying. Christianity really was embedded in the center of American government.

HEIRS TO THE FOUNDERS

Since the 1970s, America's Christian heritage has become an industry that includes publishing, entertainment, art, education, and tourism. Regardless of the medium, however, heritage makers share the same three claims about the Christian foundations of the nation. First, the nation was founded and later led by devout Christians who were evangelical in all but name. Second, those Christian leaders saw no need to separate religion from government. On the contrary, they saw a union of the two as essential to the well-being of the nation. Third, the Christian God blessed and protected the Christian leaders of the nation, especially Washington, because God himself had a stake in the survival of the United States. In the context of Christian heritage tours, guides made these claims in their stories and used D.C.'s art and architecture to corroborate them.

Together, these three claims form the core of the insider narrative, retelling American history to create a particular role for white evangelicals. By depicting the founders as proto-evangelicals, this public narrative prompts today's white evangelicals to step into the founders' role. In the process, it displaces mainline Protestants, who could make a plausible claim to the founders' legacy themselves. The insider narrative also provides a theological justification for Christians to participate in politics by highlighting the divine blessings received by the United States when Christians occupied positions of power in the past. And it makes a constitutional argument about the legality of Christian involvement in politics and government preference for Christianity by looking to the Founding Fathers' example and early legal precedents. The insider narrative tells white evangelicals that the nation is theirs in every sense: it was founded by Christians like them to be a Christian system of government with the blessing and aid of the Christian God. This custodial or proprietary attitude derives from the insider narrative, and specifically from the form it has taken over the last four decades. The purpose of the insider narrative is not merely to rewrite American history. It is to inspire white American evangelicals to take political action and thus rewrite the future.

At the same time, however, the very idea of Christian heritage is built on nostalgia. White evangelicals may be convinced that the founders were Christian and intended their successors to be the same, but they are equally convinced that the nation has strayed from its founding principles. The insider narrative is only part of the story. The Christian Right's jeremiad synthesizes the insider and outsider narratives, and its power depends on white evangelicals feeling as if they are not currently in the custodial role given by God to the nation's white Christian founders. If they play their role correctly, the script promises a return of divine blessings and protection. However, if they fail to refound the nation in its original righteous form, the nation will continue to decline. America as they know it will end, and they will be no more than exiles wandering in the wilderness.

Chapter 2 **Exiles**

....

On the first afternoon of Stacy's tour, she leads our newly assembled group straight from the airport to the Washington Monument. "I like to start here," she tells us, "because it's really the center of everything." We gather around her, panting slightly from the walk from the bus. Stacy thinks this is one of the most important sites to see if you want to understand "our Christian history." After the initial flurry of picture taking, she begins to tell us about the monument, including the tortuous history of its construction and the reasons for the visible shift in the color of the marble.[1] When it was finally completed in 1884, she says, the builders put a final flourish on top, a metal pyramid made of the most valuable metal in the world at the time. Can we guess what it was? "Gold!" says one young boy. "Steel," someone else guesses. No, Stacy tells us. It's a metal that we have everywhere now. We even drink our Coke out of it. "Ohhh, aluminum," say several people at once. They are correct: the apex of the Washington Monument is made of aluminum, once a rare and valuable metal. And it contains a very important inscription.

On the eastern side of the aluminum pyramid, Stacy tells us, is the inscription *Laus Deo*—Latin for "Praise Be to God." At 555 feet above the National Mall, it is the highest point in D.C. and the first thing the rising sun strikes each morning. The tourists around me crane their necks to gaze reverently up at the monument, as if they could see the inscription from here. "I like to remember that since 1884 the words 'praise be to God' have been declared over this city and this nation," Stacy concludes. But one of the tourists has a question. He raises a tentative hand, almost as if he regrets ruining the moment.

A replica of the Washington Monument's capstone on display in the monument's gallery level, with the inscription *Laus Deo* on the eastern face, July 2016. Photo by the author.

"But, weren't they going to take it down? Is it really still there?"

The people around him murmur in distress. Stacy pauses for a moment, choosing her words carefully. "It's still there," she finally says, *"as far as I know."* She tells us that she had heard the same thing, that "they" were going to take God off of everything, even the Washington Monument. She didn't think it had happened yet. If it were to happen, though, she couldn't help but think of what it says in the Bible, about how if the people cease to praise God, the very stones themselves will cry out.[2] With that enigmatic statement, she dismisses us to take more pictures and make our way back to the bus. The group is subdued, wondering about the fate of *Laus Deo*, and wondering, too, how they would even know if the inscription was removed.

Though Christian tourists traveled to D.C. for the express purpose of seeing America's Christian heritage, their experiences were rarely a straightforward celebration of what they found. Thanks to the outsider narrative and the metanarrative of secularization, they were convinced that, regardless of the power Christians had wielded in the past, Christians were marginalized today. As tourists explored the city, guides amplified the feeling of being marginalized by continually using the outsider narrative to frame their stories about D.C.'s sites. At every opportunity they reminded tourists that Christians were excluded from mainstream politics and culture, as well as from normative accounts of American history. "You wouldn't hear this in public school" was a frequent refrain. Throughout the tours, guides used the outsider narrative to push tourists to play the role of exiles, even as they experienced a tour telling them they ought to be running the country.

In this usage, the outsider narrative speaks to a broader sense of exile among white American evangelicals today. They feel that, like ancient Israel, they have been exiled, in their case from American public life. From their point of view, Christianity is marginalized in classrooms, courtrooms, and popular culture. However, the Israelites returned from their exile, and white evangelicals believe they will do the same. Their sense of alienation depends on their concomitant sense that they ought not to be outsiders at all.[3] They founded the nation, and they believe they will return from exile to save it. This tension between what is and what ought to be characterizes the lived history of Christian heritage tours and white evangelicals more broadly. The insider narrative constructs a nostalgic past of Christian founding and Christian glory, and when measured against it the present invariably falls short. The outsider narrative explains this discrepancy by casting white evangelicals as exiles or victims.

However, the insider and outsider narratives are inherently contradictory, and nothing revealed the tension between them more than tourists' encounters with the various Christian statues, inscriptions, and images that populate D.C.'s landscape. If secularists hold all the power in American politics and culture, as the outsider narrative suggests, one might expect that they would have erased any remnants of Christian heritage from the nation's capital, such as removing *Laus Deo* from the Washington Monument. Of course, this was not the case; plenty of Christian material culture remained for Christian heritage tours to see. These objects, in a sense, joined the conversation. They told a story about Christian presence where tourists expected to find only absence. In doing so, these objects disrupted the outsider narrative, prompting tourists to defend it in creative ways. Their most frequent response was to write the disruptive object itself into the outsider narrative by questioning the object's permanence. Even though it was not gone yet, they said, surely it would be soon. This response allowed them to see that D.C. was full of Christian objects while also maintaining that Christianity had been exiled from D.C. The disruptive objects receded into the background, no longer a contradiction.

Given that Christian heritage tours promise to prove that the United States is a Christian nation, it may seem odd that the outsider narrative is such a central feature of the experience. Their customers are paying for proof that they are founders, not exiles. This incongruity raises some important questions: Why is it so important to Christian heritage tours that their customers retain their outsider identity? What benefit is there to white American evangelicals in remaining on the margins? The outsider narrative performs two key tasks in this context. First, it carves out space for a revisionist Christian heritage history by discrediting all opposing views, including those tourists may have learned from other sources. Whatever tourists may have heard in public schools or in the media becomes untrustworthy, because those sources are anti-Christian according to the outsider narrative. Second, the outsider narrative manufactures tension between white evangelicals and what they see as "mainstream" America. That tension is itself a source of power, since both Christian tradition and American tradition tend to revere outsiders as righteous. The exile role does not supersede or replace the founder role discussed in chapter 1. Rather, it employs a different combination of narratives to offer white evangelicals a new position from which to attempt to save the nation.

FOR SALE: CHRISTIAN AMERICA

The outsider narrative comes into play on Christian heritage tours long before tourists arrive in D.C. Tour companies rely on this narrative in their advertising, using it to convince potential customers that they *need* to purchase a tour in order to repair their damaged view of American history. Advertisements juxtapose the outsider and insider narratives to set up the central theme of Christian heritage tours: something is missing in current accounts of American history. As one tour company's website put it in 2015, "Critical and necessary information has been systematically removed from the teaching of American History, creating a missing 'gap.' It so happens that the missing gap contained the legacy left to today's Christians. They have been effectively robbed of that inheritance." Another advertisement warned potential tourists that "the stories of America's beginnings involving the influence of God and Christianity have been effectively purged." Advertisements raise the alarm, often describing the missing piece in terms of a legacy, an inheritance, or even a birthright. In this view, white evangelicals are entitled to this knowledge, but it has been withheld from them.

Another key move in the marketing formula was to name the parties responsible for the sin of omission. Schools are a recurring villain in these stories, especially public schools. One tour company, for instance, promised to "clearly illustrate how God used people of faith, in critical roles, at critical times. None of these stories appear in school textbooks anymore." But schools are not the only villain. Another tour company highlighted a testimonial from a past customer who blames the media, which "will only give you one side." Several ads mentioned Hollywood specifically. The most frequent culprits, however, are "secularists," a category that encompasses any person or group that opposes a privileged position for Christianity in the United States. "Wielding misapplied separation of church and state arguments, secular groups have worked tirelessly to remove references to God and Christianity from America's public life," read one Christian tour website's introduction. Included in the ranks of secularists are academics in general and historians in particular, especially those who criticize America or Americans. One tour's sample itinerary derisively referred to "Historians" in scare quotes, and another repeatedly reminded readers of the academy's liberal bias that distorts "real" history. Not every advertisement names the parties responsible — there is no need. The outsider narrative has a familiar rotating cast of villains who can be called upon at any point, and the target audience already knows whom to blame.

Marketing materials then remind their audience of the false history that has come to fill the gap and challenge its veracity. "You've heard the stories about this being a secular nation, and the stories that the Founders were all deists," writes one tour company, "but is that the case?" The litany of hearsay goes on: "Most folks believe the phrase 'separation of church and state' is part of the Declaration of Independence or the Constitution. Is that true?" This marketing strategy primes the audience to question its received knowledge of American history, and it also separates them out from "most folks." A key feature of Christian heritage tours is the opposition between the Christian tourists who are in the know and their secular counterparts who are ignorant of the real history of the nation. Tour companies' advertisements are the first step in setting up this dynamic, and they do so by suggesting to potential tourists that they do not want to be on the side of ignorance. They want to know more than "most folks." After all, the well-being of the nation is at stake in this battle over its history.

After setting up this problem, the advertisements reveal the solution: REGISTER NOW! As with any good marketing strategy, that solution is the product for sale. Christian heritage tours of D.C. offer tourists "the rest of the story." One typical tour promises to "expose and resurrect the true history of our nation's founding as a people deeply rooted in faith, finally giving Christians everywhere an accurate portrayal of America envisioned by its founders." In a quintessentially Protestant move, that true history is said to be found in the original texts of the founders themselves. "What do the Founders' own writings (not the writings of a twentieth-century author) tell us about their beliefs?" asks one company's website. "When you see their words engraved in stone, and hear what else they had to say, it becomes clear their intent was to forge a nation built on Christian principles." Another company similarly promises to demonstrate in the founders' "actual words ... their beliefs that America would be exceptional, a blessed nation—One Nation Under God!" In all of their advertisements, Christian heritage tours promise to recover what has been lost, to fill the missing gap with the truth. Washington, D.C., is sold, literally, as incontrovertible evidence for America's Christian heritage.

This use of the outsider narrative to sell "Christian America" works because it resonates with how white evangelicals already understand their relationship to the nation. Tourists themselves consistently drew on the outsider narrative in explaining their decision to join a Christian heritage tour. In follow-up interviews and in casual conversations, they expressed their doubt that they could learn this Christian history from other sources, including secular tours of D.C. They chose a Christian heritage tour because they wanted to experience D.C. from a "Christian perspective." Some referred to a "Christian focus" or even "Christian flavor" that they found appealing. For those who had visited D.C. previously, this Christian perspective was what distinguished this trip from the others. "I just wanted to have an understanding of it [D.C.] from a Christian perspective and just see, be able to bring it all to life again," said Charlene, who traveled from Texas to take the tour with her children and her parents. Another woman, Erica, mentioned her regret that, though she and her husband had visited D.C. with their children a decade earlier, her children did not remember the "Christian aspect" of the visit. "I wish I'd have known then and paid more attention," she told me. "I want to learn this, I want to pass it on to my kids, what I know, what I learn." At the time of her interview, she was considering writing up a summary of what she learned to share with her children, who had not joined her on this trip, but didn't know when she would find the time.

Erica was one of many tourists who prioritized their tour's "Christian perspective" for the sake of the children or grandchildren who joined them in D.C. For Katherine, a middle-school teacher from the Deep South, the tour's main draw was the "Christian value and educational value" it offered the students who came with her. On the same tour, a father from the West Coast, Jacob, explained that it was a long trip for them, but something he and his wife Amy wanted to provide for their children: "It's important for them to see, here's your nation's history, its beginnings, its roots, its monuments, its government, and then also put in that Christian flavor." He later added that he hoped the trip to D.C. would "preempt" the secularist agenda his children would encounter in public school history classes: "If they hear the Christian perspective first, and then they hear the secular perspective, they're kind of in tune to a potential agenda that might go with it." For this family and several others, a Christian heritage tour was a way of defending their children against the sort of distortion of history that the tours' marketing warned about.

The outsider narrative shapes both the marketing of Christian heritage tours and tourists' own explanations for why they choose to participate. It is an ideal vehicle for advertising, and tour companies take full advantage of it. The purported loss of "Christian America" opens a space for products that promise to restore it, at least in part, by offering "Christian" versions of mainstream products. And tour companies are by no means the only businesses to take advantage of it. Christian book publishers, Christian music producers, Christian fitness classes—all these and more are predicated on the notion that Christians (specifically white evangelicals) are outsiders to mainstream culture. An entire subcultural economy depends on Christian consumers feeling excluded by non-Christian products.[4] A cynic might suggest that the outsider narrative is *only* a marketing tool, deployed to convince the gullible to make a purchase, and we should not overlook the fact that companies profit from white evangelical consumers' self-identification as outsiders. However, the outsider narrative is a complex phenomenon that cannot be reduced to a mere tool of the market. It makes for a successful marketing strategy precisely because it resonates with white evangelicals; moreover, its success leads companies to keep using it, which only strengthens its salience among white evangelicals as they hear it over and over. Marketing for Christian products is one way in which the outsider narrative is produced and disseminated as a public narrative among white evangelicals. It both turns a profit for companies that know how to deploy it and perpetuates white evangelicals' sense that they are outsiders.

EXILES FROM HISTORY

When tourists arrived in D.C. for Christian heritage tours, their guides picked up the outsider narrative where the advertisements left off. According to every guide I observed, there were essentially two kinds of American history. In the good kind of history, Christians were unimpeachable heroes of the story, and the Christian God was ultimately in control of events. In the bad kind of history, the Christian faith of American heroes was downplayed or denied, and God never entered the scene. Guides portrayed this second kind of history as mainstream, widely accepted by the academics, the media, and the government, and they used it as a foil to the Christian heritage story.[5] They made frequent references to this "bad" history as they introduced or concluded stories about America's Christian heritage. Through this pattern the outsider narrative became a frame for everything tourists heard. They could not hear about the nation's Christian history without also hearing about how that history is endangered in the present.

According to most guides, the most significant threat to America's Christian history was the public school. White evangelicals and the public schools have long been at odds over everything from school prayer to sex education.[6] Christian tour guides drew on that antagonism to fuel tourists' sense of exile, using diatribes against the public schools to frame episodes of American history. During the first bus ride of one tour, Mark asked his group why Christopher Columbus sailed to the Indies: "What motivated him?" The tourists mumbled a range of indeterminate answers. One man shouted "freedom of religion!" but was ignored. Mark waited for quiet. "We're taught that it was greed or glory," he continued, "but really it was his desire to propagate the gospel." According to Columbus's own Book of Prophecies, written after his third voyage to the New World, he was divinely inspired by God to sail in order to fulfill prophecies in Isaiah. These were Columbus's own words, Mark told us, not the distortions of biased historians. He waited a moment while the amazed tourists digested this bit of information and then delivered his punch line: "Now, were you ever taught that in American history class at school?" "No!" shouted most of the bus. "Well, you've been robbed! Someone has stolen from you the truths you need to know," Mark declared. He then segued into an overview of what they should look for in the paintings in the Capitol Rotunda the next day to recover those stolen truths. Thanks to this juxtaposition, his complaint against the public schools' depiction of Columbus worked on two levels: it framed the brief story about Columbus's motivations, and it framed the entire subsequent discussion of the Rotunda paintings, which tell the origin story of the United States. Tourists were reminded that they could not trust what they had learned from public schools or academic historians.

This pattern was repeated on every tour with a wide range of stories: tour guides would draw attention to tourists' ignorance of Christianity's role in a particular story as a way of introducing or concluding the story itself. But while the guides routinely highlighted the gaps in tourists' knowledge of history, they took care not to blame the tourists for their ignorance. It was not the tourists' fault that they knew so little about their own "birthright." They were victims of the sins of omission of the public schools and secular historians.

Tourists themselves echoed this suspicion of public schools, both in D.C. and in follow-up interviews. Russell and Jeanie were a retired couple from Texas who took Clay's tour, and they expressed their doubts about what students are learning in public schools these days. Their grandchildren were in eighth grade and twelfth grade at the time, Jeanie said, "and of course they're taught history. But is it the history that I was taught?" Russell jumped in: "No, it's politically correct." Jeanie went on, "I just don't think there's a focus on history." The kids on their tour, she said, "don't have a clue." And it's about more than knowing famous people or events, Russell added. "It's good to understand the historic information our country's based on ... but it's more important to understand the Christian perspective. Whether you knew George Washington was the first president or fifth president isn't as important as knowing what George Washington was about." Jeanie murmured in agreement. They both felt lucky to have access to the real history of the country, but they worried for generations that would grow up not knowing any better. The public schools could not be trusted to teach the truth, they felt, and they were far from alone. History education is just one more area where white evangelicals see themselves being pushed to the margins by a progressive agenda.

One phrase more than any other encapsulated this problem: the separation of church and state. Tourists and guides used this phrase sarcastically as a shorthand version of the outsider narrative, a quick way to remind everyone in earshot that Christians had been exiled from the public square in a way that the founders did not intend. As Mark's colleague Dan put it, "Separation of church and state is a phrase modern courts have misconstrued to mean 'let's kick God out of public life.'" Guides dwelled at length on the incongruity of the founders' own actions and twenty-first-century interpretations of Jefferson's famous phrase. The founders went to seminary, quoted the Bible, and supported prayer in the legislatures, but "we're told they were a bunch of atheists—who had prayer meetings! Pretty good for a bunch of atheists," said Mark sarcastically. Several guides also quoted Washington's Thanksgiving Proclamation, which begins, "It is the duty of all nations to acknowledge the providence of Almighty God, to obey His will, to be grateful for His benefits, and humbly implore His protection and favor."[7] Of course, they hastened to add, no academic historian would mention that.

Mark's tours in particular mocked today's interpretations of separation of church and state by juxtaposing them with evidence from the life and writings of Jefferson himself. During one visit to the Jefferson Memorial, he told us that Jefferson wanted to be remembered as the founder of the University of Virginia, which has been called the first secular university in the United States. In reality, he said, the school was only nonsectarian, and students still studied theology and attended chapel every day. "This is our so-called 'secular' university!" he added derisively, making a scare quotes gesture on "secular." In this case, Jefferson's actions (and those of the students at his university) spoke louder than his famous letter to the Danbury Baptists in which he first articulated the principle of separation. Mark also pointed out the references to God inside the Jefferson Memorial to corroborate this point, most notably the phrase encircling the inner dome: "I have sworn upon the altar of God eternal hostility against any form of tyranny over the mind of man." Surely no atheist would have made such a declaration!

This purported ignorance on the part of liberals or secularists when it comes to interpreting separation of church and state or other founding doctrines was a consistent frame on Christian heritage tours. Guides juxtaposed academic interpretations with selected writings or actions of the founders themselves in order to reveal the discrepancy between the two. Jonathan told his tourists about a school prayer case in which Christian heritage maker David Barton filed an amicus brief that drew on his private collection of the founders' personal papers. When Barton quoted a letter, Jonathan exclaimed, he was "reading from the original!" The judges in the case, however, rejected Barton's evidence that the founders prayed at public events, moving Jonathan to conclude that the judges must have thought "the founders were either hypocrites or they didn't understand what the Constitution said." Several tourists groaned in dismay, as Jonathan shouted at the absent judges, "You idiots! You think you know more than the men who debated it for four months?" Such stories were almost comical in their caricatures of liberals who refuse to see the text in front of them, but those same caricatured liberals were said to be the ones in power. Ironic references to "separation of church and state" reminded tourists that, regardless of the stories they heard or the sites they saw, Christianity was exiled from the public square.

TAKING BACK THE NATION

Like the insider narrative, the outsider narrative has roots in earlier moments in American history, but it gained new force and purpose in the 1970s in the hands of leaders of the Christian Right. Even as they rewrote American history to claim for themselves the role of founders and stewards of the nation, these leaders embraced their status as outsiders, casting themselves first as exiles and later as victims. They defended their position on the margins at the same time that they lamented their loss of power. This move, however, was strategic, and we should view such outsider claims with a degree of skepticism. The rhetoric of deviance is a tool, and it may be wielded by the powerful and the marginalized alike.[8] To take any group's claim to outsider status at face value, as many scholars have done with both fundamentalists and, more recently, white evangelicals, is to risk overlooking the advantage gained by strategic claims of marginality.

Outsiderhood has long been a source of power in both the Christian tradition and the American mind. The Hebrew Bible and the New Testament are replete with stories of righteous younger sons, victorious underdogs, and redeemed outcasts. The ancient Israelites were slaves in Egypt, without power yet chosen by God. The Hebrew prophets were outsiders; so were the Apostles. According to the Gospels, Jesus himself preferred the company of the socially marginalized—lepers, prostitutes, children—to the company of those in power, who ultimately crucified him. These stories resonated with the early English settlers who shaped how white American Protestants would understand their role in the New World. The Pilgrims and Puritans saw themselves as righteous outsiders fleeing the oppressive Church of England, just as the Israelites fled Egypt. And when the colonies revolted against the powerful British Empire, there was no question that the Americans were the underdogs. Since the beginning, there has been something glamorous about being an outsider in America, a nation that cheers for underdogs and vilifies establishments.

Many groups have strategically cast themselves as outsiders in American history, but few so effectively as Christian fundamentalists during the early twentieth century.[9] As they diverged from modernist (or mainline) Protestants, these white conservative Protestants capitalized on their marginality, even as they claimed to resent it. Though scholars have tended to exaggerate how marginalized fundamentalists were after the Scopes trial in 1925, their exaggerations are understandable given how loudly fundamentalists themselves proclaimed their exile. At the time, being "a beleaguered minority fighting with their backs to the wall" was theologically defensible, politically expedient, and occasionally even lucrative.[10] Fundamentalist leaders had discovered the power of appearing powerless. As a result, they highlighted their losses and made a show of their defeat at the hands of the mainline.[11] The reality of their strength within mainline denominations, not to mention corporate America, was beside the point.

Americans' reverence for the outsider grew even stronger in the second half of the twentieth century, when a wide range of white middle-class Americans began to depict themselves as outsiders. They saw in that identity an alluring sort of moral capital, the product of centuries of Christian and American tradition. This romance of the outsider, as historian Grace Hale calls it, was "a knot of desire, fantasy, and identification . . . the belief that people somehow marginal to society possess cultural resources and values missing among other Americans."[12] Hippies, Jesus People, and young political conservatives all cast themselves as outsiders, finding new meaning and power in marginality even as they retained the privileges that came with being white and middle class. Whereas fundamentalists in previous decades had lamented their (admittedly often self-imposed) outsider status, the new outsiders celebrated their distance from the mainstream. By the end of the 1970s, the romance of the outsider had worked its way into white fundamentalist and evangelical discourse as well. These conservative Protestants ceased to see their marginality as a loss and began to see it as an advantage.[13] Conservative Christians learned to claim the moral authority of the outsider, and they turned that moral authority to a duty they have always felt was theirs: saving the nation.

On July 4, 1976, Moral Majority founder Jerry Falwell celebrated the nation's bicentennial with a call to action: "This idea of 'religion and politics don't mix' was invented by the devil to keep Christians from running their own country," he said.[14] The Father of Lies had convinced conservative Christians that their place was on the political and cultural sidelines, but it was time for them to take back their rightful place at the center. This was an abrupt change of heart for Falwell, who had criticized Rev. Martin Luther King Jr. a decade earlier for being too political.[15] But now, according to Falwell, the only way America could return to God and avert destruction was for conservative Christians to return to politics. In another sermon a few years later, Falwell elaborated on this call to action:

For too long, we have sat back and said politics are for the people in Washington, business is for those on Wall Street, and religion is our

business. But the fact is, you cannot separate the sacred and the secular.... If we are going to turn this country around, we have to get God's people mobilized in the right direction and we must do it quickly....
If all the fundamentalists knew who to vote for and did it together, we could elect anybody. If every one of these people could be intelligently taught and mobilized, brother, we could turn this nation upside down for God.... We preachers have to teach some Solomons how to build a new national house. This nation has to be rebuilt.[16]

In Falwell's view, conservative Christians were outsiders, with all the attendant moral authority—but they ought to be insiders. He and other leaders of the Christian Right would go on to create a jeremiad to that effect. Like ancient Israel, they argued, they had been exiled from their homeland. Their exile was not literal but metaphorical, in the sense that they were absent from most high-profile political and cultural institutions following the Scopes trial. And they, too, wanted to take their nation back from its conquerors and rebuild. Even as conservative Christians gained political, cultural, and economic power, their dominant motif in this period was exile, playing on the dissonance between what was and what ought to be.[17]

It is worth noting here the productive tension between the exile motif and the moniker chosen by Falwell for his organization: the "Moral Majority." While Falwell's group by no means represented the whole of the Christian Right, the Christian Right did claim to represent the moral views of the majority of Americans. Richard A. Viguerie wrote in 1981, "There is a new majority in America, and it is being led by the New Right," which is "in harmony with the deepest sentiments of the American people."[18] In this respect, Falwell was conjuring up a narrative in which white Christians ought to be insiders by virtue of both tradition and sheer numbers. This majority, however, was in exile from the institutions of political and cultural power, which were held by what Falwell and others called the "godless minority."[19] We thus should not conflate the claim to numerical superiority with a claim to political dominance. The generative power of the image of an exiled Moral Majority lay precisely in its dissonance. It seemed illogical in a democracy that a minority could seize power, but the Christian Right argued that this was precisely what had happened. That dissonance justified the majority's efforts to retake their rightful place in command of the nation's political and cultural institutions.

The Christian Right's image as an exiled majority allowed them to benefit from both insider and outsider rhetoric in this period. While its leaders claimed to represent the values of the majority, they did not hesitate to draw on the language and strategies of other outsider groups. By the late 1970s, there was already a cultural script for outsider groups seeking acceptance in the mainstream, a script used by movements for African Americans' civil rights, women's rights, gay rights, and so on. Conservative Christians found that this script fit their cause as well. "It's amazing what we've learned from feminists and the other side," Falwell said in 1982. "Civil rights people had that kind of backbone to stand up for their freedom, and Christians better have that kind of backbone, too."[20] Others, like pollster George Gallup Jr., called for conservative Christians to "bring [their] religious feelings out of the closet."[21] They should not be satisfied with being "second class," according to Pat Robertson.[22] These leaders positioned white conservative Christians alongside other persecuted outsiders in mid-twentieth-century America, and it proved an effective strategy. By the end of the Reagan administration, white evangelicals had become a powerful voting bloc and a core constituency of the Republican Party. Falwell shut down the Moral Majority in 1989, saying he had succeeded in his mission of activating the Christian Right.[23] Even as they gained power, however, they continued to play the role of exile when it was expedient, adapting it to better fit their new roles in the highest echelons of government.

FROM EXILES TO VICTIMS

Under the leadership of Robertson and Ralph Reed's Christian Coalition, conservative Christians became a new kind of outsider. Previously they had imagined themselves as exiles longing for home. In the 1990s, however, they were more like exiles who had returned home only to find themselves unwelcome there. They had gained entry to the halls of power, but they maintained their outsider posture by highlighting the resistance their presence inspired. Such resistance was real—the 1994 elections in particular sparked a media frenzy over the "evangelical takeover" of the Republican Party— but it was also convenient for white evangelical leaders who had built their brand as outsiders. Reed in particular seemed to relish the opposition to conservative Christians in government, invoking it even while insisting that the Christian Right was playing by the same rules as everyone else. During the 1994 elections, he said, "Other movements have gone through phases similar to ours. Civil rights activists and feminists started in the trenches and then obtained mainstream political power. Now it's our turn. If moderates complain, they have to keep in mind that we're the ones licking the envelopes and burning the shoe leather. The only crime that the Christian

Right has committed is the crime of democracy."[24] By 1996 he would acknowledge that their efforts had paid off: conservative Christians were "no longer greenhorns throwing rocks at the castle" but were "actually inside the castle."[25] Even then, however, his characterization of his constituents as "greenhorns" reflected the useful derision directed at them by the mainstream. Reed acknowledged that he had gained power, but he seemed not quite ready to give up his posture as an exile.

At the same time, some of the Christian Coalition's rhetoric hinted at the shift in roles that was to come in the twenty-first century, as white evangelicals began to play the role of victims in addition to the role of exiles. They recast their core issues in liberal terms of rights and freedoms rather than God-given morality. They turned abortion into a debate over the "rights of the unborn" and school prayer into a matter of "students' rights"; conversely, they attacked the gay rights movement for seeking "special rights" over and above those afforded to heterosexuals. They also co-opted liberals' terms for their opponents, accusing them of "bigotry" and "discrimination."[26] They claimed to be asking only that their rights be respected alongside those of other minorities. Mike Farris, founder of the Home School Legal Defense Association, told *Newsweek* in 1994 that if black students could opt out of reading Mark Twain because of racial slurs in the text, then "religious Christians shouldn't be forced to read books that are offensive to them."[27] As he saw it, schools were discriminating against Christians by treating them differently from other protected groups. The American Center for Law and Justice was founded at Regent University in Virginia in 1990 to protect "the rights of Christians." Its chief counsel, Jay Sekulow, said at the time, "We are on the offensive. We will no longer stand for Christians being victims."[28] This was a far cry from Falwell's call to "take back America." The Christian Right of the Clinton years was slowly but surely shifting toward the language of victimization that would characterize it in the new millennium.

Yet in the 1990s this outsider rhetoric existed in palpable tension with the reality of the Christian Right's power. In 1994 Republicans took control of both houses of Congress for the first time in forty years, due in large part to the efforts of Robertson and Reed's Christian Coalition.[29] They were well funded and well organized, enough to drive the impeachment of a Democratic president later in the decade. Nonetheless, they maintained their posture as outsiders fighting for every ounce of political capital. In this they were aided and abetted by the news media: journalists routinely wrote about the conservative Christian "takeover" of the Republican Party, portraying Christians as interlopers at best. Occasionally their portrayals were openly hostile. In 1993 the *Washington Post* famously characterized the Christian Right's supporters as "largely poor, uneducated, and easy to command."[30] The leaders of the Christian Right harnessed the ensuing outrage by accusing the media of elitism and handing out buttons that read "poor, uneducated, and easy to command" to their supporters on Capitol Hill. Far from hurting the Christian Right, such disdain generated politically expedient outrage at the grassroots level. In the months before the 1994 election, political analyst Sara Diamond warned against dismissing the Christian Right as "extremists." To do so, she said, would only "increase their claimed underdog status."[31] She was right to recognize that continuing to treat white evangelicals as outsiders only strengthened them. Doing so obscured the fact that conservative Christians were no longer really political outsiders at all. Yet the Christian Right continued to benefit from the claim that it represented an exiled or victimized majority.

None of this is to say that the Christian Right did not suffer losses during the 1990s. On the contrary, they lost important battles, not least of which was the battle to remove President Bill Clinton from office over his involvement with Monica Lewinsky. That loss proved profoundly destabilizing, as it underscored the fact that if there ever had been a "moral majority" in the United States, it was now nowhere to be found. Approximately two-thirds of Americans opposed the impeachment process, and when Clinton was acquitted he had an approval rating of 73 percent.[32] In the aftermath of the impeachment hearings, some pundits celebrated what they thought was the end of the Christian Right, and some conservative Christians did exit the political arena and call for an end to the culture wars.[33] But to take these losses as evidence for the outsider narrative is to miss an important function of that narrative. As historian R. Laurence Moore argues, any rhetoric of deviance or conformity carries with it a "counterimage" that historians ignore at their peril. Declarations of marginality tend to indicate that the self-proclaimed outsiders are sure of their significance and security, and conservative Christians in the 1990s were both a significant political force and securely entrenched in the Republican Party.[34] They may have failed to impeach Clinton, but they set the topics and terms of policy debates in D.C. for most of his administration, and they made significant gains on issues like Don't Ask, Don't Tell and religious liberty in the public schools. They also consolidated power at both the state and local levels, including city councils and school boards.[35] By the end of the decade they had found their way into all levels of American political life, where they would remain for the foreseeable future.

ERASING THE EVIDENCE

The Christian Right's exile motif has been embedded in the discourse of Christian heritage tours from the beginning. Since the late 1980s, conservative Christian culture warriors have criticized the government and especially the National Park Service for erasing or obscuring the Christian features of many D.C. sites. In their view these features are endangered by the removal of artifacts, renovations of sites, and revisions to signs and guidebooks. Catherine Millard, one of the earliest Christian heritage tour guides in the city, argued in 1991 that the U.S. government was failing to preserve artifacts relevant to the Christian heritage of the nation, including presidential Bibles. She also documented changes to captions at various historical sites, including the Supreme Court, that deleted references to Christianity.[36] Since 2005 the conservative Christian website WND has reported on controversies surrounding Christian features of D.C. sites and on purported government attempts to erase Christianity.[37] A small industry of Christian guidebooks to D.C. emerged in response, many written by prominent advocates of Christian heritage history.[38] And, of course, Christian heritage tours both create and respond to white evangelicals' feeling that the nation's true Christian history is being deliberately obscured.

Christian tourists arrived in D.C. already aware of these threats. Ruth, a senior citizen from Georgia, was eager to tell me all about them at dinner our first night in D.C. She had heard there was lots of Christian history to be found in D.C., and she was looking forward to learning about it. "In Georgia, unfortunately, we have Common Core," she said apologetically, so no one learned much about American history. But she knew that we had "strayed so far from our founding." Others at the table nodded in agreement. One woman added, "I heard they're trying to take God out of the pledge [of allegiance]." Ruth went on, explaining that she wanted a Christian heritage tour because she had heard that the script for officially licensed D.C. tour guides deletes more about Christianity every year. Officially licensed guides, she said, "aren't even allowed to point out Christian things." They could mention them only if people specifically asked about them. "I heard that, too," said someone else at the table. The people we were sitting with greeted this news with disappointment but not surprise. They took for granted that Christianity was under attack and that such an attack would include an assault on any material evidence of the nation's Christian heritage in the capital.

Like Stacy's group described earlier in this chapter, many tourists I met had heard a rumor that *Laus Deo* was about to be (or had already been) removed from the Washington Monument.[39] Occasionally the guide would prompt them—"Have you heard what they're going to do to it?"—but more often the tourists would initiate the conversation. They arrived in D.C. expecting to find their God and their praise erased. Only one guide, Marian, responded to such questions with any optimism. She, too, had heard that "they were going to take God off of everything," but to do so they would have to climb to the top of the Washington Monument and erase it there—a task she declared to be impossible. "God's name is etched in stone everywhere," she said, "and it will stay there as long as our democracy survives." Her tourists responded with defiant amens.[40] Most guides, however, did little to dissuade their tourists from their pessimistic outlook.

Some guides further reinforced this pessimism in their discussions of another notable Christian feature of the Washington Monument, the inscriptions on the interior faces of its marble blocks. These stones were donated in honor of George Washington by a variety of groups and organizations, including American states and foreign countries. Each one is inscribed with messages and symbols, many of which are inflected with Christian sentiments. During the tours I observed, guides read examples of these inscriptions, particularly those donated by Sunday School societies that include direct quotations from scripture. Almost immediately, however, they added that unfortunately almost no one could see those inscriptions anymore. Because of structural instability caused by an earthquake in 2011 and concerns about vandalism to the interior of the monument, very few public tours are allowed to take the stairs. And while the elevator does slow to display some of the stones, none of those stones are the ones with Christian inscriptions.

Despite the fact that *Laus Deo* and the interior inscriptions remained intact, every element of their context worked to make them invisible.[41] Their inconvenient locations, the earthquake damage to the structure, the choices made by elevator engineers, the scarcity of tickets—together, these features of the site kept Christian tourists from seeing the inscriptions they came to see, enabling guides to make the case that the government was trying to erase Christianity from American history. No one could see them, after all, so they might as well be invisible. In fact, who was to say that they were really still there? Since tourists had no way of seeing the apex or interior of the monument, most of them typically went along with this attitude. It was a useful way to avoid the disruption that seeing these Christian inscriptions would have caused.

Christian tourists' encounters with the Washington Monument revealed how the insider and outsider narratives work together in their lived history. At first tourists were cheered by the presence of Christian inscriptions in such a prominent place. They heard an insider story about Christianity's central place in American history, a story corroborated by the monument's apex and interior inscriptions. But that story and its material evidence challenged tourists' equally strong conviction that today, at least, Christians are no longer insiders in America. The inscriptions disrupted the outsider narrative, creating cognitive dissonance. In this case, the dissonance was easily resolved by the suggestion that the inscriptions were threatened, a threat made more plausible by their invisibility. In a sense, the inscriptions were written into the outsider narrative: Christians themselves had been exiled from D.C., and any lingering material evidence of America's Christian heritage would soon follow.

The power of the outsider narrative is such that Christian tourists found a way to believe it even when they were standing in front of the objects that contradict it. In the House of Representatives' chamber at the U.S. Capitol, the front of the room is dominated by a gold inscription, "In God We Trust," over the speaker's rostrum.[42] It was impossible to miss, but our guides (and sometimes our congressional representatives) highlighted it in their talks anyway. However, their point was not to reassure visitors of Congress's piety. Downstairs in the Visitor Center, they told us, is a replica of this very room. It is perfect in every detail, except for one: "In God We Trust" was missing from it when it was initially constructed. Why? Because at the time, Democrats had control of both houses of Congress. Three tour guides and two congressmen told this story to different groups, with almost no variation. After giving the tourists a moment to groan in dismay, they continued on to describe how Representative Randy Forbes of Virginia saved the day. Forbes, a Republican and the founder of the Congressional Prayer Caucus, stopped construction on the Visitor Center entirely by blocking funding for any further work until "In God We Trust" was added to the replica. The story had a happy ending: the inscription was added and construction went on. But in some sense the worst had already happened—God had been erased, albeit on a replica—and what was to stop this from happening again?

Like the *Laus Deo* example, this story moved between the insider and outsider narratives, but it also added two important dimensions to the perceived threat. First, the heroes in the story were Republicans, and the villains were Democrats. Second, the story suggested that threats to material Christianity should not go unchallenged. Conservative Christians should, like Forbes, take action to protect material evidence of their heritage. Taken together, these two aspects of the story prompted listeners to take political action on behalf of Republicans in order to protect the capital's Christian objects from Democrats' erasers.

Elsewhere in the Capitol, Christian tourists expressed a sense of urgency to see other Christian objects while they still could. Among these objects were the many statues of Christian ministers and missionaries that populate National Statuary Hall, major hallways, and parts of the Visitor Center. Every state is allowed to send two statues of famous, deceased citizens to represent it in the national collection, and many of these have some connection to Christianity. One such figure is Jason Lee of Oregon (1803–1845), a missionary and pioneer whose statue was sent to the Capitol by his state in 1953. However, in the summer of 2015, a couple from Oregon reported to me that there were plans afoot in their state to replace Lee with someone else. Jacob and Amy were distressed that Lee might be replaced with a less godly figure, and they saw his Christianity as the obvious cause for his removal. "So here we have a Christian missionary who is instrumental to the founding of our state being removed because, let's face it, Oregon is probably one of the least churched, least Christian states in the country," Jacob told me in a follow-up interview. "And for us to go there and still see him there, for me that was kind of like, oh, let's get our picture now, because this isn't going to be our future." As it turns out, his worry was well founded: in February 2016 the Oregon House of Representatives approved a bill to commission new statues of Chief Joseph and former senator Mark Hatfield.[43] The bill was blocked by the state senate, but a 2017 bill proposed statues of Chief Joseph and women's rights advocate Abigail Scott Duniway.[44] Oregon lawmakers may be divided on whom they should honor in the Capitol, but they have made it clear that it will not be Jason Lee.

In each of these instances, Christian objects disrupted the outsider narrative simply by being present. In response, guides and tourists identified physical threats that loomed in the near future or, in the case of the House of Representatives replica, had already been carried out but subsequently reversed. This strategy allowed tourists to maintain both the insider and outsider narratives despite their contradictory claims and the cognitive dissonance created by the presence of Christian objects. Tourists could use the objects to corroborate their claims about the nation's Christian past, but they could also maintain their present role as exiles. As they saw it, no matter how many Christian objects remained in D.C., Christians themselves had been pushed to the margins. Soon enough, the objects would follow.

Bronze statue of missionary Jason Lee sent by the state of Oregon to the
National Statuary Hall of the U.S. Capitol, July 2016. Photo by the author.

UNMARKED PROTESTANTISM

If Christian heritage tours are designed to prove that America is a Christian nation, why did they spend so much time convincing tourists that American Christians are outsiders? In this context, the outsider narrative accomplished two important tasks. The first is that it made space for an alternative, Christian-centric account of American history and insulated that account from criticism.[45] Tour guides often alluded to the "wrong" history that tourists might have heard from other sources, including the public schools. This framing was more than just a convenient rhetorical device. Tourists really might have heard conflicting accounts of American history from sources they trusted. Guides could use the outsider narrative to discredit mainstream versions of American history by telling a story in which the government, public schools, and academia were working overtime to expunge Christianity from the historical record. This narrative gave tourists a reason to mistrust anything they "might have heard," challenging the legitimacy of what tourists had heard from other sources. Moreover, this use of the outsider narrative also gave tourists a story into which they could plot future challenges to the Christian heritage story. They could simply dismiss any critique they later encountered as anti-Christian bias.[46]

The second task of the outsider narrative is to maintain tension between white evangelicals and what they see as the American mainstream. This is true both in the context of Christian heritage tours and in the broader discourse of white evangelicals in the United States. Tension with the so-called mainstream confers the moral authority of the outsider on any marginalized group, and white evangelicals are no exception. Moreover, in a religiously diverse society, a religious group must make diversity work for it rather than against it in order to thrive.[47] One way to do this is for the group to incorporate its opposition to what it sees as the mainstream into its identity, positioning itself as a subculture. This, in essence, is what the outsider narrative does. It makes "tension, conflict, and threat" a defining feature of white American evangelicalism, such that mainstream opposition does not destabilize the subculture's identity but reinforces it.[48]

In reality, however, Christians (and especially white Protestants) are not outsiders in the United States in anything like the same way that African Americans, religious minorities, or other historically marginalized groups are outsiders. Christian heritage proponents are not wrong when they argue that Christianity has played an important role in many moments of American history.[49] The reason it matters here is that today's so-called mainstream has been shaped by centuries of Christian influence, to the point that its Christian features are so taken for granted that they go unnoticed. In the same way that ambient Christianity permeates D.C.'s landscape, so too do Protestant ideas and values permeate American politics and culture.[50] Sociologist Lynne Gerber notes that this implicit Christian dimension of "mainstream" America creates a convenient resemblance between it and the (white) evangelical subculture. The two agree, for instance, on moralizing discourses around weight and health because of their Christian influences.[51] Because of the historical dominance of Christianity, the values of white evangelicals and the mainstream align more often than it would first appear.[52] The result of this "unmarked Protestantism" is that white evangelicals can easily collaborate with the purported mainstream when their values align.[53]

Yet just as unmarked Protestantism enables white evangelicals' collaboration with the culture around them, so too does it complicate their efforts to distinguish themselves from what they see as the mainstream. The tension needed for the white evangelical subculture to thrive does not arise naturally, as the subculture has too much in common with the still implicitly Christian mainstream.[54] Instead, white evangelical leaders must manufacture the necessary tension through rhetorical means. This is what the outsider narrative accomplishes: it creates tension by teaching white evangelicals to see themselves as exiles or victims, always at the mercy of a hostile mainstream culture.

Studying Christian heritage tours reveals this dynamic in action. Though the tours' stated purpose is to teach tourists about Christianity's profound influence on the nation, doing so risks undermining white evangelicals' sense of tension with the mainstream. Framing every Christian heritage site or story with the outsider narrative solves this problem. Tourists hear that they are outsiders before and after they hear about the nostalgic past in which people like them were insiders. Even relics from that nostalgic past are plotted into the outsider narrative, cast as endangered artifacts that will soon be removed. The outsider narrative distances tourists from the Christian heritage stories they hear by repeatedly asserting that those stories are history. Regardless of how important Christianity was in the American past, it is said to have little or no bearing on the present. It may, however, return to impact the future of the nation.

The outsider narrative maintains white evangelicals' sense of alienation during Christian heritage tours—and beyond. It helps to shore up white evangelicals' tension with the mainstream whenever it seems that perhaps they are more insiders than outsiders. The reality is that nearly every aspect of American politics and culture is marked by the legacy of Christianity, and white evangelicals remain a powerful force in the United States today. The outsider narrative rewrites this reality by providing white evangelicals with a plot in which they play the role of exiles. It teaches them to look for ways in which they are oppressed rather than privileged. And it shifts their focus to events that fit into this story of alienation, leading them to render invisible events and objects that might cast them in a different role.

When they take on the role of exiles, white evangelicals still do not cede any power. Whereas the role of founders claims the authority of tradition, the role of exiles claims the moral high ground of the outsider. In a nation steeped in Christian reverence for the marginalized, casting oneself as the underdog is a savvy political move. In recent elections, many American politicians have capitalized on this attitude, claiming to run as outsiders even when they were working in tandem with the establishment. White evangelicals make the same move every day, to similar effect. In the twenty-first century, however, they have also found power as another kind of outsider. When being an exile fails to yield the desired results, they can cast themselves as victims.

Chapter 3 **Victims**

Perched atop Mount Saint Alban in the northwest quadrant of D.C., the Washington National Cathedral is an eye-catching silhouette in the capital's skyline. Its imposing neo-Gothic edifice brings to mind the great cathedrals of Europe, while its decorative details reflect its American context. As our tour group gets off the bus, people scatter across the front lawn to snap pictures of every angle. I kneel, trying to get the whole facade in my shot, and see several others doing the same. As we approach the main doors, people pause to admire the detailed reliefs over the door. Some look even farther up, hoping to spot the famous Darth Vader gargoyle.

Entering the cool shade of the vestibule is a relief after the July heat outside. We continue down the aisle, most of us still staring upward. Flags of the fifty states line the nave, and the stained glass windows depict stories from the Bible alongside American achievements such as the moon landing. A docent in bright purple robes comes over to greet us, welcoming us to the "National House of Prayer." She begins to tell us about the history of the cathedral, which was built in the early twentieth century, and lists some of the major events in American life that have been held here. Martin Luther King Jr. gave his final Sunday sermon from that pulpit, she tells us, pointing at it. Presidents' funerals have been held here, including Ronald Reagan's. A memorial service for the victims of the September 11th terrorist attacks also took place here. We ponder this history as we quietly follow her down to the crossing for a closer look at the pulpit and the high altar. I catch a few people looking skeptical. Our tour guide, Marian, is Episcopalian, but she may be the only one in our group accustomed to such high church aesthetics.

West facade of the Washington National Cathedral, July 2014. Photo by the author.

As the docent leads us through one of the side chapels, two women from our group pause in front of the altar. They look at each other and shrug, then kneel together at the altar rail. They shift around experimentally, as if they're just testing it out. One closes her eyes in prayer. After a moment, they stand and join the rest of us as we exit the chapel. On our way out, I ask them what they think so far. "Of all this?" one says, raising her eyebrows and gesturing around her. "Is all this really necessary? It's too much." She shakes her head. "Jesus wouldn't want this," she says with conviction. Still following our docent, we descend into the crypt for a short lecture on the damage to the cathedral wrought by the 2011 earthquake in D.C., followed by a reminder that all donations go to maintain the building. Our visit concludes the old-fashioned way, exiting through the gift shop.

Many of the tourists in this group seemed uncomfortable during their visit, which was unsurprising. Aesthetically, the cathedral was strange to them, but their discomfort stemmed from more than that. It may be the most prominent symbol of Christianity in D.C., but as far as most Christian tourists were concerned, the National Cathedral hardly represented Christianity at all, as it is affiliated with the liberal-leaning Episcopal church. Jonathan said his groups usually skip the site. The docents, he said, "take great delight in talking about all the people who preach in the cathedral. God, he's a jealous God. I don't think he wants the Dalai Lama in a cathedral." His groups' time was better spent at other sites, he explained. "It's a beautiful building, but I'm going to see it as a work of architecture rather than a place of worship."

However, the main point of contention for most Christian tourists was not interfaith services but same-sex weddings. Another guide, Dan, explained why his groups avoid the cathedral: "We're basically a conservative group of people, and the National Cathedral started marrying homosexuals. And so, they're an active Episcopal church, they made the decision to do that, so we just made the decision not to support that, you know. As soon as I tell our people that reason, they fully understand, because they're not supportive of that either." Instead of hailing the cathedral as a prominent symbol of Christian power in the nation's capital, Christian tourists saw it as emblematic of the corruption of mainline Protestantism, corruption that had been enshrined on the highest hill in Washington, D.C. "The Bible I read doesn't say God's inclusive about that, and they were pealing the bells the day they decided to do that," Jonathan said with obvious disgust. "Clearly, God has left the building."

The fact that the United States even has a national church could be taken to indicate the central place of Christianity in the nation, the ultimate proof for the insider narrative. For the Christian tourists and guides I met, however, it was the wrong kind of Christianity. Throughout the tours, they consistently excluded mainline Protestantism from their stories about the nation's Christian heritage. By their logic, Washington and Jefferson may have attended Episcopalian churches like this one, but Episcopalians were not the true heirs to the founders. On the contrary, they had betrayed the founders' legacy by conforming to the norms of secular culture. Yet while white evangelicals fought to uphold what they perceived as the founders' legacy by advocating for conservative moral values and a public presence for Christianity, the Episcopalian church occupied this prime position as the symbolic home of American Christianity. Even here Christian tourists felt like outsiders. But they were not outsiders in the sense of exiles who would someday reclaim the nation and right its wrongs. Rather, they were victims of a hostile culture, a persecuted minority at odds with everyone around them, even others claiming to be fellow Christians.

This feeling of victimization is widespread and growing among white American evangelicals. In 2016, 59 percent of white evangelical Protestants believed that America was no longer a Christian nation, up from 48 percent in 2012.[1] Seventy-seven percent of white evangelicals felt that discrimination against Christians in America was as great a problem as discrimination against racial or ethnic minority groups. Relatedly, 68 percent believed reverse discrimination against whites was a problem.[2] According to sociologist Robert P. Jones, these findings indicate that white evangelicals are mourning the demise of "white Christian America."[3] Where once they reigned unquestioned over politics and culture (or so they believe), they must now negotiate or cede territory to newcomers. In the process, they risk being mistreated by newcomers who do not share or respect their values.[4] This sense of victimization was present during Bill Clinton's administration, particularly after the impeachment proceedings that failed to remove him from office, but it was during Barack Obama's presidency that white evangelicals fully developed their role as victims. The subtle difference in language has real consequences for evangelicals' political activity. In their exile role, white evangelicals are interested in reforming the nation to conform to their values. As victims, they are ostensibly interested only in protecting themselves and their own religious beliefs and practices.

Christian heritage tours played on this sense of victimization in D.C., depicting white evangelicals as strangers in what Jerry Falwell once called "their own country."[5] Guides invoked the long tradition of Christian persecution and martyrdom, reminding tourists that to be Christian means to face opposition from worldly powers. Around the world, Christians were suffering and dying for their faith—why should American Christians expect any different? For their part, tourists readily believed that they were being treated unfairly by American society in general and the D.C. establishment in particular. Each time they had to empty their pockets to pass through security, and each time a guard scolded them for speaking too loudly, it reinforced their feelings of mistreatment. Being a tourist is inherently alienating and uncomfortable, but in this case the experience complemented the larger message of the tour. If tourists ever needed a reminder that they were mistreated, they had only to notice their aching feet.

Like the exile role discussed in chapter 2, the victim role offers white evangelicals a position from which to claim the moral authority of an outsider in tension with the purported mainstream. But it, too, can be easily disrupted when tourists encounter the myriad Christian objects, images, and inscriptions that Christian heritage tours make visible. In response to such disruptions, Christian tourists wrote these objects into the outsider narrative by suggesting not that they were about to be physically removed, but that they were threatened in a different way. They cast the objects, like themselves, as victims. These interactions illustrated the dynamic relationship between religious objects and religious identities: the same object can stabilize an identity or disrupt it. How an object acts on a person depends on the whole assemblage in which the interaction unfolds. And how a person responds depends on, among other things, what role they want to play.

In their interactions with these disruptive objects, Christian tourists demonstrated how they can move between the insider and outsider narratives by identifying different kinds of threats. In doing so, they modeled one strategy that white evangelicals can use to make similar moves in a broader context, which is to recreate their feelings of alienation by identifying threats to themselves and their values. Such threats can take many forms: sharia law, Common Core education standards, and forcing pastors to perform same-sex weddings were just a few I heard mentioned by Christian tourists. All three are familiar specters in white evangelical discourse. Hyperbolic or not, these threats serve to cast white evangelicals as victims of a hostile society in which their values have been widely deemed regressive and unconstitutional. In today's culture wars, there could be no stronger position.

Legend has it that Washington, D.C., was built on top of a literal swamp, and generations of disgruntled Americans have found it an apt metaphor.[6] Christian tourists were no exception. They had little good to say about the city in its present form, much less the Obama administration then in power. They took for granted that the federal government was the domain of secularists and that in D.C. they were trespassing on enemy territory. Their suspicions were often confirmed by the D.C. residents they met. "It's not easy to be Christian and conservative inside the Beltway," said one guest speaker, a conservative Christian lobbyist. "It's like we're the last of the Mohicans," he added, shaking his head sadly. Tourists near him nodded, unsurprised by this claim. Another guest speaker who worked in conservative media mentioned the difficulty of finding a good Bible study group near the Hill. He eventually had to start his own, but it was only for men. In response to a question from the group, his female assistant said at the time that there was no similar group for women, at least not yet. By all accounts, "real" Christians were few and far between in American government these days.[7]

For that matter, "real" Christians were hard to find outside D.C. as well, according to many tourists, guides, and guest speakers. Several indicated that the United States was moving in the direction of a "Christian minority." One congressman who spoke to a tour group in 2015 expressed deep concern about the growing threat of the "nones," which he explained was the sociological term for people who do not identify themselves as affiliated with any religion. What was "disturbing," he said, was that "70 percent of nones are Democrats."[8] His audience collectively gasped in alarm. Even though Republicans controlled both houses of Congress at that point, this congressman spoke as if conservatives' hold on power was tenuous. And while Christian tourists often expressed dissatisfaction with Republican politicians—including this congressman—they preferred even a nominally Christian Republican to a Democrat.[9]

Speaking to a different tour group, another congressman went even further, announcing that "faith is under enormous attack in the United States." The list of groups working against faith, he said, "would scare you to death. They are well-organized and well-funded. They outspend faith groups 9:1." The onslaught was going to continue, he told us, not just in courts but in legislatures, and even in big corporations pushing against "people of faith." He told a brief story about a white-collar worker in Iowa who lost his job for opposing same-sex marriage. Tourists' distress at this story was obvious from their solemn faces and serious murmurs, but they showed no sign of surprise. The idea that Christians were already being targeted for persecution was not new to them. Only one guest speaker ever tried to put a positive spin on these claims, arguing that persecution would be a welcome test for conservative Christians, separating the wheat from the chaff.[10] Everyone else—tourists, guides, congressmen, and lobbyists alike—were anxious about what would happen to them and to the nation, faced with such overwhelming odds. The biblical allegory was obvious even before tour guides pointed it out. Christians were David, and the government was Goliath.

Given this attitude toward those in power, it was unsurprising that Christian heritage tours sent mixed messages when they visited the headquarters of the three branches of government. For most groups, the heroic stories about the past were tempered with their anxiety about the present and future, and the Christian iconography and inscriptions seemed like an ironic counterpoint to what went on inside the walls. At the Capitol, for instance, guided tours always passed the Congressional Prayer Room on their way to the Rotunda. On several tours I overheard tourists joking about how it must not get much use these days. One group was invited to join their congressman for prayer in the room, which led to them muttering about how small it was. They noted that you could pack the room and still only have a tiny fraction of Congress present. The modest presence of the Prayer Room, even combined with all the other Christian material culture of the Capitol, did little to reassure tourists about the federal government. Instead, these elements highlighted the stark contrast between how tourists thought America had been and should be run—by "real" Christians—and how it is currently run. One woman told me as we exited that, as "magnificent" and "historic" as the building was, she wasn't impressed. She saw it only as an opportunity to pray for our leaders.

Visits to the White House offered similar opportunities to pray, and several tour guides explicitly directed their groups to pray for then-President Barack Obama, whether or not they had voted for him. Cathy's group actually huddled together on the corner of 15th Street and Pennsylvania Avenue, blocking pedestrian traffic to join hands in silent prayer. After a few minutes, we looked up and Cathy and a few others said "Amen!" Cathy beamed and gestured for us to join the stream of other tourists headed to Lafayette Park and the view of the North Portico's iconic white columns. Most guides also quoted John Adams's prayer inscribed over the mantle in the State Dining Room, often in an ironic tone: "I pray Heaven to bestow the best of Blessings on this House and on all that shall hereafter inhabit it. May none but honest and wise Men ever rule under this roof."[11] Each time the prayer was recited, at least a few people snickered, evidently not convinced that Adams's prayer had been granted. "We've mostly had honest and wise men there," Mark commented at one point, "but especially since the twentieth century, they've been dishonest and immoral." Every president had professed Christianity and invoked God in his inaugural address, he told us. "But if they don't respect their oaths, it's grounds to kick them out!" His tourists seemed cheered by this possibility. The reality, though, was that compared to the idealized presidents of the past, current administrations could never measure up. "I was kind of moved, sitting there looking at the White House," Charlene told me. "There've been so many good presidents, and right now I'm not too impressed by who's living in it, but it was just, it's pretty cool just staring at the house where our president of America lives." They may not have been fans of Obama, but no tourist missed a chance to take a picture of the White House.

Of the three branches of government, however, the one subjected to the most negativity and resentment was the Supreme Court. In 2014 and early 2015, when I conducted my fieldwork, the Court had not yet affirmed same-sex marriage in *Obergefell v. Hodges* (2015), but the case was on everyone's minds.[12] Same-sex marriage came up frequently in conversations among tourists at dinner, on the bus, and standing in line. When guide Stacy asked what one thing in American society her tourists would want to change, as Martin Luther King Jr. had worked to change racism, one middle-school boy raised his hand and responded, "Same-gender marriage." No one on any tour spoke in favor of it, and most tourists made it clear that they supported "traditional" marriage. But they had little hope that their view of marriage would triumph, and they held the Supreme Court and its "activist judges" responsible for the coming changes. Tourists in every group discussed same-sex marriage while visiting the Court, either in private conversations among themselves or during the lecture by the Christian guides. Many expressed their dismay that, despite all the Christian heritage visible in the building, including representations of Moses and the Ten Commandments, the Court seemed prepared to ignore biblical law. Others worried about a slippery slope to forced compliance with same-sex marriage. "If they can say I want to get married and you have to bake the cake, then they can say Pastor, we want to get married, you have to marry us," warned one guest speaker. Gladys told me that her church back in Oregon was very concerned about what would happen if the Court affirmed same-sex marriage. "If somebody asks us to marry a gay couple, we won't do it, and they're saying we may lose our tax exempt status," she said. "And we're saying, so be it, we're not going to do it, and we will not hire a gay person. Whatever it takes, we're not going to do it." She did not elaborate on what further consequences there might be, but she was adamant that her church would not comply.

During one visit to the Court, Mark gathered his group in the downstairs visitors' center to explain how today's Court had deviated from the biblical view of law the founders intended. Those in power had abandoned absolute truth for relativism. As a result, he said, "what once was legal can become illegal. And for disagreeing, you can be jailed, persecuted, or fined." Several people murmured, distressed. He continued, explaining that the laws made by our Congress, justices, and executives are not really laws at all. "These fake laws are made by men, but not all men—by the *special* ones, the *smart* ones who went to the *right schools*, because *we* can't decide what a family is." His sarcastic emphasis delighted his audience, who responded with groans, laughter, and scattered applause. "So when the Supreme Court rules later this year about what a family is, it's wrong if it's contrary to God's higher law," Mark concluded. "Two plus two is never five." The tourists responded with cheers and amens that rang through the visitors' center, until they were shushed by a security guard. As we headed upstairs to the courtroom, Erica grinned in delight and told me how much she loved that Mark was bold enough to preach such things in the hearing of "this pagan court."[13] But her sense of rebellion took for granted that the battle against marriage equality was already lost.

For many Christian tourists, the Christian inscriptions and iconography in D.C. stood in stark contrast to everything the city represented in terms of laws and government. Their conversations about present-day American politics kept them feeling alienated from the sites they visited, despite the ambient Christianity at those sites. When they visited the Capitol or congressional office buildings, or when they caught a glimpse of the White House or the headquarters of federal agencies from the bus, they did not celebrate the democratic process. Rather, they experienced it as a reminder of their status as political outsiders—to gain entry to those halls of power today, as one congressman they met said, they would have to "leave Jesus at the door."

FAITH IN THE HALLS OF POWER

Not that long ago, white evangelicals thought their days as political outsiders were over. At the start of the new millennium, Americans had elected a president who named Jesus Christ as his favorite philosopher, strongly encouraged White House staff to attend Bible studies, and opened Cabinet meetings with prayer.[14] George W. Bush had been cultivating his ties to the Christian Right since his days as coordinator for evangelical outreach during his father's 1988 presidential campaign, but the real key to his success with white evangelicals was simpler: he was one of them. He spoke their language, shared their concerns, and believed, as they did, in the saving power of both Jesus Christ and the United States. Bush also believed in the power of religion to improve society, a belief reflected in his establishment of the White House Office of Faith-Based and Community Initiatives and his support for "charitable choice," which allowed faith-based agencies to be considered for federal funding regardless of their missions.[15] Prominent evangelicals occupied key positions in this Bush administration, including attorney general John Ashcroft, national security adviser Condoleezza Rice, and lead speechwriter Michael Gerson. Roughly a quarter of a century after the Moral Majority's founding, white evangelicals had gained a remarkable degree of power and respectability inside the Beltway. Recognizing this shift, the National Association of Evangelicals released a statement prior to the 2004 election telling its constituents, "Never before has God given American evangelicals such an awesome opportunity to shape public policy in ways that could contribute to the well-being of the entire world."[16] The exiles had recaptured D.C. and, with it, the nation.

During George W. Bush's administration, however, white evangelicals suffered significant culture war losses, most notably on issues of sexuality and marriage equality. These losses gave an authentic ring to their occasional outsider rhetoric. Beginning in 2003, the movement for LGBTQ+ rights made significant advances at the state and federal levels, despite white evangelicals' efforts to intervene. Vermont recognized same-sex civil unions, while Massachusetts went even further, becoming the first state to recognize same-sex marriage. That year also saw the Supreme Court declare antisodomy laws unconstitutional in *Lawrence v. Texas*.[17] In response to these changes, white evangelicals made a series of failed attempts to persuade Congress to pass the Federal Marriage Amendment, which would have amended the U.S. Constitution to define marriage as being between one man and one woman.[18] James Dobson, the founder of Focus on the Family, called that failure "our D-Day, our Gettysburg, our Stalingrad."[19] Conservative Christians had, in his view, suffered a devastating loss. As the movement for marriage equality gained momentum, this defeatism would become commonplace. Conservative Christians saw the nation's rejection of traditional marriage as an attack that they were powerless to stop, despite holding some of the highest offices in the land.

When white evangelicals spoke as outsiders during Bush's presidency, they tended to sound more like victims than exiles. After the election of President Barack Obama in 2008, that language of victimization increased sharply. Obama came to embody everything that white conservative evangelicals opposed. It was not just that he was black and a Democrat; he was also accused of being a socialist, a Muslim, and a Kenyan.[20] During the 2016 presidential campaign, Donald Trump accused Obama of being in league with terrorists working to destroy the United States.[21] The absurdity of such accusations was irrelevant. For many white American evangelicals, Obama was the Other. Every policy he advocated was interpreted by the Christian Right as an attack, not just on them but on America itself. Shortly after Obama's inauguration, the Tea Party grew out of white conservatives' sense of disenfranchisement, this feeling that the nation that was rightfully theirs had been stolen from them.[22] By the end of his first term, Obama was accused of waging both a "war on whites" and a "war on religion."[23] This claim of victimization was not the strategic ploy Ralph Reed used in the 1990s to position Christians as outsiders fighting for equal rights. Rather, it was a genuine cry of outrage at being on the losing side.

When white evangelicals accused Obama of waging war on religion, they often pointed to his signature health care reform, the Affordable Care Act.[24] The act mandated that employers provide their employees with insurance plans that cover contraceptives. Numerous religious institutions, groups, and businesses protested, and they framed the issue as an assault on religion. A series of lawsuits argued that the mandate violated the 1993 Religious Freedom Restoration Act by substantially burdening the free exercise of religion of employers whose religious beliefs prohibited the use of contraceptives and abortion.[25] In one such case, *Burwell v. Hobby Lobby* (2014), the Supreme Court ruled in favor of such employers, reversing what many white evangelicals saw as a dangerous trend of subordinating their religious beliefs to the will of the government. In their view, the ruling was a victory for a victimized religious minority. Negotiations ensued over how to accommodate business owners' religious objections while still providing no-cost contraceptive coverage to their employees.[26] What was striking about white evangelicals' approach to this issue was their purported willingness to compromise. Unlike the Christian Right of the 1980s, they were not on a crusade to ban abortion or denounce contraceptives. They had seemingly abandoned the founders' role as guardians of national morality.

In their role as victims, they took aim at a more modest goal: protecting their own religious liberty as they defined it.

White evangelicals took a similarly defensive position on same-sex marriage after it was affirmed by the Supreme Court in June 2015. They did not entirely abandon attempts to reinstate "traditional marriage" as the law of the land, but they shifted their efforts toward protecting the consciences of individuals who objected to same-sex marriage on religious grounds. In Indiana, then-governor Mike Pence signed a state-level Religious Freedom Restoration Act into law, which allowed businesses to refuse services based on the religious beliefs of the owners.[27] Tennessee and Mississippi both passed laws in early 2016 allowing counselors and therapists to refuse service to patients on the grounds of religious conscience.[28] And North Carolina passed a law forbidding cities to pass more comprehensive nondiscrimination policies than the state's own policy, which, at the time of the bill, did not prohibit discrimination based on sexual orientation or gender identity.[29] These legislative efforts made conservative Christians out to be the victims in these scenarios.[30] The language of religious liberty and freedom of conscience allowed them to seem only to want to live and let live; it was their intolerant opponents who were imposing their beliefs on others. Once again, white evangelicals had found a way to claim the moral high ground of the outsider, as well as the sympathetic stance of the victim.

There is no better exemplar of white evangelicals' new role as victims than Kim Davis, the Kentucky county clerk who went to jail rather than issue marriage licenses bearing her signature to same-sex couples. Davis and her legal team argued that the case was about protecting her rights, not denying the rights of same-sex couples.[31] After she lost in district court and the Supreme Court refused to hear her case, Davis issued a statement positioning herself as the wronged party: "I never imagined a day like this would come, where I would be asked to violate a central teaching of Scripture and of Jesus Himself regarding marriage. To issue a marriage license which conflicts with God's definition of marriage, with my name affixed to the certificate, would violate my conscience." She called the matter "a Heaven or Hell decision" and claimed that she had no animosity toward gays or lesbians. What she wanted, she said, was "what our Founders envisioned—that conscience and religious freedom would be protected."[32] Despite her legal losses, Davis continued to defy a judge's order to issue marriage licenses. On September 3, 2015, the judge held her in contempt of court and remanded her to custody. By sending her to jail, the judge elevated her in the eyes of her supporters from a mere victim to a modern-day martyr.

With Davis incarcerated, the media frenzy around her case reached its peak, and many conservative Christian leaders and politicians took advantage of the spotlight. Davis was being persecuted for standing by her Christian beliefs, they said, and her case represented what Republican presidential primary candidate Mike Huckabee called "the criminalization of Christianity."[33] Ted Cruz, another Republican presidential primary candidate, argued that "those who are persecuting Kim Davis believe that Christians should not serve in public office. That is the consequence of their position. Or, if Christians do serve in public office, they must disregard their religious faith — or be sent to jail."[34] The American Family Association called for "states to protect Christians since the Supreme Court did not."[35] Support for Davis was by no means unanimous among conservative Christians, but her supporters made the most of this opportunity to advance the narrative of Christian victimization.[36] When Davis was released from jail after five days, she was celebrated as a hero. Huckabee hosted a press conference turned victory rally that Davis entered to the accompaniment of "The Eye of the Tiger," raising her arms in triumph. To outside viewers the whole affair seemed almost farcical; but to white evangelicals Davis's persecution was proof that Christians had become victims in the nation they had founded. Like the apostles in the New Testament, they were being jailed for defying the government and following their conscience.

Three years after Kim Davis's saga, white evangelicals once again deployed the rhetoric of victimization to resist same-sex marriage, this time with more success. The Supreme Court ruled in favor of Jack Phillips, the owner of Masterpiece Cake Shop who refused on religious grounds to bake a wedding cake for a same-sex couple. In the majority opinion, Anthony Kennedy sidestepped the thorny question of whose rights would prevail in a clash between LGBTQ+ rights and the rights of conservative Christians who objected to same-sex marriage. Instead, Kennedy focused on the question of whether the Colorado Civil Rights Commission displayed hostility toward Phillips's religious beliefs during its investigation. Phillips's legal team argued that the Commission was not neutral or respectful toward his sincerely held religious beliefs about marriage. Kennedy agreed, writing that the Commission showed "clear and impermissible hostility" and that one member of the Commission in particular had "disparaged" Phillips's religious beliefs during a hearing.[37] Phillips was made out to be the real victim of bigotry and discrimination in this case.

The *Masterpiece Cake Shop* decision was an important victory for white evangelicals who oppose same-sex marriage, the culmination of a legal and rhetorical strategy that had been years in the making. They had indeed learned a lot from the other side, as Jerry Falwell had once said.[38] They had learned that seeking equal protection could yield more results than attempting to take back the whole nation. What is most significant about this case, however, is how it expanded the definition of religious hostility in a way that will allow white evangelicals to more easily position themselves as the wronged party in future cases. Kennedy's opinion highlights two statements from the Commission's hearings on the matter that, in his view, are impermissibly hostile. In the first, a commissioner suggested that if someone wants to do business in the state but has a religious objection to a law, that person might need to consider a compromise.[39] In the second, another commissioner stated that "freedom of religion and religion has been used to justify all kinds of discrimination," including slavery and the Holocaust. Kennedy found the first statement "dismissive" and the second "disparaging."[40] But compromise is a fact of life in a religiously diverse society in which government seeks to balance its own compelling interests and the needs of society with the individual rights of citizens. And the historical reality is that religion has indeed been used to justify horrific acts of violence, including violence against LGBTQ+ people. Both statements are reasonable points to raise in discussions of how the United States will navigate shifting sexual norms that are not agreed upon by all. If the suggestion of compromise and a statement of historical fact now constitute hostility, white evangelicals will have no trouble casting themselves as victims in future debates on this issue.[41]

MAKING AMERICA GREAT AGAIN

During the 2016 presidential election, many observers were shocked by how strongly white evangelicals supported Donald Trump, no matter how many scandals came to light about his behavior. A pattern emerged in articles and op-eds, in which the author would recite the litany of Trump's sins—gambling, divorce, profanity, greed, adultery, pride—followed by expressions of dismay and disbelief that white evangelicals could support someone who so openly rejected their "family values."[42] At worst, white evangelicals were depicted as hypocrites who sold their values for thirty pieces of silver and a Supreme Court appointment. At best, they were depicted as dupes who put their trust in a fraud. The real discrepancy, however, was not between white evangelicals' family values and their political activity. Rather, it was between how white evangelicals were expected to behave by many Americans and how they actually behaved. Since the 1980s scholars have understood evangelicalism to be a set of theological commitments, most notably those articulated by Bebbington.[43] In a similar fashion, the American public has understood evangelicalism to be strict adherence to the traditional moral values that make up the conservative side of the culture war.[44] But neither of these understandings explained white evangelicals' overwhelming support for Trump.[45]

Trump's message did not resonate with white evangelicals because it conformed to their theological principles or moral values. Rather, it resonated with them because it mapped onto their narratives about who they are and what the United States should be. His campaign slogan, "Make America Great Again," encapsulated their jeremiad. Much as the Moral Majority once did, it argued that the nation is in decline from an idealized white Christian past but that recovery remains possible.[46] At key moments in the campaign he elaborated on what recovery would look like under a Trump administration. For instance, he famously and repeatedly promised that "we're all going to be saying Merry Christmas." This claim played to both to white evangelicals' sense of marginality and their sense that their norms and values—including their holiday greetings—should be universal in American culture.[47]

What Trump did most effectively, however, was cast himself as a victim, even as he validated white evangelicals' sense of victimization. Throughout his campaign he claimed to be persecuted by both the media and the D.C. establishment, claims that he continued to make as president. Congressional investigations into his dealings with Russia and Ukraine and other ethical violations only confirmed his supporters' belief that he, like them, was being unfairly maligned by the Left. They sympathized with him, and he with them. A few months after his inauguration, he promised an audience at Liberty University, "As long as I am your president no one is ever going to stop you from practicing your faith or from preaching what's in your heart. We will always stand up for the right of all Americans to pray to God and to follow his teachings."[48] Whether a real threat to these practices existed was beside the point. Trump spoke to white evangelicals' deep sense that they were on the verge of outright persecution. He indirectly confirmed that they were right to be afraid, all while positioning himself as their savior.[49]

Even after Trump took the White House and Republicans took both houses of Congress in 2016, white evangelicals continued to position themselves as outsiders. At the state and local levels in particular, they have focused on finding ways to protect themselves from being forced to conform to progressive values. Since the legalization of same-sex marriage nationwide, many state legislatures have considered or passed bills that allow religious individuals or businesses to refuse service to same-sex couples, exclude LGBTQ+ people from nondiscrimination protections, or prohibit transgender people from using the bathroom corresponding to their gender identity.[50] Not all of these efforts have been successful, but many have, and more will come. The Project Blitz campaign, led by the Congressional Prayer Caucus Foundation and WallBuilders, provides a variety of templates for legislation prohibiting the government from penalizing people or businesses who deny the validity of same-sex marriage.[51] These templates employ the language of discrimination, but not in the context of same-sex couples, transgender individuals, or other sexual minorities. Rather, they position religious objectors to same-sex marriage as the targets of discrimination for their sincerely held beliefs. This inversion of roles demonstrates the extent to which the Christian Right has embraced an outsider position and learned to deploy the rhetoric of minority groups to the advantage of white evangelicals. It is a masterstroke of political strategy, one that liberals and progressives have yet to counter effectively. Any successful counter-move will require curtailing white evangelicals' ability to cast themselves as victims, which will continue to be difficult so long as the conversation is framed in terms of discrimination and competing rights.[52]

Like their exile role, white evangelicals' victim role does not entirely depend on the degree of political power they wield at any given moment. Rather, this role is constructed in opposition to the idea of a Christian America that exists only in nostalgic imagination. The present will always fall short compared to that mythical past, no matter how many conservative policies become law. The lost golden age evoked in recent American jeremiads is a strategic fiction, created by the Christian Right in the 1980s to further its political agenda, and it continues to serve that purpose today. As long as being an outsider comes with moral authority and legal advantages, white evangelicals will continue to cast themselves as victims, regardless of who is in power.

STRANGERS IN A STRANGE LAND

Visiting the Supreme Court is an uncomfortable experience. This discomfort has little to do with politics, however, and everything to do with the intensive security and design of the space. After picking their way through the protestors who often camp out on First Street, tourists must cross an open plaza to line up at one of the visitors' entrances on the ground level. Since 2010, no one has been allowed to enter through the massive bronze doors that once served as the main entrance. At least one police officer is always stationed on the marble steps to redirect wayward visitors who want to use the front door.

Stacy's group had just finished their visit to the Library of Congress before walking the short distance to the Supreme Court next door. The tourists in the lead veered toward the right-hand entrance, and the rest of us followed, dutifully obeying a sign's instruction to FORM LINE HERE. No sooner had we organized ourselves than a guard emerged from the building, visibly annoyed. We couldn't all enter here, she said in exasperation. Half the group had to go around to the other side. Right now. We looked at each other, nonplussed, and sorted ourselves into two groups. I joined the group that trekked across the plaza to the left-hand entrance, where we reformed our line and resumed waiting.

By this point we were all sweating from the walk over and ready to be inside with air conditioning. Instead, we stood dutifully in line as the sun beat down on us and heat radiated up from the stones of the plaza. At last another security guard emerged and instructed us to remove everything from our pockets before going through the metal detector and to put our belongings in the X-ray machine. Yes, we could keep our water bottles. We were old hands at security procedures by now, so most of us made it through without a hitch. As usual, though, a couple of men forgot about their belts, earning the disapproval of the security guards and an extra trip through the metal detector.

Beyond the security screening room, we rejoined the rest of our group, all of us thankful to be out of the sun. Stacy instructed us that we had forty-five minutes before the next curator's talk in the courtroom, but we should be upstairs and lined up at least fifteen minute early. More would be better, because seating was limited and it was crowded that day. In the meantime, we should explore the exhibits in the visitors' center. Only a few people took her up on that suggestion, though. Most were more interested in using the restroom, refilling water bottles, and purchasing snacks in the cafeteria. It had been a long day, and it was only early afternoon. I took a brief lap of the exhibits with one family and headed upstairs with them to get in line for the courtroom talk.

Unfortunately for us, the Great Hall of the Supreme Court is one of the most spartan rooms in D.C. For all its elegant marble and historic portraits of past justices, it lacks important creature comforts, including places to sit down. Even sitting on the floor was forbidden. All we could do was stand in line, trying to entertain ourselves with conversation about what we'd seen

The Great Hall of the U.S. Supreme Court, looking from the entrance toward the courtroom, November 2011. Collection of the Supreme Court of the United States.

so far. But even that was too much—every five minutes or so a security guard came around to ask us to lower our voices, speaking in a whisper. All around me exasperated tourists rolled their eyes but complied, not wanting to get kicked out. "Don't I pay for this?" muttered one aggravated taxpayer. By the time we made it into the courtroom itself, tempers were short, and no one was in a mood to hear about what a special place this was. The final indignity came when the curator reminded us at the beginning of her talk that we were not allowed to take photographs in the courtroom—a prohibition that, for tourists, verged on blasphemy.

All tourists, by definition, are outsiders. A tour is a liminal experience that takes tourists away from their ordinary lives. Far from home, they are surrounded largely by strangers and, in the case of D.C., living in a big city that they cannot easily navigate on their own. Christian heritage tours featured packed schedules so that tourists could see as many sites as possible in a few days. Invariably, this left them exhausted and resentful of the hot sun, long walks, and crowded venues, not to mention the high prices for food and souvenirs. Even something as mundane as the lack of tour bus parking sparked complaints. In some ways it seemed like the city itself was oppressing them. They felt like victims in a way that has nothing to do with the place of Christianity in America's past or present.

Nothing, however, made Christian tourists feel more irritable and mistreated than the constant experience of security in D.C. The Supreme Court was just one of countless examples. Most buildings involved some sort of security procedure, from simple bag checks at the National Gallery to the airport-style screening at the Capitol. The process was tedious, especially for larger groups, and tourists understandably resented being continually required to take off their jackets, belts, and nametags and to allow a stranger to rifle through their bags. And security extended well beyond the entry point to any building. Guards and docents could be found in almost every room, admonishing tourists not to get too close to the artwork or to keep their voices down. Each of these moments of friction acted as a bonding ritual for the group, uniting them against the invasion and the government responsible for it. They grumbled about the good old days, when a citizen could wander the halls of the Capitol unhindered by post-9/11 concerns. Simply put, tourists felt that the government did not trust them anymore than they trusted it, and this feeling reinforced their sense of being victims every time they entered a building.

Tour guides sometimes played on tourists' irritation with security by "joking" that they themselves were a security threat and in danger of being removed. As we walked up Capitol Hill one day, Dan shouted, "I'm here to repeal laws! Oooooh, are they coming to get me?" Tourists laughed while he dramatically looked over his shoulder, as if expecting Capitol police to arrive at any moment. On another tour, Mark delivered a fiery condemnation of the current court's jurisprudence in the Supreme Court's visitor center. After he finished, he told me in an aside, "If the thought police ever come for me, they won't let me say this anymore, especially here." Jokes like these suggested that the guides saw security not as protecting visitors and government workers from terrorist threats, but as protecting the government from dissenting voices. Tourists occasionally made similar comments, joking about having to leave their guns on the bus (concealed carry permits are invalid in D.C.) or wanting to jump the White House fence. For one group, the latter option became unexpectedly real, when someone did jump the fence not long after the tourists had stopped for a photo op. The next day several of them reported that family and friends had texted them asking, "Was it you?!" Whether it was an X-ray machine, a bag check, or an iron fence, security put a barrier between tourists and the city they had come to see, reminding them that they were only visitors. They did not belong.

HIDING IN PLAIN SIGHT

Tourists' encounters with security, combined with their general physical discomfort, played an important role in maintaining their sense of victimization. But once they made it through security, cooled off, and rested their weary feet for a moment, they found themselves in buildings full of the Christian objects they had come to see. These objects held the potential to disrupt the outsider narrative, suggesting that Christians were not so marginalized as all that. Their presence prompted tourists and guides to respond by looking for ways in which the objects were threatened. As discussed in chapter 2, many tourists expressed anxiety about the possibility that *Laus Deo* would be erased from the Washington Monument or that statues of Christians would be exiled from the Capitol. But there were other ways to make Christian objects invisible. The most common strategy was for tourists or guides to suggest that, though the object remained present, it was grossly misinterpreted by everyone else, especially those in power. This approach cast Christian tourists and Christian objects as victims together.

Perhaps unsurprisingly, the Supreme Court was a site where this sort of interaction frequently took place. The building features prominent images from biblical tradition, including a sculpture of Moses that dominates the East Pediment. This imagery continues in the courtroom itself: Moses and Solomon are both featured as great lawgivers on the South Wall Frieze, and images of the Ten Commandments are carved into the bottom panel of the main doors. In addition to all this, there are countless portraits and statues of former justices that Christian guides identified as "strong Christians" whose view of the law was formed by the Bible. Of course, according to most Christian guides, the Supreme Court's Office of the Curator did far too little to draw visitors' attention to these features. Their real concern, however, was

Replica of the central courtroom frieze on display in the U.S. Supreme Court visitors' center, August 2016. Photo by the author.

Engraving of the Ten Commandments on the lower panel of the doors to the courtroom at the U.S. Supreme Court, July 2016. Photo by the author.

the East Wall Frieze in the courtroom. Directly above the justices' bench is a depiction of two seated men representing the Majesty of Law and the Power of Government. Between them is the tablet inscribed with Roman numerals one through ten under a rising sun. Given the prominence of Christian iconography elsewhere in the building, it is perhaps not unreasonable to expect that those numerals stand for the Ten Commandments. But the Office of the Curator's current official interpretation, given during all public talks in the courtroom and in official literature, is that the numerals represent the first ten amendments to the Constitution, the Bill of Rights.[53]

When Christian guides explained this interpretation, most tourists reacted with overt disgust. They knew the Court did not share their values—that much was evident from recent rulings. But they saw this interpretation of the courtroom frieze as a blatant denial of the biblical foundations of American law, in defiance of all common sense. To them it was a powerful example of intentional government actions aimed at reinterpreting Christian objects to fit a secularizing agenda. Tourists took for granted that the government was secularist and anti-Christian, and because the government controlled the sites they visited in Washington, D.C., they expected to find this sort of "anti-Christian" revisionist interpretation everywhere. As a result, they continually looked for something wrong, something incomplete. They never had trouble finding it.

The U.S. Capitol was another site that most Christian tourists approached with suspicion, in part because of how Capitol tours are set up. Private tours are permitted only by invitation from members of Congress, so most visitors must take the official "redcoat tour," so named for the bright red jackets worn by Capitol guides. Given how little Christian tourists trusted the government to get American history right, it was no surprise that they expected this tour to ignore Christianity altogether. Christian guides reinforced this attitude on the bus ride to the Capitol, giving tourists lists of paintings and statues to look for since the government's guides could not be trusted to point them out, much less properly explain how each one demonstrated the central place of Christianity in America.

Tourists themselves reported mixed reactions to the official tour. Some experienced it exactly as the Christian guides predicted, complaining that they were rushed past the things they wanted to see even as the official guides told lengthy stories about topics that did not interest them. Ashley, a middle-aged woman from Indianapolis, compared the official tour unfavorably to her previous experiences of the Capitol, when tourists could freely wander the halls of power. To make matters worse, the Capitol dome was undergoing structural repairs at the time, and the Rotunda was full of scaffolding that did not quite block the paintings but certainly distracted from them. She said in her follow-up interview:

> Our tour guide was horrible, she wouldn't let us walk around, you know.... I wanted to stand and look at all those paintings that are in the Rotunda, but no, she wouldn't let us go there.... I was very disappointed, and that was the one place I was really excited to go to! Because it's a grand, wonderful, beautiful place, that is such an homage to our history, you know, and the paintings in the Rotunda are all about the Lord, and you can't see them because they were covered up!

Ashley's reaction was typical, echoed by many of her fellow tourists in both follow-up interviews and informal conversations.[54] They felt rushed by their guides, constrained by the rules, and annoyed by the construction, not to mention the crowds.

Even when Christian tourists were on private Capitol tours, their experiences were framed by references to the many omissions and failures of the official public tour. Two of the tours I joined took private tours led by conservative Christian congressmen.[55] Both congressmen pointed out many Christian features of the building—missionaries in the National Statuary Hall, Moses in the House Chamber, paintings of prayers and baptism in the Rotunda—and frequently reminded tourists that this was privileged information that they would not hear otherwise. This was, of course, at least in part an effort to dazzle their constituents with the specialness of the private tour. But it also cast suspicion on the official, government-sponsored tour that "everyone else" had no choice but to take. Tourists were impressed, especially those who had previously taken the public tour. "The [public] tour we were on was so darn fast," one woman said, "they don't say anything about that, in fact they hardly said anything about the Bible in past ones." In contrast, her congressman "gave it so much more meaning" by linking features of the building to the Bible. Even though those taking the private tour heard what they considered to be the "real story," they were continually reminded that this experience was not typical. Elsewhere, the story was being officially rewritten to showcase secularism instead of faith.

Another frequent complaint I heard from both tourists and guides was that the government minimized Christianity in order to spotlight more "politically correct" topics. In the Capitol's National Statuary Hall, some tourists grumbled that their official guides spent too long talking about statues of abolitionist Sojourner Truth, civil rights leader Rosa Parks, or female suffragists Elizabeth Cady Stanton, Susan B. Anthony, and Lucretia Mott. In the tourists' view, their time would have been better spent talking about the Christians in the room, like Marcus Whitman or Jason Lee. It is worth noting, however, that all of these women were Christians, and it is no exaggeration to say that their faith informed the achievements for which they are honored in the Capitol. For Christian tourists, though, these women were the wrong kind of Christian—they were not white conservative evangelicals. As a result, the statues' religious connotations remained invisible.

On several other tours, visits to the Library of Congress sparked similar complaints. Despite the prominence of the Gutenberg Bible and the Giant Bible of Mainz in the Great Hall, tourists found that official guides to the library spent more time advertising another religion: Islam. Longtime guide Stacy privately informed me that the Library of Congress puts far more emphasis on Islam today than it did when she first started fifteen years ago. During the introductory video on our visit, she said, they mentioned the Quran "four or five times, but not the Bibles in the main hall!" She added that she had once asked an official guide if Thomas Jefferson owned any Bibles; the man responded, yes, he did—but he also had five Qurans.[56] Nor were these complaints limited to sites in Washington, D.C. Jacob and Amy had traveled to other cities besides D.C. on their East Coast tour, and they said in Philadelphia they were disappointed to find discussions of Christianity had been pushed out to make room for more "trendy" topics such as civil rights and economic reform. They also visited Williamsburg, where they reportedly found similar "subtle agendas," including ones that "mocked" colonial Christianity for being intolerant. In each case, tourists' perception was that the sites' "real" message about the significance and centrality of Christianity in American history had been distorted, minimized, or silenced in order to further a politically correct, anti-Christian agenda.

DISAPPEARING RELIGION

Most Christian tourists approached D.C. with this suspicious attitude, which was encouraged by their guides. This attitude served an important purpose: it allowed Christian objects that might otherwise have been disruptive to recede into the background. Christian tourists and guides could have chosen to engage these objects differently, as evidence for the dominance of Christianity in American history—which they are. Instead, tourists and guides chose to render these objects invisible, neutralizing their potential to disrupt the outsider narrative.

Though Christian objects are present all over D.C., they are not always seen. Like many objects in public spaces, they do not invariably draw the gaze of passerby. Sometimes they recede into the background, blurring together with other elements of the scene. This quality, what Matthew Engelke has termed "ambience," allows an object to move between visibility and invisibility.[57] Whether or not it comes into view depends on a number of interrelated factors, including how the object is placed in the space; what other elements might obscure, distract, or reveal the object; whose gaze is being captured and what their identity narratives and embodied experiences are; and the historical moment, or what recent events have put a spotlight on an object that may have long gone unnoticed.[58] The ambience of Christian objects in D.C. means they are seen by some passersby and ignored by others, and they may come in and out of focus over time. One of the purposes of Christian heritage tours, of course, is to bring these Christian objects into the foreground. Guides directed tourists' gaze to these objects so that the objects could reinforce the link between Christianity and the nation in the viewer's mind. They typically did so, however, only in moments when the objects would be stabilizing to tourists' religious identity.

The capacity of religious objects to stabilize religious identity has been well documented by scholars. Such objects are often analyzed in terms of their expressive function: by analyzing an object (or a series of objects), we gain a window into the identity of the object's creator, viewer, or user.[59] Objects that express a religious identity may also serve to cultivate desired interior dispositions through disciplining the body.[60] In addition, David Morgan argues that material objects mask the instabilities inherent in our socially constructed world.[61] Popular devotional images like Warner Sallman's *Head of Christ* give material form and the illusion of permanence to things that are essential to maintaining the viewer's world, in this case the existence and authority of the historical Jesus.[62] This relative stability of objects enables them to transmit religious identity from one generation to the next, often through children's toys.[63] And more recent scholarship has explored the blurred boundaries between religious practitioners and religious objects, as these objects mediate and make possible religious experience.[64]

Religious objects can also give form to contestations over identity, particularly when they are publicly displayed. In this context, objects may provoke and respond to instability in the identity of their public(s). Sally Promey argues that such objects are likely to be unstable in their meaning, since different groups will "activate" them in different ways. To limit the possibility of misinterpretation, artists or creators may employ minimalist symbols that are unlikely to be read the wrong way.[65] But not all public displays of religion are equally visible. Recent discussions of ambient religion have shown how religious objects in public spaces can stabilize religious identity while moving in and out of focus. In Engelke's study of a Christmas market in Swindon, the abstract angels decorating the market were at least intended to surface spirituality among Britons doing their Christmas shopping, offering a brief connection to the transcendent.[66] The Quebecois roadside crosses in Hillary Kaell's study, meanwhile, inspired *pensées* of God among French Catholics who encountered them.[67] Ambient religion is also political. Both Engelke and Kaell highlight how the objects they study subtly infuse Christianity into the public square, resisting the secular demand that religion remain private and hidden. Even when they are invisible—in some cases, especially when they are invisible—ambient objects can operate in the background to maintain the authority of a particular tradition.[68]

The Christian objects encountered by Christian tourists in D.C. do perform some of these stabilizing functions, insofar as they amplify and elaborate the insider narrative.[69] They express the custodial relationship that many white evangelicals feel toward the United States by infusing the nation's most public spaces with Christianity.[70] Sites like the Congressional Prayer Room or the Washington National Cathedral indicate an expectation of Christian piety from American leaders and citizens alike, and numerous inscriptions offer collective praise to God or request divine blessings on the nation. Even when they recede into the background, these objects discipline viewers to link Christianity and the nation's institutions. Unlike Christian tourists, most visitors to D.C. do not notice, discuss, or photograph the representations of the Ten Commandments carved into the doors of the Supreme Court and inlaid in the outer vestibule floor of the National Archives. Nevertheless, these objects foster a link in a casual viewer's mind between biblical tradition and American law.[71] In addition, Christian inscriptions work to mask the instability of an increasingly diverse nation. Religious differences are elided under the sweeping claims "In God We Trust" and "One Nation under God." In these respects, the Christian objects in the capital stabilize at least one piece of white evangelicals' identity, their conviction that Christians are America's rightful insiders.

At the same time, these Christian objects disrupt the outsider narrative. American public life has been de-Christianized in important ways over the last fifty years, allowing white evangelicals make a plausible claim to marginality.[72] Yet D.C.'s ambient Christianity persists. At each site they visited, Christian tourists encountered relics of the long history of white Protestant power in the United States. Those objects suggest that Christianity remains at the very least the default language for the nation's collective expressions of memory. Moreover, their materiality lends these objects the illusion of absolute facticity. It is difficult to argue with something that is literally written in stone.

In response, Christian tourists acted to restabilize their identity. They expanded the outsider narrative to include the objects themselves, telling stories in which the objects were threatened with removal or misinterpretation. In some cases, such as their concern for the statue of Jason Lee, their responses drew on verifiable threats, while in other cases they appealed to rumors or an intangible sense that the nation was in decline. But the facticity of the threat was not what made it salient. It had only to seem plausible enough to serve as a mechanism for tourists to recast themselves as outsiders. Moreover, the objects and their surroundings often cooperated with tourists in making this narrative shift. Minor flaws and infelicities in an object's presentation—poor lighting, insufficient captions, unkempt grass—could work to amplify the outsider narrative in this context, helping tourists drown out the disruption caused by the object's more obvious Christian features.[73] Here, too, D.C.'s omnipresent security and inaccessibility supported this story, suggesting that those in power wanted these objects to be out of reach. With the help of all of these factors, Christian tourists capitalized on the ambient potential of D.C.'s Christian objects and, instead of bringing them into focus, shifted focus away.

Though guides would sometimes prompt them, most Christian tourists already knew how to respond to disruptions to the outsider narrative. As discussed in chapter 2, the outsider narrative is a rhetorical strategy that creates tension with the mainstream in order to maintain white evangelicals' position on the margins. But it is not just D.C.'s landscape that has been marked by the historical and contemporary dominance of Christianity. Many aspects of American culture, material and otherwise, have been shaped by Christianity, and these, too, disrupt the outsider narrative. White evangelicals then face the same problem faced by tourists who encountered Christian objects in D.C.: they appear to be more insiders than outsiders, despite their protestations. In identifying threats to D.C.'s Christian objects, tourists were adapting a broader script drawn from the white American evangelical repertoire. Most white evangelicals are well practiced at identifying threats to Christianity in the United States. Some of these threats are hyperbole, like "creeping sharia" and the annual War on Christmas. Changes to policy and legislation, like Common Core and same-sex marriage, also serve as threats. In the broader American context, these threats function in much the same way as the purported threats to Christian objects in D.C.: they recast white evangelicals as outsiders, despite the significant power they still wield in American politics and culture.

Christian tourists' encounters with disruptive objects in D.C. offer an opportunity to observe not only how a subject may regain stability after an encounter with a destabilizing material object, but also how white evangelicals may deal with such disruptions in a broader context. Christian tourists identified threats to Christian objects in order to quell their disruptive potential. In doing so they demonstrate one strategy for negotiating the conflicting narratives that constitute white American evangelicals' identity. This process transforms their experience of touring D.C. into one of alternating celebration and lament that parallels their view of American culture more broadly. They celebrate the Christian heritage they came to see, written in stone before them as advertised. But they also learn that what really matters are not these dusty artifacts of the past but the present-day activities of a largely secular mainstream bent on persecuting Christians for their faith. White evangelical tourists thus depart D.C. having seen what they came for. They are certain of their role as founders, but they are equally certain that they are exiles and, above all, victims. In spite of this pessimism, however, Christian tourists did not seem to despair for themselves or their nation. They still had one role left to play.

Chapter 4 **Saviors**

···

The U.S. Capitol after dark is a quiet place. The tourist hordes that overrun it during daylight hours have departed, taking with them their clicking cameras and chattering headsets. The red-coated Capitol tour guides have gone home for the night, and no one calls for us to keep up or move along. The security guards are even more visible for the lack of crowds. In halls where just a few hours ago we would have shouted to be heard, we whisper.

The congressman hosting our visit strides into the center of the group, beaming in welcome. We're in for a treat, he tells us, something very few people get to do. We follow him out of the Rotunda and into National Statuary Hall, then past a sign telling us DO NOT ENTER. Several hallways later, we emerge into the ornate comfort of the Speaker's Lobby, where we are asked to leave our cell phones and cameras. As we empty our pockets, several people gawk at the plush couches, wood paneling, and sparkling chandeliers. Others gather around the portraits of past Speakers of the House, murmuring about those they recognize. Newt Gingrich seems to be a favorite. Soon a security guard opens a door and the congressman beckons us inside, onto the floor of the House of Representatives chamber.

We slowly fan out in front of the rostrum, turning around and gazing upward. A woman near me mutters that she wishes she had a camera. The cavernous space looms over us as we gaze up at the gallery where people like us would normally sit. The change in perspective is striking. "Come in, sit down, make yourselves comfortable," invites our congressional host. We hesitate, but only for a moment. It was a long walk up Capitol Hill from the bus drop-off, and the first thing

View of the Capitol Rotunda painting *The Apotheosis of Washington* from below the statue of George Washington, September 2016. Architect of the Capitol.

a tourist learns in D.C. is to take every opportunity to sit down. The group surges toward the far side of the chamber—no one wants to sit on the left side of the aisle—and we sink gratefully into the wide leather seats.

As we twist in our seats to admire the architecture, the congressman regales us with stories about the Capitol Building. Its very existence is a miracle, he says, sliding effortlessly into the rhetoric of his audience. During the War of 1812, the British captured the city of Washington and set fire to the newly constructed Capitol. But though the damage was significant, it was not total, thanks to a sudden torrential rain sent by God to quell the fires and drive the British out.[1] God had a plan for the new nation, and it involved this very room.

The congressman goes on to tell us about John Quincy Adams, whose strong Christian faith and correspondence with fellow Christian William Wilberforce led him to oppose slavery while he served in the House of Representatives. The people around me perk up at the name Wilberforce, and I see several others nodding. They recognize the name and story from the 2006 film *Amazing Grace*, which had been popular among white evangelical audiences. Adams was unsuccessful, of course, but it was all part of God's plan, the congressman assures us.

Speaking of God's plan, do we know that we are sitting in one of the first churches in Washington, D.C.? Thomas Jefferson himself attended church here while he was president, the congressman says, and he even paid for the Marine Corps Band to play at services. How's that for separation of church and state! We laugh together, scoffing at those who would kick God out of government. But the congressman quickly sobers and tells us, as if we haven't heard, that all our founders were strong Christian men, and it was their faith that led them to found this nation. As evidence, he reads us the closing prayer in George Washington's letter of resignation as commander-in-chief of the Continental Army, which he presented to Congress in 1783: "I consider it an indispensable duty to close this last solemn act of my Official life, by commending the Interests of our dearest Country to the protection of Almighty God, and those who have the superintendence of them, to his holy keeping."[2] A few people say amen, and others murmur appreciatively.

The congressman gives us a moment to ponder the words, then asks if we have any questions. In the front row, an eight-year-old girl raises her hand. When the congressman invites her to speak, she asks, "If George Washington could pray like that, why can't we pray in schools?"[3] The crowd gasps and erupts in chatter. "That's a very, very good question," the congressman tells her. The adults around her praise her for her insight. People near me murmur about what a good question it is. To this group it seems obvious—so obvious a child can see it—that we should pray just as Washington prayed. The fact that we do not is a sign of crisis, one visible even to an eight-year-old. Her question cut to the heart of white evangelicals' anxiety about the nation. Why, if our founders were such devout Christians, do we not follow their example?

Most white evangelicals today feel that the United States has deviated from the course the founders set for it.[4] School prayer is just the beginning. Everywhere they look they see signs of decline, the result of concerted efforts by secularists to exclude Christians and their God from the nation in defiance of the founders' example. However, as in any jeremiad, there is still hope. Like ancient Israel, Americans can repent and return to their old, righteous ways. But doing so requires knowledge of how things used to be—one cannot make America great *again* without knowing what great-ness looked like the first time around. Since the 1970s conservative Christian leaders have embraced history as a solution to contemporary crises, developing a restorative nostalgia that offers the past as a prescription.[5] At the same time, they see American history itself as endangered by those who seek to exile Christians from the history books.

On Christian heritage tours of D.C., white evangelical tourists learn how to be saviors of both history and the nation. Their experience of D.C. is not a vacation but an initiation. They join the ranks of those who know the real story and who have seen the evidence for themselves. Armed with this knowledge, they are called to take action, usually in the form of becoming politically involved themselves and supporting efforts to promote Christianity in the American public square. They are also reminded at every turn that their duty may involve sacrifice. In a city full of war memorials, it is impossible to forget how many people have already given their lives to save the nation. Christian heritage tours hold up American soldiers as exemplary saviors, second only to Christ, and tourists' encounters with war memorials, Arlington National Cemetery, and especially veterans reinforce their sense of solemn obligation. Their own fight may not be on a battlefield, but the safety and survival of the nation are nonetheless at stake.

STANDING IN THE GAP

On the Christian heritage tours I observed, celebrations of America's Christian past were continually tempered with concern for the present and future. A sense of crisis lurked just beneath the surface of tour guides' monologues and tourists' conversations among themselves. The problem was not just that Christians had been exiled and victimized, in their view. Their concern went beyond themselves. As they understood it, their removal to the margins meant that the whole nation was in grave danger. They feared that American government would collapse, that the American military would be defeated, and that chaos would reign. As one Christian lobbyist told a tour group, "We are living through the absolute greatest threat to our constitutional order in the history of our country. . . . To quote Dick Cheney: This is big time."

After returning home, tourists echoed this sense of crisis and pessimism about the nation. In follow-up interviews, I asked participants to describe the United States in three words or a phrase, and a surprising number were negative. "I'd like to say godly," Gladys sighed. "But I can't, you know." Amy was equally pessimistic. "We are going to start getting what we deserve," she said darkly. Several tourists asked if I wanted them to describe the nation in the past or the present, and their choices were sharply divided among positive terms for the past and negative terms for the present. Annie, an eighteen-year-old history lover from Louisiana, described her country as "unappreciative." She explained, "We're not taught to appreciate really how much work and effort has gone into everything we enjoy, how much death has resulted so that we can maintain freedom, how much . . . some people really, really care and work very hard to keep this nation Christian, for lack of a better term. Moral, I guess you could say. . . . But on the whole, I'm rather disappointed in my country. But I do hold out hope for the next genera- tion, or, I guess, my generation." Annie also chose "gullible" as one of her three words, meaning that Americans believe whatever they are told with- out doing the work to learn it for themselves. In her view, Americans are ignorant about the past and reluctant to learn, and those attitudes keep them from seeing the true history of the nation that could help get it back on track.

Other tourists made similar points about how history can save the na- tion, if only Americans would let it. Russell and Jeanie, the retired couple from Alabama who took Clay's tour, expressed their anxieties throughout their joint interview. Russell was particularly concerned with the limited audience on his tour and wished that more people could hear Clay's mes- sage. He wondered out loud, "Are there other tour guides that know the things, that have this information, but tend not to do it?" It was a shame, in his view, that only the select few on his tour could see and hear these things. He went on to add,

I guess what I brought away from this whole thing is how many people go to Washington, D.C., as tourists would go to an amusement park as opposed to really looking and feeling what I've felt and what other people there feel, what we felt as a group, I think. The majority of people may not feel that way, but I think a lot of 'em just go there and . . . I feel sorry for the children. They go there and they say, "Oh, yeah, he was a hero and he fought these guys. They won a war and we got free- dom from England as a result of that and that was it. That was George." "Okay." "And then we had a battle over slavery and there's Lincoln. Yeah, okay," and they don't know anything about the people. They don't know what their beliefs were. They don't know that they were primarily or almost all Christian, some stronger than others, but Christian any- way, and they don't know that. . . . And how many of their parents are telling them, "Hey, this country was founded on Christian principles and we're straying away from that now." We need to look at these things. We individuals are the only thing that can bring this back where it should be, get it back on track.... It makes me concern myself sometimes with the generations behind me, what hope is there because [Clay's] doing everything he can. Other people are, too, and we are too, I think, but there's a gap. There's a big gap.

But as Russell and Jeanie and other tourists recognized, not everyone can make it to D.C. for a Christian heritage tour. Other measures can help, to a certain extent. Midwestern mom Erica admitted, "I think it's probable more people are reached, obviously, by movies like *Monumental*," the Kirk Cameron film about the Founding Fathers and Plymouth Rock. In terms of expediency, Christian heritage tours are not the most feasible choice. But across the board, participants agreed that all Americans need to learn this Christian history, one way or another. In the meantime, it was up to those in the know to act upon their knowledge—to stand in the gap.

GETTING BACK INTO POLITICS

Whenever Mark led tours, he called his audience to action on the very first bus ride. As we cruised down the George Washington Memorial Parkway one evening, just ahead of rush-hour traffic, he took up the microphone to welcome us and introduce himself. "I'll be your inspirer, informer, and agitator if you need it," he told us. "My goal is to teach you how the Christian gospel liberates nations." ("Amen," called a woman in the back.) During the next three days, we would see proof, etched in our buildings and monuments, that this nation puts its faith in God, which is what makes America exceptional. "But not perfect," he added. He continued in this vein for a few minutes, firing up the sleepy crowd as if they were at an old-time revival. By the time we reached our destination—dinner at a seafood restaurant in Alexandria—most of the audience had shaken off the fatigue of travel and was responding with cheers, amens, or, when appropriate, shouts of dismay. As Mark wrapped up, he made his closing pitch: "Without God and the Bible, there would be no America. We have to understand these biblical principles we were built on if we're going to turn this nation around." From the sound of it, most of my bus mates agreed with him.

Two days later, when we visited the Supreme Court, Mark gave his audience a more concrete task. Now that they knew the biblical foundations of the nation, it was their job to vote accordingly. Standing in the hallway just past the visitors' entrance, he gestured at a painting of the first Chief Justice, John Jay. From memory, he recited a quotation from Jay's writings: "Providence has given to our people the choice of their rulers, and it is the duty as well as the privilege and interest of our Christian nation to select and prefer Christians for their rulers."[6] He added that only Christians have moral authority and the moral vision to govern in accordance with God's law. "Now, could Jay say something like that today?" he asked sarcastically. The tourists around me snorted or laughed in derision, shaking their heads at the idea. "No, of course not," Mark said. But we should remember that the morality of a democracy depends on the Christian character of its voters and elected officials.

Of the tour guides I observed, Mark was the most upfront about the political implications of his tours, but all of the tours were punctuated with explicit and implicit calls to action. Tourists were expected to take their newfound knowledge about American history home with them and use it for more than a scrapbook. They should stand in the gap by becoming politically involved through voting, grassroots activism, and financial support for conservative Christian candidates. Paraphrasing the famed nineteenth-century revivalist Charles Finney, Jonathan told his group, "Politics are a part of religion in a country such as this. God will bless or curse this nation based on how Christians act in politics."[7] Political activism was not just an option but an obligation. Dan made similar remarks on his tours, including one set of closing remarks on the final bus ride. "Christians need to be involved in politics and government, because we need good people," he said. "We're the salt and light on the front lines."

For Clay's tour group, their political involvement started during their trip. On their first night in D.C., they attended a rally for soon-to-be Republican presidential primary candidate Ben Carson. Carson himself was not in attendance, but political operatives hoping to persuade him to declare his candidacy ran the event to drum up support. It was an unexpected highlight for Barbara, a retired home economics teacher: "Oh, I enjoyed that. I had never been to anything like that and even if it had been one in my hometown, I might not have gone." But she found it compelling, enough to consider a donation to the campaign. "Today I got something in the mail from Run, Ben, Run," she told me during her follow-up interview.[8] "Give a little money. They have nine million, and [if they had] ten million they would have more than Hillary [Clinton], and would I like to give a little something? Fifteen dollars or a small amount of money." She did. The group had also watched a film about Carson to pass the time on the long bus ride back to Missouri, and Russell and Jeanie were impressed, too, particularly by Carson's prayer habits. "He has no problem at all giving glory to God for his hands and how he can do the surgery he does," said Jeanie. "He started praying at a very young age," Russell added. It was too early for them to have a favorite for the 2016 presidential race, but they would be paying attention to Carson.

Other guides were less explicit—and less strident—about how they hoped their tours would affect their audiences' political engagement, but they still saw a connection. Stacy identified two key messages that she hoped her tourists would remember. First, she said, "I'm going to help fill in some of the gaps that people aren't being told anymore. I mean a lot of people now are starting to say we're not a Christian nation, we weren't founded as a Christian nation, things like that, so my hope would be to fill in some of those gaps." Second, she hoped that if people knew about the founders' faith, they would grow in their own faith. Then, she said, "Hopefully they would want to participate in our government and our history in some meaningful way. You know, not just sit back on the sidelines and watch it all happen around them." Throughout her tour of D.C. she encouraged us to reflect on how we could contribute to our country, and her morning devotions highlighted exemplary Biblical characters whose righteous behavior saved their people, from Queen Esther to Naaman's unnamed slave girl.[9] On the final morning of our tour she read us an "old-fashioned" poem about how we have only one life to live, and only what is done for the cause of Christ will last. She then passed out red, white, and blue rubber bracelets inscribed with "Only One Life" for us all to take home as a souvenir. Katherine, the young middle-school teacher who accompanied several of her students on the tour, praised Stacy for her approach. Being a Christian nation, she said, is about "going back to the original mind-set people had, to be passionate about making sure our faith is lived out through what we do through our jobs and in our communities." For her and her students there was a clear connection between what they learned about the nation's heritage and how they ought to live their lives.

At the same time, tour guides knew some members of their audience might be squeamish about mixing religion and politics, or at least have friends or family who might be resistant to the idea. Several tour guides raised and responded to these potential objections through their stories. As the bus crawled through traffic on Constitution Avenue one afternoon, Jonathan regaled us with stories about the founders, including the Muhlenberg brothers. Peter Muhlenberg was a Virginia pastor who accepted a commission as a colonel in the Continental Army during the American Revolution. According to a popular (though likely apocryphal) story, he preached a sermon on Ecclesiastes 3:8, "There is a time for war and a time for peace." Declaring that this is a time for war, he stepped from behind the pulpit and began removing his clerical robes, revealing an army uniform underneath. His dramatic performance inspired the men of his congregation to take up arms themselves, and clergy became known as the "black-robed regiment."[10] Peter, however, was criticized by his brother and fellow pastor Frederick for getting involved in a political dispute, at least until Frederick's own church was burned down by the British Army—after that he joined the army himself. Both brothers went on to represent Pennsylvania in the first session of Congress in the new United States (1789–1791), and Frederick served as the first Speaker of the House. "He was the *Speaker of the House*," Jonathan emphasized. Moments later he had moved on to talking about how on the day Congress ratified the First Amendment members asked President Washington to declare a day of prayer and Thanksgiving. "So much for separation of church and state!" he scoffed.

Mark also talked about the Muhlenbergs on his tours, and the moral of the story was much the same. Frederick Muhlenberg's objections to a pastor being politically involved rang a bell for Mark and his audience: "Sounds like some people today who say Christians should stay out of politics!" quipped Mark. Most of his audience laughed or rolled their eyes, knowing full well by now that "some people" were wrong. But they should look for the statue of Peter Muhlenberg in the crypt of the Capitol during their tour, Mark told them. It depicts Muhlenberg in uniform but with his clerical robe still around one shoulder, as if he were in the act of removing it. Apocryphal or not, the story of his dramatic costume change has been immortalized in this statue, sent to the Capitol by Pennsylvania in 1889. And many tourists sought it out in the crypt, snapping pictures to take home with them as proof that a pastor had been a politician.

Beyond the Muhlenberg story and others like it, tour guides also sought to persuade tourists that not only had the founders themselves been Christians involved in politics, but they also had expected future generations to do the same. That expectation was built into the very nature of democracy. Dan asked his group on the bus, "Would the Bible tell us to obey the laws and then expect us not to care about electing lawmakers? Of course not." He echoed Jerry Falwell, adding, "Where we got this idea Christians shouldn't be in politics, I don't know, but it's a bad one."[11] And Mark explicitly connected this argument to the nation's founding charters at the National Archives, which establish a democracy that relies on the righteousness of its people for its survival. He quoted an unnamed historian who said, "People made the laws, but the churches made the people." The task of reforming the nation begins with developing moral citizens. "The laws themselves aren't enough," Mark added. "We need good people to execute them and live under them." In other words, Christians should involve themselves in government in order to ensure the nation's laws are moral, but citizens themselves should also be Christians in order to be trusted to abide by the laws in the first place.

These stories and arguments pushed back against a wide range of opponents who think that religion and politics should remain separate. Within conservative American Christianity, leaders like Russell Moore and Rob Dreher, among others, have called for the "Benedict option" of Christian families removing themselves as much as possible from a culture that is beyond redemption.[12] They reject the role of saviors, at least in the political sense that Christian heritage tours advocate. The same is true of younger white evangelicals today, who, like young Americans more broadly, are resistant to the Christian Right's particular fusion of Christianity and Republicanism.[13] They may hold conservative positions on some (though not all) social issues, but most do not favor the strong Christian nationalism that Mark, Jonathan, and other Christian guides preached. And, of course, the majority of liberals and progressives oppose fusing church and state. These were the easiest targets for guides to attack, and they frequently served as foils in guides' stories about how the founders' intentions have been misunderstood and distorted. During Christian heritage tours, however, these objectors are drowned out by the stories and sites of D.C., which in the guides' hands provide precedent for Christians to become politically active. When they return home, tourists are armed not only with the knowledge of America's Christian heritage but also with theological and historical arguments for why they should step into the role of saviors.

CHRISTIANITY IN THE PUBLIC SQUARE

Saving the nation, however, requires more than infusing politics with Christianity. Tour guides also argued that Christianity must be returned to Americans' public and private lives more broadly. D.C.'s Christian iconography provides a literal representation of this claim, serving as evidence that Christianity was once a dominant feature of American public life.[14] It was the rule, rather than the exception, that the art and architecture that collectively expressed the ideals of the nation would employ the symbols, figures, and texts of the Christian tradition. Christian heritage tours present this material culture as the last remnant of a better time, when Americans were so devoutly Christian they thought nothing of proclaiming it on their buildings. At the same time, several tour guides seemed to believe that if there were more Christian iconography on buildings—or at least if more people knew about it—it would influence people to return to the Christian foundations of the nation.

During one tour group's visit to Capitol Hill, they met with a member of the Congressional Prayer Caucus, who called on them to join his group's campaign to post signs saying "In God We Trust" in public places across the nation. The Congressional Prayer Caucus was founded in 2005 by Representative Randy Forbes of Virginia, and its members meet weekly to pray for the nation. They also try to ensure that legislation coming out of Congress reflects Christian values. According to the congressman who spoke with the group, the In God We Trust campaign started in response to the omission of the phrase on the replica of the House of Representatives Chamber in the new U.S. Capitol Visitor Center.[15] While that omission was rectified after a Republican outcry, members of the Congressional Prayer Caucus wanted to go further. They wanted to post the phrase in every congressional office. "We need to put God back up on our walls—people are ripping him down from the wall and out of history," the congressman said. So the caucus sent signs to most members of Congress, and its members were delighted when many recipients actually put the signs up. "If we can put it back in the U.S. Capitol," the congressman concluded, "we can put it back in the minds and hearts of Americans." He invited his audience to join him by posting the phrase in their own homes and offices, an invitation they enthusiastically accepted.[16]

Tour guides and guest speakers also called on tourists to pray for the nation and its leaders and to share the gospel with their fellow citizens. Even if they disagreed with then-President Obama, they ought to pray for him, according to Cathy, who stopped her group near the White House to offer prayers. Dan made a similar argument to his group, telling them that part of being a good Christian citizen is praying for the nation's leaders. Before lunch one day, Clay took a full ten minutes with his group to pray for the president. "Instead of talking about him, let's pray," he said. "We always talk, but we don't pray. So let's pray for him and our political leaders." Juxtaposed with the unrelenting criticism directed at President Obama at other moments in the tours, this call to prayer might seem insincere or performative. But for many in these groups it was the only logical response—at least, until the next opportunity to vote.

For each tour group, prayer was an essential tactic for turning the nation around. In fact, prayer for the nation, its leaders, and its citizens was assigned value similar to that of political activism, and the two were consistently linked in the tours' prescriptions for how to save the nation. The clearest example of the connection came from the same congressman who introduced the In God We Trust campaign. During his talk on Capitol Hill, he directed the group to the website PrayUSA, another initiative of the Congressional Prayer Caucus that began in 2015. It brings together pastors, government leaders, and citizens to pray for the nation and "challenge the growing antifaith movement" in the United States, he explained. He then read from the website's mission statement: "People of faith can no longer sit idly by and passively watch as our nation's history and Judeo-Christian heritage are being rewritten with a false narrative. As the first unified step together, these government leaders are passionately calling on God's people to unify with one heart and one voice to pray and take action for the United States and those who lead her."[17] Most of the audience murmured in agreement or nodded along—to them the connection between prayer and political action was obvious.

However, the participants in Christian heritage tours prayed for much more than God's guidance and protection on the nation's leaders. They also prayed for the individual salvation of their fellow citizens. Claudia, a self-proclaimed prayer warrior from Southern California, told me in an interview that she and her travel companion "prayed at many stops. . . . We're prayer warriors and believe in the power of prayer." Included in their prayers were both the nation's leaders and its citizens, as well as the tour guides, her fellow tourists, and even me. "I believe that God founded our nation and that he's not done with us," she said. What she was learning on the tour was in service of her ultimate goal: making sure that every person in the world was saved. Another tour heard a similar call from their congressman when they visited the Capitol. In his talk he quoted Jesus's Great Commission: "Go and make disciples of all nations."[18] He then modified Jesus's words slightly, telling tourists that it is their duty to "disciple the nation," meaning the United States. Saving the nation, it seemed, required more than just voting Christians into office. Christian tourists were called to reclaim every level of American society for Christianity, from the White House to their neighbor's house.

HISTORY AS A PRESCRIPTION

When Christian tourists drew connections between American history and the nation's salvation, they echoed a long-standing claim of the Christian Right. When white conservative Protestant leaders began rewriting American history in the 1970s, they did so out of concern for the present and future, not the past. Their nostalgia has always been the restorative type, longing to recreate a mythical golden age that has taken on the status of truth and tradition.[19] This type of nostalgia is a common feature of nationalist movements, and it helps explain why history was such a focal point for the founders of the Christian Right, and why American history was so entwined with policy and values in their discourse. Their aim was not simply to recognize the achievements of previous generations of American Christians. They had to create—or, as they saw it, preserve—the past that was to be restored. Without that model, the nation's decline would continue, with no possibility of redemption.

Restorative nostalgia is the reason that proponents of Christian heritage start not at the beginning of the story but at its climax: the Fall. Jerry Falwell begins his 1980 jeremiad *Listen, America!* with a dire diagnosis of the nation: "America, our beloved country, is indeed sick," he warns the reader. "It is time that we come together and rise up against the tide of permissiveness and moral decay that is crushing in on our society from every side."[20] His purpose in writing is to recount American history not as an academic exercise but as a desperate effort to slow the nation's decline. Peter Marshall and David Manuel made a similar argument in their 1977 bestselling classic *The Light and the Glory*, an argument they reiterated when they published a revised edition in 2009.[21] The things they feared in the 1970s, they said, had only become worse in the intervening years, from rising divorce rates to apathy about abortion, and from the legalization of same-sex marriage to increased cheating in elementary schools. "We could go on," they write, "but you get the idea. We are in desperate shape. American morality has no firm footing; it is precariously perched on the shifting sands of the latest trend in lifestyles."[22] Current books, films, and media make similar arguments, from *Monumental* to *The Founders' Bible*. The historical question of America's Christian heritage is urgent because the nation has lost its way.

But history itself is under attack, say the heritage makers. If anti-Christian academics and other elites have their way, Americans will not even know that there once was a Christian America to which they might return. D. James Kennedy, for instance, writes, "In the last fifty years, our nation has drifted from the biblical moorings on which America was built. So much so, that the mere assertion that ours is a Christian nation invites an argument from academic and media elites. Today, Americans have largely forgotten—or never learned—about the profound and deeply embedded role of biblical Christianity in America's rise."[23] David Barton adds that, if Americans today are ignorant of the role of Christianity in American history, it is because the academy, the media, and the government have worked overtime to erase it.[24] White evangelicals must take action to protect this history, since the mainstream will not.

This opening strategy introduces the audience to not one but two threats: the first is to the nation; the second, to its history. The audience is tasked with learning the nation's Christian history and using it to restore the nation to its previous Christian ideals. Barton goes so far as to compare his second book, *The Myth of Separation*, to the biblical book of Malachi. The prophet Malachi describes his own writing as a "book of remembrance."[25] In Barton's interpretation, this means it is a historical record of ancient Israel that showed subsequent generations what is right and what is wrong, inspiring them to reject the wrong and turn back to God. Barton suggests that his own book is also a book of remembrance, through which "the hearts of the nation may again be turned back toward their fathers—their Founding Fathers."[26] The key to the nation's salvation lies in its true history, and by reading, watching, or listening to Christian heritage media, white evangelicals can prepare themselves to step in as saviors.

This particular expression of restorative nostalgia also informs the work of white evangelical activists seeking to reform history and social science textbooks to bring them in line with the Christian heritage version of history. After the battle over Texas's state history standards, board of education member Bob McLeroy told a Tea Party audience that he and the his fellow Christian conservatives on the board had "stood up for true American history" against what he perceived as leftist bias in the academy.[27] True American history, according to McLeroy, recognizes that "our nation was founded on biblical not secular principles. Secularism says there is no truth, there is no God, and that we just evolved. The Declaration [of Independence] clearly states that truth exists, that there is a Creator, and that we are created."[28] McLeroy argued that if Americans forget this, they forget "what it means to be an American."[29] Rewriting textbooks and state standards is perhaps the most effective way of preserving this message for the next generation.

FOR GOD AND COUNTRY

During their time in D.C., Christian tourists joined in a battle for the nation and its history that has been ongoing since the 1970s. They learned the nostalgic arguments that originated with the Christian Right and that have been disseminated through a variety of media in the decades since. At the same time, however, they saw themselves as entering a much longer war, the same war to defend Christianity and freedom at home and abroad that American soldiers have been fighting since the nation's founding. The countless war memorials in D.C. offered ample opportunity for Christian tourists to contemplate the sacrifice of the men and women who have already laid down their lives for their country. As they did so, they connected that tradition of sacrifice to their own calling to save the nation.

In the stories told by most Christian heritage guides, the American military served as God's proxy in defending the cause of freedom around the world. At the Iwo Jima Memorial, Mark told his group that the very first military engagement of the newly formed United States was with the Barbary pirates, who were Muslims. While European nations settled for paying tribute, President Jefferson sent the newly built American navy to fight back in the Battle of Tripoli. Victory in that war was not just for America but for all nations oppressed by the Barbary pirates and, in Mark's view, Islam.[30] It was but the first of many battles in which American soldiers would fight and die to fulfill the nation's Christian duty to eradicate "evil" wherever it was found. According to Mark, that sense of duty still drives the wars of the twentieth and twenty-first centuries. "The Devil uses false ideologies like Muslim terrorists to attack us," he told one group. In this cosmic war between good and evil, the United States is always on the side of God and freedom, while the side of evil is populated by a rotating cast of military opponents.

To further underscore the idea that God and the American military are on the same side, Christian tour guides told stories of divine protection and intervention at key moments in battle. Every guide I observed told the story of George Washington's miraculous survival and victory during the Battle of Monongahela in the French and Indian War.[31] Similarly, every group that visited the Marine Corps Memorial heard that God miraculously intervened on behalf of the United States during the battle for the island of Iwo Jima. That victory is memorialized by the iconic statue of six Marines raising the American flag to signal that the Americans had captured the island. But tour guides told their groups that, according to legend, the sculptor included thirteen hands, even though there were only six Marines.[32] Most told this story with a wink, allowing tourists to draw their own conclusions about whose hand it might be. "I think we all know who the extra hand belongs to," one guide, Paul, told his group. Jonathan, on the other hand, went straight to the point. "We're among friends," he said as he finished the story. "We all know that God is involved in these things."

This sanctification of the American military came up at many points during the tours I observed, but the most striking expressions of it took place at Arlington National Cemetery. Arlington, in some ways, carries a kind of double meaning for Christian heritage tours. On the one hand, tourists and guides rarely understand it as an explicitly Christian site. "It's more patriotic than Christian," said veteran guide Sheila in an interview. Beyond the white tombstones marked with small crosses and a few larger memorials with biblical inscriptions, there is little Christian iconography to be found. Yet at the same time, the whole site evokes the theme of sacrifice, which resonates deeply with the Christian tradition. As Jesus died on behalf of humanity, so too did these soldiers.

That idea made a powerful impression on Russell and Jeanie, who said they felt a strong sense of reverence as they walked through Arlington. Russell explained, "It does make you think very, very deeply of sacrifices of so many, not just the individuals that are buried there but so many hundreds of thousands, millions of men and women have made to protect our freedom and our rights and our right to religion, and without those people who over these centuries, we wouldn't have these rights." Jeanie added, "As a Christian, I don't think you can walk through Arlington without a sense of deep reverence." Other tourists expressed similar feelings of awe and gratitude, though some were surprised by how moving they found the experience to be. "Arlington blew me away," Annie said. "I just kinda thought it would be just a lot of white gravestones.... [But] you think about all of the other men and women who died that aren't honored, and all you can see is graves everywhere you look. It just blows you away when you think that's almost double this number that has died so you can be free." Guide Stacy went so far as to say Arlington had to be a priority for her groups, even on a short tour: "I just feel like it's so important to see the sacrifice that's been made." In a way, Arlington was personal for many of the tourists I encountered, even though only a handful knew someone buried there. The acres of white markers commemorated a sacrifice made for them, so that they could live in peace and freedom.

For Clay's tour group, the aura of sacredness at Arlington was amplified by the fact that they visited on a Sunday morning. On most of Clay's tours to other destinations, the group attends a local church service together. In D.C., though, he told them that their visit at Arlington would be their worship time. One member of the group, Loretta, was traveling with her husband, a Vietnam veteran. She said Arlington was one of her favorite sites. "We went Sunday morning. I thought that was a very fitting time for it. That was a beautiful morning, too," she told me later. "That was our worship service, I guess." The combination of a sunny morning and the peaceful atmosphere of Arlington put the group in a contemplative mood, even as we walked six long miles around the cemetery. "The beauty and serenity of Arlington is just . . . what can you say?" Jeanie mused in an interview. "To me, that was the perfect day to do Arlington, on a Sunday morning. It was almost like a worship service."

This sense of reverence for the sacrifice of fallen soldiers extended beyond Arlington to the many war memorials on the National Mall. Like Arlington, most of these sites have little or no explicitly Christian iconography.[33] But for Christian tour guides, the most important aspect of the memorials is that they honor individual soldiers who gave their lives for the nation. Jonathan explained that their Christ-like sacrifice is what matters most on his tours:

> I can't say anything at the Vietnam [Memorial] about its design. . . .
> There are maybe some individual stories that we can talk about, the
> man who fought in the war was a righteous man, was a believer. But
> things I would normally point out, even in most Christian tours, would
> be more about the sacrifice and then tying that into how God sent
> his son and was sacrificed for us. A lot of them are, it has to be about
> the man. Jesus isn't in the wall, per se, the memorial. Jesus isn't in the
> reliefs at the World War II Memorial. But Jesus is in the men who died,
> who fought, and it's their stories that are going to personalize it.

Stacy drew similar connections for her group on the bus ride to the Korean War Veterans Memorial. She spoke about compassion, or "understanding the suffering of others and wanting to do something about it." That compassion, she said, inspired American soldiers to fight for people they had never met. She then read us the Bible verse for the day, John 15:13: "Greater love has no one than this: to lay down one's life for one's friends." Both memorials made a strong impression on tourists. Charlene from Texas was struck by the lists of names of the fallen in Vietnam, saying she was amazed by "how many soldiers fought and how many died, and it's just incredible numbers, just thousands and thousands of soldiers that gave their lives for us." Barbara was similarly awed. At each memorial she found herself thinking "back to that time in history and what's going on in the world and how the men fought for our freedom to help people in different situations in the world. So many people died as a result, but that's just moving to me." At each war memorial, tourists expressed their gratitude for what they saw as the ultimate Christian act in service of others.

Veterans, too, were greeted with reverence when Christian tour groups encountered them. In some sense, American veterans are the incarnation of the sacrifice commemorated at Arlington. They are themselves Christ figures in Christian tourists' theology of the nation. Their presence made the war memorials come alive for many tourists. Gladys said the Vietnam Veterans Memorial became significant to her only through this sort of encounter. "I got there and I thought, oh, okay, that's it, just a wall. You know?" she told me. "But then the last time I went there, I saw a couple of veterans come up and find a name and just start crying and hugging each other, and then it became meaningful to me." Oregon dad Jacob felt the same way, to his surprise. At the memorial he said, "I think it was because there were so many, you know, men who had served who were being pushed around [in wheelchairs], and it was just very solemn.... I had no expectation of that. I kind of thought I'd just be bored there. But that one was kind of moving for me, actually." Katherine reported that she and her eighth graders were also deeply moved at the Vietnam Veterans Memorial because they had the opportunity to talk with visiting veterans about where they served and whose names they were tracing from the wall. "It made it seem more alive in that sense, to see such a solemn place and to just know that thousands and thousands of names on those walls, just made it more present.... It's still affecting people to this day, and we saw that firsthand." For most Christian tourists, no story told by a tour guide could equal meeting the people who had fought on their behalf.

In most cases Christian tourists' conversations with veterans were impromptu, the natural interaction of visitors to the same site: they swapped cameras to take each other's pictures, shook hands, shared their names and where they were from. When I traveled with a group of eighth graders from the South, however, we happened to arrive at the World War II Memorial at the same time as a group of WWII veterans, flown in for the day by the Honor Flight Network. As we spilled off the bus and milled around, waiting for the word to walk over to the memorial, the veterans' bus pulled in behind us, and men in wheelchairs were slowly assisted off of it. The stu-

Young visitors tracing the engravings on the wall of the Korean
War Veterans Memorial, July 2016. Photo by the author.

dents stared, and a few asked the chaperones what was happening. Their attention was short-lived, though, as their eyes wandered to the towering columns and bubbling fountain of the memorial. The tour guide, Mark, launched into his usual lecture about how Franklin Delano Roosevelt, despite his moral failings, led the nation in prayer the night before the United States entered the war. Roosevelt knew the war was necessary to "defend liberty and property from the evil in the heart of man." The students fidgeted, eager to go explore. Meanwhile, the WWII veterans had finished disembarking and, with the help of their aides, were moving slowly toward the entrance to the memorial.

Mark kept going, hitting his standard talking points for this site. We are still fighting the same war as the men who fought in WWII, he said, the ultimate battle between good and evil. We may not have to take up arms in the same way today, but the war continues. On that note, he dismissed the group to view the memorial at their own pace. Students quickly peeled off in groups of two and three and vanished into the crowded colonnade, without a backward glance for the group of veterans moving down the nearby sidewalk. Their chaperones followed at a more leisurely pace. I watched them go, stunned by how the scene had unfolded. For the last two days I had heard this group praise the nation and its military, speaking reverently of the sacrifices made to keep us free. Now, with some of the last living veterans of World War II only a few feet away, I expected Mark to skip the spiel about Roosevelt. I expected students and their chaperones to rush to honor these men however they could. Instead, it was business as usual.

I walked in the opposite direction, taking the opportunity to fill my water bottle while I tried to shake off my frustration. They were only eighth graders, after all, I thought, and they had been cooped up on a bus in traffic and corralled as a captive audience for Mark's talk. No wonder they wanted to run around in the sun, splash in the fountain, and take a selfie with their state's pillar. It was unfair to expect them to behave any differently from other tourists, even if the gap between how they spoke and how they acted was jarring. I made a few notes and went to rejoin the group at the memorial—only to stop and stare once again. While I was at the water fountain, someone in the group had noticed the veterans and summoned the students back to meet them. I watched from a short distance away as the students and chaperones shook the men's hands, hugged them, and took pictures with them. At one point the whole group applauded. It all felt simultaneously contrived yet sincere. Somehow, this veneration was no less authentic for its very public performance.

I stayed where I was. This was the scene I had expected, even wanted, but I could not bring myself to join it. Without question, I was moved. I found myself thinking of my late grandfather, who served in the Korean War and never spoke of what he saw in Korea to anyone, even his family. I would have given anything for him to experience this sort of honor. But the tour group's collective adulation felt alien to me. I wrote at the time that my reluctance to join them felt similar to my reluctance to pray with them. It was like being invited to take communion at a church to which I did not belong. Participating in this heightened emotional experience would make me part of the group in a way that I was not, nor did I wish to be. So I remained at a distance until it was time to board the bus and head off to dinner.

Most of the conversation on that bus ride was about getting to meet the veterans and what a nice bonus that was for the students' visit. I was struck by how the students spoke of the veterans as another sort of museum exhibit or historic site. They were living artifacts, something to be seen and consumed by the tourist gaze. As we approached our destination, the lead teacher took the tour guide's microphone to share her thoughts on the experience: "God planned this," she said, her voice shaking with emotion. "I love you guys, and God's timing is perfect." None of Mark's history lectures could compare to the experience of meeting real veterans at the memorial honoring their service. In the same way that the students could now say they had seen the Declaration of Independence for themselves, or walked the halls of Congress for themselves, they had now met American heroes on holy ground.

ONWARD CHRISTIAN SOLDIERS

Sacrifice was a central theme of Christian heritage tours, largely due to the prominence of war memorials in D.C. and tourists' encounters with veterans, but the theme extended beyond the specific context of the American military. Tour guides connected the sacrifices of American soldiers both to Jesus and to other biblical heroes and Christian martyrs, further linking American history and the Christian tradition. Their key message, however, was that the time for sacrifice on behalf of God and country had not yet passed. Having established that the nation is in crisis, they called on Christian tourists to step up and risk their own lives, fortunes, and sacred honor for the sake of Christian America.

Despite their conviction that the nation was in crisis, Christian tourists and guides retained the hope embedded in the jeremiad. They felt that the window of opportunity was quickly closing, but their call to political action was predicated on a sense that the nation could still be turned around. What was required was for "real" Christians to claim their rightful place as stewards of the nation, no matter the odds or the sacrifice required. The biblical story of David and Goliath was a popular analogy. On the bus one morning, Stacy admitted to us, "I've personally felt hopeless for the nation. But then I felt the Holy Spirit say, 'I'm not hopeless.' To be hopeless is to think that God has removed his hand from this nation." She let the group think about that for a moment as she opened her Bible to the story of David and Goliath (1 Samuel 17). She read us a few abridged verses, emphasizing that the battle against the Philistines seemed unwinnable for the ancient Israelites, and that young David seemed the least likely of heroes. But David's power came from God, she explained, and just as God used David to defeat Goliath against the odds, God can still use American Christians to restore the nation. "We can't give up hope for our nation yet. We need to remember the challenges God has brought us through, on both a national and a personal level," she concluded. "God is not done with us yet." I saw several tourists nodding in agreement. My later conversations with them confirmed that they felt that it was not too late for the nation to return to righteousness, fight for freedom, and proclaim the gospel. Though the current state of crisis was overwhelming, their faith told them that God could use anyone to bring about change.

Some of the most optimistic notes of Christian heritage tours arose at moments like this, during discussions of who God will use to save the nation. On almost every tour, the answer was children.[34] During the eighth graders' visit to the Capitol, their congressman gathered them around him in the Rotunda. He looked at them solemnly. "God is preparing you kids for life for his purpose," he told them. "And you should cooperate with him, not resist." One parent said amen, while the children in the group were serious and silent. It later became clear from their conversations that the group understood this visit to the Capitol and D.C. to be part of God's preparation for the students' future leadership. At the same time, most of them also expected saving the nation to be dangerous. Sheila, too, made this clear to her group during one morning devotion on the bus; she told the story of Esther and admonished the young people in the group to pay special attention. After reading a brief summary of the biblical story, she paraphrased what Mordecai tells Esther as she is deciding whether to risk her life by approaching the king: "You were born for such a time as this."[35] She let us ponder that for a moment and then reminded us also of what Esther says when she agrees to go to the king: "If I die, I die."[36] At that we all fell silent. Sheila told us that God has a plan for each one of us and that we, too, were born for such a time as this. "Do you have a vision for how you want to impact your community? Your nation? Your world?" she asked. "What are you unhappy with in our nation? What would you change?" The adults were included in this discussion, but it was aimed at the children. The familiar story of Esther reminded children of their responsibility and warned them that fulfilling it might be hard, even dangerous.

The possibility of danger loomed large in these conversations about saving the nation, as the language of victimization merged with the idea of sacrifice. Tour guides regularly brought up the persecution of Christians in other parts of the world, particularly the Middle East, in part as a foil to highlight the greatness of the United States and the privilege of religious freedom. Like many elements of Christian heritage tours, though, this praise for the United States often segued into a warning about the nation's imminent decline. On our way to the U.S. Holocaust Memorial Museum, Clay urged his group to spend some time on the second floor, looking at exhibits about current genocides. "More Christians are being killed now than ever before in history," he told us, specifically by the terrorist group known as the Islamic State (ISIS). American Christians were blessed to be able to practice their faith freely for the most part, he said, but we should not take it for granted or forget our brothers and sisters who are persecuted and killed for their faith. If the nation continues on its present course of decline, he suggested, American Christians might soon face similar persecution.

During our last lunch together on Paul's tour, a guest speaker made this argument in even stronger terms. We had gathered in the upper room of an old D.C. restaurant where, we were assured, members of Congress regularly dined. No familiar faces appeared during our short walk through the main floor, except in the photos on the walls. We were wrapping up the main course when our guest speaker arrived to talk with us about what it means to be a Christian in these challenging times. He started off with a story that had previously circulated widely among white evangelicals. In February 2015, twenty-one young men were beheaded by ISIS on a beach in Libya, all of them Coptic Christians from Egypt and Ghana. The video of the execution was released online, prompting international outrage.[37] But what we did not hear from the media, our speaker said, was how the men's families reacted. "They wept with joy," he said. He looked around the room, making eye contact with each one of us. "They wept with joy at the honor of their sons and brothers dying for Christ." These families were poor and illiterate, he continued, not powerful people like the ones here in D.C. But we should be impressed by them and their response, not by the trappings of power around us. By then many people were nodding, visibly moved by the story. One older white woman at my table wiped her eyes. The speaker continued his talk, which touched on more familiar themes in white evangelical discourse: the threat of same-sex marriage, the need for prayer in schools, the decline of the family. In each case he pleaded for compassion for the other side, without ceding any moral ground. He also asked us to embrace the loss of power and even persecution as biblically ordained. "If we end up as a minority group without the power we once had, we will be stronger for it," he said. "We have to rejoice that a family member is chosen to die. We need to rejoice when we lose a bill. We are suffering for Christ."

While not every group shared this positive outlook on the subject, tourists in each group I observed indicated that they did expect that either they or their children would be actively persecuted for their faith. For Jacob's wife Amy, that was precisely the reason she brought her ten-year-old son and thirteen-year-old daughter to D.C. As we walked together from the bus to the Jefferson Memorial, she told me, "My children are here because I truly believe they will be persecuted in their lifetime. And it will start with economic persecution." She wanted them to learn the nation's history so that when that day comes they will know what they are fighting for. Others brought up Masterpiece Cake Shop owner Jack Phillips as an example of how Christians were already oppressed in the United States, suggesting that these are only the first of many such cases. And tour guides made similar observations. "I think the Christians of America are realizing it's costing a little more to stand up and be accounted for," said Sheila. Jonathan was more direct: "Jesus said that's what's going to happen. We will be persecuted, duh." These conversations were reminders that it is dangerous—even deadly—work to be a savior.

At first glance it would appear that white evangelicals' battle to restore the nation has little in common with the battles fought by American soldiers overseas. Yet in the world of Christian heritage tours, these battles are all part of the same war. Christian guides and tourists portrayed the American military as God's proxy, fighting to defend a Christian nation and its righteous way of life from the forces of evil. Their narrative had no room for other motivations, much less the complex history of American imperialism and its effects on the world. There was only one reason for American soldiers to fight and die for their country: to preserve the conservative Christian values that define America. In other words, soldiers gave their lives not for America as it is in reality, but for America as seen through the lens of restorative nostalgia. By the logic of Christian heritage tours, that makes them the tourists' brothers and sisters in arms.

For Christian tourists, Arlington National Cemetery and the war memorials honor the kind of sacrifice they are called by God to emulate. They, too, had to be willing to give their all for the sake of restoring America to its Christian foundations. Their lives were not in danger—at least not yet—but they expected to meet resistance and even persecution. That might take the form of academic ridicule for their revisionist history, or the destruction of the evidence of America's Christian heritage. It might take the form of legislation condemning their conservative values, or hostility from their neighbors. But they learned they should count these trials as joy. Their beloved country was in crisis, and it was up to them to reverse the decline. Their time in D.C. was their boot camp, their training ground to learn America's real history. When they returned home, it would be their turn to join the battle, to use that history to save the nation.

Conclusion   Invisible Grace

....

When visitors enter the new Museum of the Bible, they walk into the Bible itself, at least in a sense.[1] The museum's massive bronze doors are engraved with the text of Genesis 1 from an early edition of the Gutenberg Bible. Visitors do not get far, however, before encountering a sophisticated security apparatus that is also ornamented with scripture. The experience is pleasant compared to security at the Capitol, but it is no less intense. Evidently something here needs protection, though it is not clear what it might be. After security we traverse part of the museum's great hall, staring upward at the changing images on the LED ceiling panels that stretch as far as the eye can see. Museum greeters direct us to the elevators, suggesting we start at the top of the museum and work our way down.

As the elevator doors open on the sixth floor, we emerge into a glass-encased gallery with views of the D.C. skyline. To our right is the Capitol dome, and the Washington Monument is to our left. It is an impressive sight, even if the sea of roofs immediately around us is somewhat distracting. I see other visitors snapping pictures, and I do the same. But the view is just the beginning. What follows is an overwhelming series of exhibits on everything from ancient Near Eastern archeology to twenty-first-century "Bible-based" businesses. One whole floor is dedicated to bringing the narratives of the Hebrew Bible and New Testament to life through multimedia experiences. Another floor explores the history of the Bible's composition, translation, and dissemination around the world, with a particularly elaborate display about the King James Version. At every turn some new technology offers an opportunity to "engage with the Bible."

The Gutenberg doors at the Museum of the Bible, December 2017. Photo by the author.

The Museum of the Bible opened in November 2017, the culmination of nearly a decade of planning by Steve Green, its founder. Green is the CEO of the Hobby Lobby chain of craft stores, which made national headlines by successfully challenging the Affordable Care Act's birth control mandate before the Supreme Court in 2014.[2] He is also a conservative evangelical Christian and the owner of one of the largest collections of biblical manuscripts and artifacts in the world, many of which are now on display at the Museum of the Bible. The museum takes a scholarly approach, focusing on the history, narrative, and impact of the Bible across many times and places rather than evangelizing for one perspective over others. But Green has also expressed a political vision for the museum that echoes Christian heritage arguments and influenced the choice of location: in D.C. the museum can attract both tourists and political leaders. "As many people as we can educate about this book, the better," Green told the *Washington Post* in 2014. "I think seeing the biblical foundations of our nation—for our legislators to see that, that a lot of that was biblically based, that we have religious freedoms today, which are a biblical concept, it can't hurt being there."[3] This vision becomes clear in a variety of places in the museum, as the exhibits make sweeping claims about the influence of the Christian Bible on the United States.[4]

One example of these claims is Washington Revelations, an attraction inside the museum worthy of an amusement park. For a small fee visitors to the museum can "fly" over D.C. in a multisensory experience. According to the ride's introductory video, we were about to see evidence of the Bible's influence on great Americans, including artists, architects, and presidents. Inside the ride I followed the staff's directions to stand on a small platform ("flyboard") and hold on tightly to the handlebars. The flight began with a rush, as the platforms began to move. We soared above the D.C. skyline, then plunged down to see features of the city that I knew well from Christian heritage tours: Moses on the East Pediment of the Supreme Court, the statue of Paul and a quote from the biblical book of Micah in the Library of Congress, the mention of God in the inscriptions at the Jefferson Memorial. Wind blew on us, and water splashed in our faces, adding to the dramatic effect. Eventually we hurtled toward the base of the Washington Monument, turning sharply upward at the last moment. When we reached the top moments later, *Laus Deo* appeared before us, the final image of the ride.[5] The museum hoped, however, that it would not be our final encounter with Christian objects in D.C. The introductory video encouraged visitors to explore the sites featured on the ride for themselves during their time in the capital. The gift shop even sells a *Washington Revelations* photo album to inspire visitors to document and remember what they find.[6]

Long before the museum opened, Christian heritage tour guides were anticipating how to incorporate it into their tours. The location was convenient—a few blocks off of the National Mall, it is not as out of the way as the National Cathedral—and it would obviously be of interest. The challenge was how to fit one more site into an already packed agenda. Dan mused at one point that he might skip the National Archives to free up an afternoon for the Museum of the Bible. The lines at the Archives were so long in the summer, and he was unsure it was worth the wait. Other guides said they would at least strongly recommend it to tourists as an option for their free time in D.C., even if they were unable to visit as a group. By the time the museum had been open a year, nearly one million people had visited it, and most Christian heritage tours' websites advertised it as one of D.C.'s main attractions.[7]

Much like Christian heritage tours, the Museum of the Bible brings D.C.'s ambient Christianity into focus. The *Washington Revelations* ride does this in an explicit way, bringing visitors literally face to face with Christian images and inscriptions around the city. But the sheer existence of the museum itself also raises the profile of Christianity in the nation's capital. Its monumental size, its prime location, its proximity to the Smithsonian museums, its state-of-the-art design, its massive collection—all of these components make it impossible to ignore. The museum's exhibits consistently resonate with the arguments of Christian heritage makers, particularly the "Impact" floor. A dizzying array of objects, text, and interactive technology demonstrates how the Bible has influenced everyone from American abolitionists to fashion designers. The subtext is that the Bible is embedded in all aspects of culture, even in the supposedly secular United States. When visitors enter the exhibit about the Bible's impact on America, they are greeted by a passage from the 1620 Mayflower Compact, rendered in bronze and suspended over the central display in a spotlight: "Having undertaken for the glory of God and advancement of the Christian faith and honour of our king and country, a voyage to plant the first colony in the northern parts of Virginia, do by these presents solemnly and mutually in the presence of God and one of another, covenant and combine ourselves together into a civil body politic." This is the starting point for the exhibit and for the museum's story about the United States, which highlights the Christian faith of mostly white, mostly Protestant American heroes through Bibles, artifacts, videos, holograms, and interactive screens.[8] Nothing could be further from the sterile exhibits at the Supreme Court. Here, the Bible comes alive.

SHARED STORIES, DYNAMIC IDENTITIES

This book has explored the stories white evangelicals in the United States tell about themselves in relation to the nation. Christian heritage tours are a good place to eavesdrop on these stories, but they are not unique to this context. White evangelical tourists from all over the country arrived in D.C. already knowing these stories. They shared a sense of simultaneous belonging and alienation that was reinforced by their experiences in D.C. And they shared a way of talking about the United States that mimicked the jeremiad created by the Christian Right and disseminated through a variety of media since the 1980s. When tour guides pointed out Christian objects as evidence of America's Christian heritage and, in the next breath, warned that these objects were endangered or even already lost, tourists nodded along in agreement. These dissonant claims resonated with the stories they already knew.

These stories fell into two narrative arcs, what I have called in this book the insider and outsider narratives. The insider narrative described a nostalgic past in which Christians—specifically, white conservative evangelical Protestants—dominated American politics and culture and infused American laws with conservative Christian values. The United States was a nation in covenant with the Christian God, and as long as its citizens and leaders honored that covenant, God blessed the nation with economic prosperity and military might. The outsider narrative, in contrast, described how Americans in the more recent past abandoned the covenant with God, removed Christians from positions of power, and turned away from Christian values. The nation fell into decline as a result, plagued by drug use, rising poverty, broken families, and impotence in global politics. Together, the two narratives set up the biblical jeremiad's call to repentance: if Americans could be persuaded to turn back to righteousness, God's blessings would return and the nation would be saved. Underlying the jeremiad were three metanarratives that shaped how these stories were told and made them believable to this audience: the idea of American exceptionalism supported the idea that the United States was chosen and blessed by God and that the nation's demise would be catastrophic; the basic plot of Christian salvation history amplified the themes of sin, repentance, and sacrifice already present in these stories; and a simplistic form of the theory of secularization provided an antagonist.

During Christian heritage tours of D.C., guides and tourists alike told these stories over and over as they talked about the United States in the past and present. They varied somewhat in terms of characters and details, but the plots remained recognizable. Some guides were more strident in their narration, while others were more circumspect. Some tourists eagerly jumped in to tell their own stories, while others hesitated to share. Across the nine tour groups I observed in 2014 and 2015, however, these stories remained surprisingly consistent. Moreover, most tourists said that what they learned in D.C. were the details, the supporting evidence for the stories they already knew how to tell. Taylor, a single man in his thirties, said he had not learned anything really new about Christianity in America, even though he was excited about many of the sites he saw and the stories he heard. "It's like I sort of knew it already.... Nothing was really eye-opening," he said in a follow-up interview. "I guess I kind of expected it." Like Taylor, many tourists came to D.C. not to learn something wholly new but to experience what they expected to find. Because the overwhelming majority of them were white evangelicals, they already knew the stories. Thanks to the efforts of the Christian Right and the prevalence of white evangelical consumer culture, the insider and outsider narratives were routine frameworks for how they talked about their relationship to the nation.

These narratives do more than entertain or educate. They are public narratives, shared stories that members of a group use to explain who they are and what they are doing. In a sense, identity itself is a story, one that we all continually retell to incorporate new events and experiences. As we do so the story shifts—past events that were once prominent become less relevant in light of new developments, and past minutiae take on new significance in the plot. These stories are never singular or static. We can choose from a range of available narratives at any given point, some shared and some individual, and combine them in creative and dynamic ways. Among white American evangelicals, the insider and outsider narratives are dominant shared stories that intersect with the stories of individuals' own experiences as well as the metanarratives of modern American society. In their various combinations, these narratives offer plots in which white evangelicals play a distinct set of roles. They can be founders, exiles, victims, or saviors, depending on which stories they tell about themselves and the nation in a given moment.

These roles and the narratives that produce them are mutually contradictory, but this is not unusual. Embedded in any insider claim is the claimant's anxiety about being perceived as an outsider, while an outsider claim, by contrast, may work to disguise how much of an insider the claimant is. In other words, people cast themselves as powerful when they fear they are powerless, or about to become so. And people cast themselves as powerless in order to downplay the power they do possess. Insider and outsider rhetorics are thus inextricable from each other; where one is present, the other lies just below the surface.[9] This means that when we look at the outsider or insider claims of white evangelicals, we must be attentive to what those claims mask or reveal about the group's relationship to the purported mainstream, and what advantage is gained by either claim. The outsider narrative works together with the insider narrative to give white evangelicals the option to claim either position. Sometimes white evangelicals find it expedient to be insiders, to call on the authority of tradition to legitimize their arguments. At other times they gain an advantage by claiming to be outsiders, even if that claim fails to reflect the reality of how dominant white Christians have been and remain in the United States.

Together, these narratives form an interpretive framework for white American evangelicals to understand their relationship to the nation. Christian heritage tours are a place to observe them in action and to witness how they can reinforce one another, frustrate one other, and combine in different ways to produce different roles. The role of founders, for instance, emerges from the combination of the insider narrative and the metanarratives of American exceptionalism and Christian salvation history. Tour guides told stories of the great white Christian men who founded the nation and expected their successors to be similarly Christian. They argued for the implicit Christianity of the nation's founding documents and the central role of the Bible in shaping the American form of government. They also told stories about the Christian God's interventions on America's behalf as part of a broader plan for the salvation of the world. The Christian objects tourists encountered in D.C. amplified and reiterated these stories, offering corroborating evidence of America's Christian heritage.

Underlying these stories, however, was the outsider narrative, as tourists continually heard how the nation had strayed from these Christian founding principles. Throughout the tours they were made to feel the disjuncture between the Christian founders' experience as insiders and their own experience as outsiders. That disjuncture made way for two other roles: exiles and victims. In creating their role as exiles, Christian tourists and guides relied on the outsider narrative along with the metanarrative of secularization. In these stories Christians had been exiled from the public square and stripped of the political and cultural power they once had. Secularists had erased God from monuments, textbooks, and laws in the name of the separation of church and state. The nation was on the verge of forgetting its Christian heritage and forfeiting God's protection. In this context, the outsider narrative generated nostalgia for the past the insider narrative depicts. Christian tour companies capitalized on this nostalgia in their marketing, calling on tourists to visit D.C. in order to recover that idealized past. If they did so, they could return from their exile and rebuild a Christian nation.

Christian tourists and guides combined narratives in a slightly different way to cast themselves as victims. While this role, too, relied heavily on the outsider narrative and the metanarrative of secularization, it treated the insider narrative as an account of a lost cause rather than an aspirational past. In discussing current events, they revealed their sense that the country had irrevocably abandoned their values, particularly on the issue of same-sex marriage. They commented on the absence of "real" Christians in D.C., and they told stories about Christians who had been persecuted for standing up for their faith at home and abroad. Their experiences with D.C. security confirmed their sense of alienation, as did D.C.'s inhospitable landscape. Even the Christian objects that populated that landscape became part of the outsider narrative, threatened by the same forces that threatened Christians themselves.

The fourth role that emerged during Christian heritage tours was the role of saviors. This role combined all of these narratives to establish that the nation was in decline and to offer the past as a prescription for how it can be saved. Tourists, guides, and guest speakers were all convinced that Christianity needed to be returned to the public square in every sense. More public displays of Christianity would influence the American public for good, they argued, and Christian values should inform laws as the founders intended. If more Americans knew the Christian heritage of the nation, they would not see such things as unconstitutional favoritism of white Christianity. Instead, they would see that this was what America was intended to be all along: a Christian nation. Christian heritage tours of D.C. initiated tourists into this battle for the soul of the nation, arming them with the historical arguments they would need to spread the word. Like the American soldiers who fought for the nation overseas, Christian tourists would fight for the nation at home, sacrificing whatever was needed. Their sacred duty was to share what they had learned, to pray for the nation, and, of course, to vote.

Christian tourists moved easily among these roles during their time in D.C., just as white evangelicals move among them in a broader context. When they wanted to play an insider role, they appealed to the prominent place of white Christians at key moments in American history, and their claims were validated by the Christian inscriptions, images, and objects found in the capital. When they wanted to play an outsider role, they identified potential threats to American Christianity and amplified those threats in order to position themselves on the margins. This move was especially visible in their interactions with Christian objects, which disrupted the outsider narrative with their material presence. Identifying a threat to such objects neutralized their disruptive potential, as they joined Christians themselves on the margins. Both strategies are familiar features of white evangelicals' political discourse, and the benefits of this dynamic identity are endless. As outsiders, white evangelicals can claim the moral high ground of the outsider and elicit Americans' sympathy for the underdog. But in reality, white evangelicals are as much insiders as outsiders in the United States today. They benefit from the historical and contemporary power of white Christians in American law, politics, and culture. As insiders they can claim the authority of tradition and the benefit of laws made in their image. They can choose whichever position offers the most advantage in a given moment.

SPREADING THE GOOD NEWS

When the Christian tourists I met returned home, they were eager to share what they had learned in D.C. with their families, friends, and churches. Everyone I interviewed reported taking hundreds or even thousands of photos during their trip, both to aid their own memories and to show the folks back home. Many also bought postcards and small souvenirs for family members. And some bought Christian heritage books and movies, which they planned to share with as many people as possible. "I bought a copy of *Monumental* and took it in to our Christian school so they could show it to the kids," Erica told me. She also suggested that her guide, Mark, ought to make a video of his talk about the Gutenberg Bible at the Library of Congress. "And if that ended up in the hands of Christian schools, at the very least, wouldn't that be a blessing," she said. Constance, too, bought two books and a film on Christian heritage to accompany her pictures. When I asked her if she had shared them with anyone, she replied, "Oh gosh, have I ever!" She had shown pictures to her friends and everyone at church, and she was planning to ask her pastor if her women's Bible study could use excerpts from the Christian heritage film when they finished their current series.

For Loretta, this was her second time in D.C., but she was excited that her husband, an Army veteran, was able to see the sights with her for the first time. She also said she appreciated the experience much more with a Christian guide to help her know what to look for. "I think before when I was there, I didn't realize all of this, the writings and things on the wall and so forth, that didn't really sink into me," she said. "I didn't realize how much of this stuff was based on Christianity." She was particularly taken with the Christian inscriptions she noticed for the first time. "I told some of the people around here and at church, I said, they're trying to take God out of everything nowadays, but it's going to be hard to take it out of all those buildings in Washington," she said, laughing. "It is there. They'd have to do a lot of scratching to get rid of it!" She spoke with authority, confident now that she had been there and seen it for herself.

Some tourists also marveled that they had been in the places they saw on television and in the news. Charlene's tour took place in June 2015, not long before the Supreme Court affirmed same-sex marriage in *Obergefell v. Hodges*. In her follow-up interview, she reflected on how close she came to witnessing that piece of history: "I thought it was really moving, sitting in the Supreme Court, listening to the nice lady [curator] talk about the Supreme Court and the justices, and what their roles are. Then when we got back, right after that, a week later, the ruling on gay marriage happened!" she exclaimed. "And I was like, oh my gosh, we were just in that room. I mean, if we'd just stayed seven more days we really would've been there. That was kind of cool. I mean, it was not cool the result, but, you know." Though she disagreed with the ruling, Charlene was amazed to have been in the room where it happened, even if not at the same time. Eighteen-year-old Annie had a more mixed reaction to on her time in the halls of power. During her tour she sat in on discussions in both the House of Representatives and the Senate. "That was awesome and comical at the same time, because I was severely disappointed in the lack of participation of our elected representatives," she said in frustration. Only a few representatives were present, and she was not impressed with their level of discourse. "I'm expecting extremely smart people, like very intelligent conversation," she told me. "And I was like, well, I could keep up with y'all rather easily. It was a little disappointing." Like many tourists I met, Annie was torn between the glamour of being in the Capitol and the letdown of seeing the prosaic reality of our political system. But she was considering running for office someday.

Most tourists I interviewed spoke highly of their guides and fellow tourists, and they were please by how much they learned. Barbara's most memorable moment was the stories her guide, Jonathan, told at Signers Island. "I didn't take any notes," she said, "but the stories he told really show how the Constitution does not say anything about the separation of church and state, and how these men, with their religious background and their knowledge of the Bible, they're Christians." The tour more than met her expectations in terms of providing the information she sought about the nation's Christian heritage. Jacob, too, was pleased and encouraged by what he and his family learned. "I actually found the trip to be really encouraging to my faith," he said. "It was just really encouraging to hear about America and about our Christian heritage. . . . It was really obvious that because of our Christian foundation, and the fact that our laws and rules and foundation were on biblical reasoning, that led to the success of our country. And then our country, you know, was—is—a world power." He continued to explain his key takeaways, saying, "Our rule is God given, it's based on God's laws, and God knows what's best for us. God has a plan not just for individuals but for societies, and God has chosen to use America." Right on cue, however, he moved seamlessly into the language of the jeremiad. "Of course, it's concerning to see us turning away from biblical values, because there's definite consequences that go along with that. But so much of our success that we've been riding on through the years, even as we're now rebelling, was based on what our founding fathers did, but also just the Bible." Like many tourists, Jacob had already known this narrative arc, and he had articulated similar ideas to me early on in the tour. His guide, Stacy, confirmed what he expected to find.

In follow-up interviews, I did hear plenty of complaints, many related to security and too much walking. ("People my age *cannot* walk that much," said seventy-six-year-old Barbara emphatically.) Some tourists thought the guides were too professorial, particularly Mark. But in terms of the content of the tours, everyone I interviewed was satisfied. They felt they had witnessed sufficient evidence of America's Christian heritage to be persuaded or, perhaps more accurately, to persuade others once they returned home. Their experiences of the tour granted them an extra measure of authority. They had been there. They had taken the photos. They had met the guides and politicians. They were not taking anyone else's word for it that Christianity is everywhere in D.C.—they had seen it for themselves. With the authority of experience, they could confidently evangelize in their communities, spreading the good news of America's Christian heritage.

MAKING CHRISTIANITY VISIBLE (AND INVISIBLE)

In order to save the nation, Christian tourists and guides sought to make Christianity visible, both in American history and in the D.C. landscape. In both contexts Christianity can be understood as ambient: ever present, but not always noticed. In D.C. certain objects came into focus as Christian based on how they were positioned in a space, the movement of crowds around them, signage and symbols, tour guides' talks, tourists' own interests, and countless other factors. These factors could also shift focus away from the object so that, rather than being a visible example of Christianity, it faded into the background, becoming part of the blur of sensation tourists experience in D.C. Similarly, Christianity is always a factor in accounts of American history, given how dominant white Protestants have been and how deeply embedded Protestant language and values remain in American society, even in this supposedly secular age.[10] Depending on how the story is told, by whom, and in what context, Christianity may become more or less visible in the American past.

The foundational premise of Christian heritage tours is that most Americans do not "see" Christianity, either in D.C. or in American history, and their stated goal is to reveal the nation's Christian heritage on both fronts. They do not always adhere to this goal—sometimes they go to great lengths to make Christianity invisible instead. But their commitment to raising the visibility of Christianity in these ways also raises a question about what they expect to happen if more Americans do see Christianity in public spaces as well as in the past. The opening of the Museum of the Bible is already a major step in this direction in D.C., as it draws attention to Christianity on a massive scale. What is the purpose of making the invisible visible?[11]

On the one hand, the biblical jeremiad provides a traditional answer to this question. If Americans see Christianity embedded in the nation's capital and woven through its history, they will also see the error of their ways. Like the ancient Israelites, they will repent and return to righteousness. Americans will collectively turn back to God, realign American laws with biblical laws, and embrace public displays of Christianity as the founders did. God, in turn, will bless the nation, which will once more become a beacon of economic prosperity and military power. This, in a sense, would be salvation.

On the other hand, it is unlikely that these efforts will yield such a result. The Christian Right has been seeking to raise the profile of Christianity in American history and the American public square for over forty years, with mixed results. A more likely outcome is that, upon noticing ambient Christianity in D.C., for instance, many Americans would try to make it invisible again. They would put Christian objects in museums, hedging them about with captions that provide historical context at a comfortable distance. In the most extreme scenarios, the objects might be removed or destroyed. Such outcomes are, of course, exactly what Christian tourists said they feared. Yet Christian tourists spent much of their own time in D.C. rendering disruptive objects invisible by identifying real or imagined threats. They embraced the opportunity to contest the rightful place of the objects and, by extension, of Christianity in the United States. The visibility of Christian objects seemed ultimately less important than their ability to prompt intense responses from tourists as the objects moved in and out of focus.[12]

At the same time, these contests over select Christian objects worked to make something else invisible: by focusing so intently on the material legacy of conservative white Protestants, Christian tourists overlooked the myriad other varieties of Christianity that also appear in D.C. White conservative Protestant men are not the only people whose faith has inspired them to heroic actions on behalf of their fellow citizens. Sojourner Truth, for instance, was the first African American woman to be recognized with a bust at the U.S. Capitol. She was a Christian preacher, abolitionist, and advocate for women's rights. Rosa Parks, too, is honored with a statue commissioned by Congress, which sits in National Statuary Hall not far from missionary Marcus Whitman, a favorite of Christian tour guides. Parks was also a devout Christian, and she credited God with giving her the strength to refuse to give up her bus seat to a white man in 1955.[13] Yet she never came up in Christian tour guides' directions on which statues to see. Tourists in one group even complained to me that their official Capitol guide, a black woman, spent too long telling them about Parks's statue instead of the statues of Christians—that is, white male Protestants—they wanted to see. Christian tourists did tend to like the statue of Father Junípero Serra of California, who raises an eye-catching cross over the room in a public display of religion that appealed to them. Many tourists I observed stopped to photograph the statue once they saw the cross, but Christian guides never mentioned the Catholic Serra in their discussions. Any tour must necessarily choose to highlight some things and ignore others, but it was striking to observe how Christian tourists and guides engaged with some objects

Bronze statue of civil rights leader Rosa Parks commissioned by Congress for the National Statuary Hall at the U.S. Capitol, July 2016. In the background is the marble statue of suffragist Frances Willard, president of the Woman's Christian Temperance Union, sent by the state of Illinois. Photo by the author.

as "Christian" and ignored others. In doing so, they rendered invisible the countless ways that Christians who are women, people of color, mainline Protestants, non-Protestants, and advocates for progressive causes have mattered in American history.

A similar phenomenon takes place in broader public discussions of both American history and religious freedom. When white evangelicals advocate for Religious Freedom Day, or Christian Heritage Week, or the Year of the Bible, they tend to use terms that sound fairly inclusive: *religion* rather than Christianity, *Christian* rather than Protestant, and *Bible* rather than the King James Version. This allows their acts and legislation to pass constitutional muster. In practice, however, those terms almost always signify people, texts, and stories that feature white conservative Protestants.[14] This approach narrows the field of vision for what is even recognizable as Christianity to many Americans, whether it is in the past or in the present. Likewise, in the context of debates about the limits of religious freedom, *religion* has come to be nearly synonymous with conservative Christianity. Other religious traditions have long struggled to win the First Amendment protections that white Protestants take for granted.[15] But the cases that currently dominate American discourse about religious freedom revolve around white conservative Christians' objections to same-sex marriage, constraining what can be imagined as the freedom of religion or even religion as a category.[16] Religion, in this usage, is equated with conservative sexual mores, despite the strong support for same-sex marriage and other LGBTQ+ rights among many religious groups who are not white evangelicals, and even among younger white evangelicals.[17] To be "more religious" is to be more socially conservative, while to be more socially liberal is seen as less religious.[18] The religious-secular binary maps onto the conservative-liberal spectrum in American politics, erasing expressions of religion that do not fall into the straight and narrow path of conservative white evangelicalism.

This sort of erasure was such a routine feature of Christian heritage tours that even though I noticed it during my fieldwork, it rarely moved me. At most, I felt annoyed. But during my first visit to the Museum of the Bible two years later, the visceral wrongness of it struck me. Midway through the exhibit on the impact of the Bible on the United States, I encountered one of the museum's many interactive displays, in this case one on American music inspired by the Bible. A touch screen allowed me to choose a song to play from a menu of options, starting with genre. I selected gospels and spirituals, then scrolled through the available songs, landing on "Amazing Grace." To my surprise, the screen gave me the option to hear a version sung by Barack Obama. I glanced at the white visitors around me and decided, why not? I pressed PLAY.

His baritone voice filled the space around me, drowning out the competing hum of other exhibits nearby. I saw the person closest to me startle. Like me, he did not expect to hear Obama's voice in this room. I let the words wash over me, words so familiar I cannot remember a time I did not know them: "Amazing grace / how sweet the sound / that saved a wretch like me." Without knowing why, I began to cry. I had spent all day exploring this museum, and it was both exactly what I expected and profoundly alienating. To hear this song, in this place, was like a moment of rest. It struck me that I was hearing the first black president of the United States, whose Christian faith had been continually attacked, singing with the congregation of Charleston's Emanuel African Methodist Episcopal Church as they mourned the deaths of nine of their brothers and sisters at the hands of a white supremacist. For a moment, I glimpsed another face of American Christianity, one that offered comfort and hope—even grace.

That face is nowhere to be found in the Christian heritage story of America. And we are all the poorer for it.

TAKING HISTORY SERIOUSLY

In the aftermath of the 2016 presidential elections, scholars of American Christianity experienced a crisis of explanation as we struggled to explain why the overwhelming majority of white evangelicals voted for Donald Trump. Turning to theology did little good. Where in Bebbington's famous quadrilateral (biblicism, conversionism, crucicentrism, and activism) did one find an endorsement of a "baby Christian" who said "two Corinthians?"[19] Even less helpful was the discourse of family values that dominates white evangelicals' discussions of politics. Why would advocates for traditional morality throw their support behind a twice-divorced gambler who bragged about sexually assaulting women?

Efforts to make sense of this quandary have done much to illuminate the current attitudes and emotions of white evangelicals in the United States. John Fea argues that white evangelicals who supported Trump did so out of a combination of fear, lust for power, and nostalgia for an imagined past.[20] Similarly, Rebecca Barrett-Fox argues that Trump spoke to white evangelicals' feelings of fear and resentment in a way that allowed them to write him into their story as a "plot twist," despite his own lack of convincing evangelical credentials.[21] These themes resonate deeply with what I found in studying Christian heritage tours and white evangelicals' identity narratives. At the same time, it has been all too easy for scholars and other observers to explain white evangelicals' support for Trump as a manifestation of racism, class anxiety, or misogyny, dismissing religion altogether as a meaningful factor in their political decision making. This approach prematurely forecloses on the possibility that white evangelicals voted for Trump and support his policies not in spite of their faith but because of it.

More is at stake in this debate than a satisfactory explanation for why Trump won 81 percent of the white evangelical vote in 2016. That statistic has catalyzed a broader interrogation of how we understand white evangelicals' political behavior, particularly when it surprises us. But that discussion was ongoing before 2016, and it will continue after Trump's presidency ends. The evangelical tradition in the United States, like any religious tradition, is continually evolving and changing, and our interpretive frameworks are changing with it.

This book has argued for thinking about white evangelicals' identity in a way that takes seriously their understanding of American history. Indeed, there is room in religious studies for more scholarship on how history and religion are imbricated in people's daily lives regardless of which religion they practice.[22] For white evangelicals in particular, if we hope to make sense of their political behavior, whatever form it may take in the future, we need to examine how they see themselves vis-à-vis the nation. How they talk about history reveals how they plot themselves into the American story. This in turn tells us how they will tend to respond to certain events, based on the available narratives and how they have deployed those narratives in the past. History is not the only factor in their political decision making, of course, just as race, class, or gender is not the only factor. But their understanding of the American past shapes their behavior in ways that merit our attention.

History is not just something scholars do. It is also something ordinary people do to make sense of their lives. Stories about the American past are an integral part of how white evangelicals understand themselves. Their dynamic identity derives from the shifting relationship of white Protestants to the nation throughout American history, which has given them the ability to play both insider and outsider roles. They can be founders, exiles, victims, or saviors, depending on what role best suits a given moment. On Christian heritage tours and beyond, white evangelicals do history as they plot themselves into narratives about their communities and their country. And as they do so, they come to understand who they are and how they can save the nation.

Notes

INTRODUCTION

1 President John Adams, November 17, 1800, 6th Cong., 2nd sess., *Annals of Congress*, 723.

2 The United States did pay tribute to the Barbary States beginning in 1795. It was not until 1801, when the Pasha of Tripoli demanded additional tribute and declared war, that the U.S. responded with military action by the Marine Corps. The resulting Treaty of Tripoli is famous in atheist circles for Article 11, which states that "the government of the United States is not in any sense founded on the Christian Religion." The Christian heritage tours I observed never mentioned the treaty. See Office of the Historian, "Barbary Wars, 1801–1805 and 1815–1816," U.S. Department of State, history.state.gov/milestones/1801-1829/barbary-wars (accessed August 17, 2017).

3 This new variety of Christian tourism was part of the booming Christian leisure industry that began in the 1950s and included other forms of travel such as pilgrimages to the Holy Land. See Kaell, *Walking Where Jesus Walked*, 5–7, 199.

4 By *Christian Right* I mean the political alliance of conservative Christian groups that emerged in the 1970s and 1980s to advocate for conservative social policies on religious grounds. This group was not limited to white evangelicals but also included fundamentalists, charismatics, Catholics, Mormons, and others. It is sometimes known as the Religious Right in deference to the small number of non-Christian groups involved.

5 In the twenty-first century some of the best-known proponents of the Christian heritage story are Republican activist David Barton, actor Kirk Cameron, and television host Dave Stotts.

6 This calculation is based on my own observations of the tours I participated in and the published capacity of other publicly available tours, as well as tour guides' estimates for private tours organized for Christian school groups.

7 In my use of *lived history*, I follow the approach of scholars of lived religion. See Orsi, *Madonna of 115th Street*; and Hall, *Lived Religion in America*.

8 Like any other tradition, white evangelicalism is internally diverse, and white evangelicals hold a range of positions on both Donald Trump and his policies. Statistically speaking, however, the majority favor him. See Gregory A. Smith and Jessica Martinez, "How the Faithful Voted: A Preliminary 2016 Analysis," Pew Research Center, November 9, 2016, www.pewresearch.org/fact-tank/2016/11/09/how-the-faithful-voted-a-preliminary-2016-analysis/; and Jones et al., *Partisan Polarization Dominates the Trump Era*, 11, 15–17.

9 During the five tours in 2014, I was living in D.C. and did not need to stay at a hotel. The tour companies I observed that year graciously allowed me to join them without paying a fee, something I greatly appreciated on a student budget. I paid for all my meals and any site tickets separately. During the four tours in

2015, I paid the list price for a solo traveler (most companies offered discounts for couples and families based on room occupancy). I am grateful to Boston University's Graduate School of Arts and Sciences for funding that supported these costs.

10 Bebbington, *Evangelicalism in Modern Britain*, 2–3.

11 This is the language used, for instance, by the National Association of Evangelicals, which endorses Bebbington's definition. See National Association of Evangelicals, "What Is an Evangelical?," www.nae.net/what-is-an-evangelical/ (accessed August 16, 2019).

12 Gloege, *Guaranteed Pure*, 12–13.

13 Kristen Kobes Du Mez, "There Are No Real Evangelicals," Religion News Service, February 6, 2019, religionnews.com/2019/02/06/there-are-no-real-evangelicals -only-imagined-ones/.

14 Wong, *Immigrants, Evangelicals, and Politics*, 21.

15 See, for instance, Glaude, "The 'Trump Effect' and Evangelicals," 63; Campbell Robertson, "A Quiet Exodus: Why Black Worshipers are Leaving White Evangelical Churches," *New York Times*, March 9, 2018, www.nytimes.com/2018/03 /09/us/blacks-evangelical-churches.html; and Eliza Griswold, "Evangelicals of Color Fight Back Against the Religious Right," *New Yorker*, December 26, 2018, www.newyorker.com/news/on-religion/evangelicals-of-color-fight-back -against-the-religious-right.

16 Butler, "African-American Religious Conservatives in the New Millennium," 61.

17 Brekus and Gilpin, *American Christianities*; Albanese, *America: Religions and Religion*; Ahlstrom, *Religious History of the American People*.

18 The data I gathered on household income during qualitative interviews was too limited to be anything more than illustrative, but more than half of the tourists I interviewed reported a household income greater than $100,000 per year.

19 Smith, *Hosts and Guests*, 1.

20 Smith, *Hosts and Guests*, 1–2.

21 The majority of that growth took place in evangelical denominations, especially among Baptists and Methodists, who in 1776 made up only 19 percent of all American church members but by 1850 accounted for 55 percent. David Sehat qualifies this figure by noting that, with better networks as the nation expanded, more people were logistically able to be included in membership rolls. See Sehat, *Myth of American Religious Freedom*, 51–52; Noll, *America's God*, 179–86; and Finke and Starke, *Churching of America*, 22–24.

22 Religion was disestablished at the federal level in 1791 with the passage of the Bill of Rights, and at the state level by 1833. Massachusetts was the last state to end establishment.

23 Noll, *America's God*, 5. See also Fessenden, *Culture and Redemption*, 34–83; and Fraser, *Between Church and State*, 8–105.

24 Sehat argues that they did so in response to anxieties about "the anarchic tendencies of democratic capitalism" in which each person is out for themselves. See Sehat, *Myth of American Religious Freedom*, 53–55. See also Fessenden, *Culture and Redemption*; and Fraser, *Between Church and State*.

25 Sehat, *Myth of American Religious Freedom*, 69. See also Fessenden, *Culture and Redemption*; Jakobsen and Pellegrini, "World Secularisms at the Millennium"; and Brekus and Gilpin, *American Christianities*, 1–28.

26 Fessenden, *Culture and Redemption*, 60–83; Prothero, *Why Liberals Win the Culture Wars*, 55–138; Flake, *Politics of American Religious Identity*; Moore, *Religious Outsiders and the Making of Americans*.

27 On the Scopes trial's lingering impact on white conservative Protestants, see Marsden, *Fundamentalism in American Culture*, 184–95; and Larson, *Summer for the Gods*. Liberal and mainline Protestants retained significant power immediately following the trial, but they faced a sharp decline in numbers and influence in the mid-twentieth century that some scholars attribute to an increasing concern for ecumenism and diversity among the leadership, a concern that was not shared by the laity. See Hedstrom, *Rise of Liberal Religion*; and Hollinger, "After Cloven Tongues of Fire."

28 Marsden, *Fundamentalism in American Culture*, 184–95, 231–57; Carpenter, *Revive Us Again*. For an overview of recent correctives to this historical narrative, see Sutton, "New Trends in the Historiography of American Fundamentalism."

29 Schäfer, *American Evangelicals and the 1960s*, 3–16.

30 Recent scholarship proliferates with studies of the links between white conservative Protestants and business leaders in this period. See Dochuck, *From Bible Belt to Sunbelt*; Dochuk, *Anointed with Oil*; Gloege, *Guaranteed Pure*; Kruse, *One Nation under God*; Sutton, *American Apocalypse*; and Williams, *God's Own Party*.

31 Carpenter, *Revive Us Again*; see also Williams, *God's Own Party*.

32 Hale, *Nation of Outsiders*, 3.

33 According to *Newsweek*, the year of the U.S. bicentennial, 1976, was also the "Year of the Evangelical." Jimmy Carter was running for president as a born-again Christian, a term that was new to many Americans at the time. White evangelicals were a fascinating (and soon to be intimidating) force in national politics.

34 *Engel v. Vitale*, 370 U.S. 421 (1962); *Abington School District v. Schempp*, 374 U.S. 203 (1963); *Roe v. Wade*, 410 U.S. 113 (1973).

35 Prothero, *Why Liberals Win the Culture Wars*, 183–94; Balmer, *Thy Kingdom Come*, 11–16; Balmer, *Evangelicalism in America*, 109.

36 Prothero, *Why Liberals Win the Culture Wars*, 189; Balmer, *Evangelicalism in America*, 109–22.

37 Peter Marshall said so explicitly in an interview about history education in Texas: "We're in an all-out moral and spiritual civil war for the soul of America, and the record of American history is right at the heart of it." See Stephanie Simon, "The Culture War's New Front," *Wall Street Journal*, July 14, 2009, www.wsj.com/articles/SB124753078523935615. See also Chancey, "Rewriting History for a Christian America." John Fea succinctly summarizes political stakes of the battle over history for the Christian Right: "If America was not founded as a Christian nation, the entire foundation of their political agenda collapses" (*Believe Me*, 155).

38 Prothero, *Why Liberals Win the Culture Wars*, 229–30; Thomas and Dobson, *Blinded by Might*.

39 Wuthnow, *Restructuring of American Religion*; Putnam and Campbell, *American Grace*; Hunter, *Culture Wars*. Just as white evangelical priorities to some extent reshaped the Republican Party, so too did this union reshape white evangelicals' identity. See Bean, *Politics of Evangelical Identity*, 13.

40 Sutton, *American Apocalypse*; Williams, *God's Own Party*.

41 Pew Research Center, "Nones on the Rise," October 9, 2012, www.pewforum.org /2012/10/09/nones-on-the-rise/.

42 Smith and Martinez, "How the Faithful Voted."

43 Jones et al., "Partisan Polarization Dominates the Trump Era," 11, 15–17. Trump did draw strong public opposition from some prominent white evangelical leaders, including Russell Moore, president of the Southern Baptist Convention's Ethics and Religious Liberty Commission. See Russell Moore, "Why This Election Makes Me Hate the Word 'Evangelical,'" *Washington Post*, February 29, 2016, www.washingtonpost.com/news/acts-of-faith/wp/2016/02/29/russell -moore-why-this-election-makes-me-hate-the-word-evangelical.

44 Here they are alluding to Esther 7:1–7, in which Queen Esther risks her life by revealing she is Jewish in order to persuade her husband, King Ahasuerus, to stop Haman from murdering Jews.

45 Scholars who study identity have long recognized the challenge of capturing its dynamic nature. See Scott, "Evidence of Experience"; and Bauman, "From Pilgrim to Tourist," 18, 23–24.

46 Somers, "Narrative Constitution of Identity," 606; Ammerman, "Religious Identities and Religious Institutions." See also Mackenzie, "Embodied Agents, Narrative Identities"; and Schechtman, *Constitution of Selves*.

47 Ammerman, "Religious Identities and Religious Institutions," 214. See also Somers, "Narrative Constitution of Identity," 619.

48 Ammerman, "Religious Identities and Religious Institutions," 212–14.

49 On the contributions of businesses in particular to the construction of the public narrative of Christian America, see Kruse, *One Nation under God*, and Dochuk, *From Bible Belt to Sunbelt*.

50 Progressives have their own public narratives, of course; in this instance, the cup was read as part of the grand narrative of pluralism and inclusivity by avoiding explicitly Christian symbols, even though it was red (still a "Christmas color") and released for a holiday season clearly revolving around Christianity. It is also important to note that news media and social media greatly amplified this story, which made for clickable headlines.

51 Somers, "Narrative Constitution of Identity," 619.

52 Somers and Ammerman both identify two other types of narratives that contribute to identity: autobiographical and conceptual narratives. An autobiographical narrative is the internal, private narrative a person tells herself about who she is. This kind of narrative is largely inaccessible to researchers, though qualitative interviews often aim to bring it to the surface. Conceptual narratives are

the narratives that social scientists and other scholars use to make sense of the phenomena we observe. We plot social forces into coherent stories, much as individuals plot the events of their lives. See Somers, "Narrative Constitution of Identity," 618; and Ammerman, "Religious Identities and Religious Institutions," 213–14.

53 "Shining" was Ronald Reagan's addition. The first use of the "city on a hill" metaphor is attributed to John Winthrop as he and his fellow travelers on the *Arbella* sailed from England toward what would become Massachusetts Bay Colony. In Winthrop's usage, it is clear that the Puritan covenant with God is conditional: "For we must consider that we shall be as a city upon a hill. The eyes of all people are upon us. So that if we shall deal falsely with our God in this work we have undertaken, and so cause Him to withdraw His present help from us, we shall be made a story and a by-word through the world." Winthrop indicates that there are consequences for failing to fulfill the covenant, not that God will bless whatever America chooses to do, which is how the idea of a covenant or city on a hill has come to be used today. See Fea, *Believe Me*, 76–84; and Prothero, *American Bible*, 34–38.

54 Berger, "Desecularization of the World." Here I refer to the theory of secularization in its most simplistic form, which is how it typically appears in white evangelicals' public discourse. Secularization is, of course, far more complex, and certain elements of it remain useful. See Casanova, *Public Religion in the Modern World*, 11–39.

55 Edward Gunts, "The Site and the Symbols of the World War II Memorial," *Baltimore Sun*, May 27, 2004, www.baltimoresun.com/news/bs-xpm-2004-05-27 -0405270076-story.html.

56 Mackenzie, "Embodied Agents, Narrative Identities," 162–63; Ammerman, "Religious Identities and Religious Institutions," 214; Dings, "Dynamic and Recursive Interplay of Embodiment and Narrative Identity," 186–90; Menary, "Embodied Narratives," 63–84.

57 Dings, "Dynamic and Recursive Interplay of Embodiment and Narrative Identity," 203. See also Mackenzie, "Embodied Agents, Narrative Identities," 162–63.

58 Here they are alluding to Luke 19:40.

59 Engelke, "Angels in Swindon," 155, 158–59.

60 Activation can occur through the rhythms of practice at a site where an ambient religious object is located; see Whitford, "Activating Sacred Objects in Public Space," 343. In the case of D.C.'s ambient Christian objects, tourist rhythms— tour guides speaking, tourists taking pictures, the tourist gaze consuming even the most mundane aspects of the site—were the main means of activating objects. As Sally Promey notes, though, different groups can activate different meanings in the same object ("Public Displays of Religion," 39). For instance, an American Atheists tour might make the verses on Union Station visible, but with an entirely different purpose. See Promey, "The Public Display of Religion," 39.

61 Much like the roadside crosses in Kaell's study, D.C.'s Christian objects could act on observers, visually striking them so that they paid attention. The object's

ability to do so depended on its location in the whole assemblage, not just the arrangement of the object in space, but also the tourist's movement through it and the tourist's own feelings and experience. See Kaell, "Seeing the Invisible," 142–45.

62 In many studies of lived religion or religion and material culture, objects are understood to express or shape identity, or to stabilize an unstable, socially constructed world. See Morgan, *Visual Piety*; Tweed, "Mary's Rain and God's Umbrella"; and Baker, "Robes, Fiery Crosses, and the American Flag." The ability of material culture to discipline the body has also been examined; see Mahmood, *Politics of Piety*, 118–52.

63 See Orsi, *Madonna of 115th Street*; and Hall, *Lived Religion in America*. On the need to add the consideration of material culture to the study of lived religion, see Morgan, *Religion and Material Culture*, 1–18, 55–74.

CHAPTER 1

1 Lowenthal, *Heritage Crusade*, x.

2 Lowenthal, *Heritage Crusade*, 3–5.

3 Lowenthal, *Heritage Crusade*, 121. In Birgit Meyer and Marleen de Witte's terms, heritage "is the outcome of a selection of certain cultural forms which are— more or less persuasively—canonized" ("Heritage and the Sacred," 276).

4 I noted that this assumption of sincerity extended only to founders and leaders prior to the twentieth century. President Barack Obama, for instance, was assumed to be insincere in his public expressions of Christianity.

5 Washington's faith is subject to debate. For an introduction to the various points of contention that typically arose on tours, see Mount Vernon Historical Society, "George Washington and Religion," www.mountvernon.org/library /digitalhistory/digital-encyclopedia/article/george-washington-and-religion/ (accessed June 9, 2019).

6 Many of the blocks of the monument are inscribed on the interior faces with the names of those that donated them—the American states, foreign countries, and a variety of private organizations—along with commemorative messages. Blocks donated by some states as well as by Sunday School societies are inscribed with biblical verses and phrases like "In God We Trust."

7 See, for instance, Chernow, *Washington: A Life*, 127–36.

8 Many conservative Christian writers and leaders use these quotations as proof texts. These quotations and many others like them have been identified and disseminated by Barton's WallBuilders organization, which archives them on its website and features them in publications and documentaries.

9 Bellah, "Civil Religion in America."

10 Only one group made a point of all watching the film together; other groups gave tourists the option, and one group discouraged it.

11 Prothero, *Why Liberals Win the Culture Wars*, 23–53.

12 Unitarianism was a nineteenth-century American religious movement that rejected the Trinity and recognized God as a singular deity.

13 The Library of Congress's records confirm that both Jefferson and Madison attended church services in the U.S. Capitol during their terms as president. See Library of Congress, "Religion and the Founding of the American Republic," www.loc.gov/exhibits/religion/rel06-2.html (accessed August 26, 2017).

14 This was Jefferson's second attempt to separate the teachings of Jesus from what he saw as superstition. The first was "The Philosophy of Jesus of Nazareth," compiled while he was president. See discussion in Prothero, *American Jesus*, 23–25.

15 Noll, *History of Christianity in the United States and Canada*, 320–23. In *America's God* (430–32), Noll points out that Lincoln held two theological views that were, at least at the time, unconventional: that the United States was not uniquely chosen and that God's plan can be difficult to see in human events. These views are certainly at odds with how Christian heritage tours depict Lincoln and with how they understand the relationship of God and the United States.

16 Washington's will stated that his own slaves were to be freed upon the death of his wife, Martha Custis Washington. However, many of the slaves at Mount Vernon were part of Martha's inheritance from her first marriage, and they were not (and could not be) freed in Washington's will. See Morgan, "'To Get Quit of Negroes': George Washington and Slavery," 403–4.

17 Scholars dispute whether this line was in the original draft of the Constitution. Daniel Dreisbach argues that it is no more than a "scrivener's flourish" added later ("In Search of a Christian Commonwealth," 947).

18 Most guides also told a story about Benjamin Franklin asking for prayer on a contentious day at the Constitutional Convention. As the story goes, after they prayed together, the delegates were able to resolve their differences and move forward with drafting the Constitution. The story was intended to demonstrate God's hand in the writing of the Constitution. The records of the Constitutional Convention show that, while Franklin did propose prayer as a means of unifying the delegates in June 1787, other delegates, including Alexander Hamilton and Roger Sherman, felt it would be seen as a sign of weakness. The convention adjourned without voting on Franklin's motion, and Franklin himself later wrote that "the Convention, except three or four persons, thought Prayers unnecessary." See Fea, *Was America Founded as a Christian Nation?*, 151–52.

19 Historian Pauline Maier criticizes these displays as "mummified paper curiosities lying in state" that contribute to the mythology around the Declaration of Independence in particular (*American Scripture*, 215). Treating the Declaration as a sacred text, she argues, hinders the ongoing work of democracy.

20 The doors are thirty-eight feet and seven inches high, eleven inches thick, and ten feet across. Since 2003, they have opened only on special occasions such as Independence Day. Until 2017, they were the largest bronze doors in the city. That record is now held by the Museum of the Bible, on the southeast side of D.C. Its doors are forty feet high and inscribed with the text of Genesis 1 from the Gutenberg Bible.

21 Gretchen Buggeln notes that putting something in a museum display like this validates it. See Buggeln, "Religion in Museum Places and Spaces," 63.

22 Though the Gutenberg Bible itself is in Latin (Vulgate edition), subsequent translations into the vernacular were printed using Gutenberg's technology.

23 This is a key function of heritage making. See Lowenthal, *Heritage Crusade*, x–xi.

24 See Stephen Prothero's discussion of Winthrop's sermon on the *Arbella* in *American Bible*, 34–38.

25 Haselby, *Origins of American Religious Nationalism*; Green, *Inventing Christian America*.

26 Kruse, *One Nation Under God*; Dochuk, *From Bible Belt to Sunbelt*; Williams, *God's Own Party*.

27 John Fea also gives a helpful list of the common features of Christian heritage accounts of the founding. See Fea, *Was America Founded as a Christian Nation?*, 59.

28 On the far-reaching influence of this text, see John Fea, "Thirty Years of *The Light and the Glory*."

29 Marshall and Manuel, *The Light and the Glory*, 22.

30 Marshall and Manuel, *The Light and the Glory*, 23.

31 Marshall and Manuel, *The Light and the Glory*, 22. They also produced children's versions of these books.

32 Heritage often takes the form of "secret history," knowledge given to a privileged few. See Lowenthal, *Heritage Crusade*, 129. Christian heritage tours function as a kind of initiation ritual into this secret knowledge. See chapter 4.

33 Barton's book *The Jefferson Lies* covers everything from Jefferson's faith to his relationship with his slave Sally Hemings, and Barton paints Jefferson as a devout, quasi-evangelical Christian who was morally unimpeachable. Academic historians found fault with nearly all of Barton's claims. Warren Throckmorten and Michael Coulter, both professors at evangelical Grove City College, responded with a thorough debunking in *Getting Jefferson Right: Fact-Checking Claims about Our Third President*. The backlash was so strong that Barton's publisher, Thomas Nelson, withdrew the bestseller less than six months after publication. See also Garrett Epps, "Genuine Christian Scholars Smack Down an Unruly Colleague," *Atlantic*, August 10, 2012, www.theatlantic.com/national/archive/2012 /08/genuine-christian-scholars-smack-down-an-unruly-colleague/260994/.

34 Barton, *Myth of Separation*, 245.

35 Barton claims to speak to over four hundred groups a year. See WallBuilders, "David Barton's Bio," wallbuilders.com/bios/ (accessed June 9, 2019).

36 WallBuilders is "dedicated to presenting America's forgotten history and heroes, with an emphasis on the moral, religious, and constitutional foundation on which America was built—a foundation which, in recent years, has been seriously attacked and undermined." The organization, originally named Specialty Research Associates and renamed in 1988, claims that its resources are used not only by churches and Christian schools but also by public officials and even in public schools. See WallBuilders, "About Us," www.wallbuilders.com /ABTOverview.asp (accessed June 9, 2019).

37 Thomas S. Giles reported in *Christianity Today* on the proliferation of specialty Bibles as early as 1992, listing some of the new options and raising concerns that

Christians might cease to have "a common biblical language" if the trend continued. See Giles, "Pick a Bible—Any Bible."

38 For instance, WallBuilders produces Christian heritage films for use in churches and Christian schools. Titles include *America's Godly Heritage* (1993) and *Exceptional: America's Keys to Greatness* (no date). A popular television series with similar themes is *Drive Thru History*, with Dave Stotts (see watch.tbn.tv/drive-thru-history), which features episodes on American history, the Gospels, ancient history, and the Holy Land.

39 "Film Synopsis," Kirk Cameron Presents *Monumental*, www.monumentalmovie.com/ (accessed August 30, 2017).

40 The monument features a central figure, Faith, holding a Geneva Bible and pointing to the sky; Faith is surrounded by four seated figures representing Morality, Law, Education, and Liberty. According to Cameron, the five principles form a "matrix of liberty" that is the key to America's success. See Andrew Thompson, "Kirk Cameron's 'Monumental' Issues," *Christianity Today*, March 26, 2012, www.christianitytoday.com/ct/2012/marchweb-only/monumentalissues.html.

41 Marshall and Manuel's *The Light and the Glory* is also often used as a textbook by Christian private schools and Christian homeschoolers. See Fea, *Was America Founded as a Christian Nation?*, 59.

42 Fea, *Was America Founded as a Christian Nation?*, 60–61; McDowell and Beliles, *America's Providential History*, 5.

43 Chancey, "Rewriting History for a Christian America," 326; see also Fea, *Was America Founded as a Christian Nation?*, 60–61.

44 The Texas State Board of Education also included seven conservative Christian members, including Cynthia Dunbar and Bob McLeroy, both prominent Christian heritage activists.

45 As of 2010, Texas distributed forty-eight million textbooks annually. The only state that rivals Texas in size, California, had a smaller budget for textbooks, giving Texas greater influence. See Chancey, "Rewriting History for a Christian America," 326; Russell Shorto, "How Christian Were the Founders?," *New York Times Magazine*, February 11, 2010, www.nytimes.com/2010/02/14/magazine/14texbooks-t.html.

46 Religious studies scholar Mark Chancey has demonstrated how each of the 2010 changes to the Texas state social studies standards is linked to the Christian heritage agenda. He argues that the activists' goal was transparent: "They were staking claims not only to what happened in the 1700s but also to what they hoped would happen in the 2000s; the lessons they sought to teach about the past were in reality lessons about who counts as an American in the present" ("Rewriting History for a Christian America," 352).

47 Congressional Prayer Caucus Foundation, *Report and Analysis on Religious Freedom Measures*, 58–101. See additional discussion of these strategies in chapter 3.

48 Congressional Prayer Caucus Foundation, "Project Blitz," cpcfoundation.com/first-freedom-coalition-project-blitz/ (accessed February 20, 2019). Following negative publicity in early 2019, the Congressional Prayer Caucus Foundation renamed this page "Toolkit," though the original name remains in the URL. See

John Fea, "Project Blitz's Bible Literacy Act and the 2019 Bible Course Bills," Bible and Interpretation, June 2019, bibleinterp.arizona.edu/articles/project -blitzs-bible-literacy-act-and-2019-bible-course-bills#_edn15 (accessed August 20, 2019).

49 For instance, the suggested templates for the "Religion in Legal History Act," the "Proclamation Recognizing Religious Freedom Day," and the "Proclamation Recognizing Christian Heritage Week" replicate the core arguments of Christian heritage makers. See Congressional Prayer Caucus Foundation, *Report and Analysis on Religious Freedom Measures*, 15–18, 24–29.

50 Examples include Kramnick and Moore, *Godless Constitution*; Allen, *Moral Minority*; and Porterfield, *Conceived in Doubt*.

51 Fea, "Using the Past to 'Save' Our Nation," 10.

52 Fea argues that their "present-mindedness" prevents them from attending to the principles of good historical writing, including attention to the complexity of the past. These principles are the "five Cs": change over time, context, causality, contingency, and complexity. See Fea, *Was America Founded as a Christian Nation?*, xxiv–xxv.

53 Throckmorten and Coulter, *Getting Jefferson Right*; Epps, "Genuine Christian Scholars Smack Down an Unruly Colleague," *Atlantic*, March 10, 2012, www.the atlantic.com/national/archive/2012/08/genuine-christian-scholars-smack -down-an-unruly-colleague/260994/.

54 Stephen P. Miller writes of proof-texting, "This approach to history writing—one hesitates to call it scholarship—elevates the significance of isolated statements over context, rhetorical usage, or a lifetime of written work." He refers to this approach as "law office history," which infers the legal implications of a historical event without regard for its context. See Miller, *Age of Evangelicalism*, 11. Fea offers a similar critique of this approach in *Was America Founded as a Christian Nation?*, xxvi. Barton himself takes the opposite view of this approach, priding himself on using the best "legal standard" by letting the texts speak for themselves. See the foreword and editor's notes in Barton, *Original Intent*.

55 Miller, *Age of Evangelicalism*, 13.

56 David Lowenthal writes that "heritage is immune to critical reappraisal because it is not erudition but catechism; what counts is not checkable fact but credulous allegiance" (*Heritage Crusade*, 121). Meyer and Witte note that it is the process of sacralization that makes heritage products "incontestable" ("Heritage and the Sacred," 277).

57 They specifically name and respond to arguments from Christian heritage writers Francis Schaeffer, Jerry Falwell, and Peter Marshall and David Manuel. See Noll, Hatch, and Marsden, *Search for Christian America*, 141.

58 On a historical level, Noll, Hatch, and Marsden claim that "a careful study of the facts of history shows that early America does not deserve to be considered uniquely, distinctly, or even predominantly Christian.... There is no lost golden age to which American Christians may return" (*Search for Christian America*, 17).

59 Noll, Hatch, and Marsden argue that "the idea of a 'Christian nation' is a very

ambiguous concept which is usually harmful to effective Christian action in society" (*Search for Christian America*, 17).

60 Noll, Hatch, and Marsden, *Search for Christian America*, 23.

61 Fea, "Using the Past to 'Save' Our Nation," 9.

62 David Austin Walsh, "What Is the Least Credible History Book in Print?," History News Network, July 16, 2012, historynewsnetwork.org/article/147149. Nevertheless, in 2015–16 Barton led the Keep the Promise Political Action Committee, which supported Ted Cruz in the 2016 Republican presidential primary.

63 In order to protect the anonymity of my sources, I do not name individual tour companies in this book, whether or not I observed them directly. The advertisements quoted here and in chapter 3 are taken from a mix of tour companies, including some that I observed.

64 Not every guide was able to lead a private tour, only those groups with congressional connections. Other guides told the same stories but on the tour bus.

65 Gretchen Buggeln puts this succinctly: "Emplacement validates" ("Religion in Museum Places and Spaces," 163).

CHAPTER 2

1 The cornerstone was laid in 1848, but construction halted in 1854 due to a variety of political factors, not least of which was the American Civil War. When construction resumed in 1877, marble could not be acquired from the original quarry, and builders had to source it from elsewhere, where it was a different shade.

2 Luke 19:40.

3 Greeley and Hout, *Truth about Conservative Christians*, 67; Gerber, *Seeking the Straight and Narrow*, 6–7; Carpenter, *Revive Us Again*, 11, 241.

4 See Miller, *Age of Evangelicalism*; Hendershot, *Shaking the World for Jesus*; and Frykholm, *Rapture Culture*.

5 To be fair, most academic historians do reject the Christian heritage version of American history, but they do so because they reject supernaturalism, not because of antagonism toward Christianity. See discussion in chap. 1, n. 4.

6 Fraser, *Between Church and State*, 130–237; Prothero, *Why Liberals Win the Culture Wars*, 191–206; Petrzela, *Classroom Wars*.

7 George Washington Papers, Series 8, Miscellaneous Papers -99, Subseries 8A, Correspondence and Miscellaneous Notes: Correspondence and Miscellaneous Notes, 1773 to 1799, Library of Congress, www.loc.gov/item/mgw8a.124/.

8 Moore, *Religious Outsiders and the Making of Americans*, 164–65.

9 Others include Mormons, Jews, Catholics, black Christians, and new religious movements such as Christian Scientists. See Moore, *Religious Outsiders and the Making of Americans*.

10 Moore, *Religious Outsiders and the Making of Americans*, 163.

11 Moore, "Insiders and Outsiders in American Historical Narrative," 405; Moore, *Religious Outsiders and the Making of Americans*, 163–65.

12 Hale, *Nation of Outsiders*, 1.

13 Hale, *Nation of Outsiders*, 9.

14 Harding, *Book of Jerry Falwell*, 22.

15 Harding, *Book of Jerry Falwell*, 23–29; Prothero, *Why Liberals Win the Culture Wars*, 191.

16 Harding, *Book of Jerry Falwell*, 127. In this passage, Falwell is fusing two biblical stories: the story of Solomon, who built the First Temple (1 Kings 6: 1–38), and the story of the rebuilding of Jerusalem's temple and walls (described in Ezra and Nehemiah).

17 For an account of the inroads white evangelicals made into American institutions in this period, see Lindsay, *Faith in the Halls of Power*. For examples of the outsider motif, see Helms, *When Free Men Shall Stand*, 120–21; Lienesch, *Redeeming America*, 157–58; Neuhaus, *Naked Public Square*, 37; Miller, *Age of Evangelicalism*, 88; and Wuthnow, "Political Rebirth of American Evangelicals," 178.

18 Viguerie, *New Right*, 7, 16.

19 Falwell, introduction to Viguerie, *New Right*, iii. See also Liebman and Wuthnow, *New Christian Right*, 1–9.

20 Quoted in Harding, *Book of Jerry Falwell*, 9. See also Schäfer, *American Evangelicals and the 1960s*, 6.

21 Miller, *Age of Evangelicalism*, 19.

22 Quoted in Lienesch, *Redeeming America*, 46. Falwell made similar remarks about Christians being "second-class citizens." See Hale, *Nation of Outsiders*, 256; and Harding, *Book of Jerry Falwell*, 24–25. This rhetoric was also prevalent among white evangelicals quoted in Smith, *American Evangelicalism*, 142–44.

23 "Scrapping the Moral Majority," *Time*, June 26, 1989, 26. Arguably, his real motive for shutting it down was that it was ineffectual by that point; see Prothero, *Why Liberals Win the Culture Wars*, 224.

24 Quoted in John F. Persinos, "Has the Christian Right Taken Over the Republican Party?," 23.

25 Reed, *Active Faith*, 244. Even that comment, however, encapsulates the purported disdain of the mainstream for evangelicals ("greenhorns"), and it carries at least a hint of class anxiety ("castle"). See also Hart, *From Billy Graham to Sarah Palin*, 137.

26 Moen, "From Revolution to Evolution," 352. See also Donna Minkowitz, "The Christian Right's Antigay Campaign," 100.

27 Leslie Kaufman, "Life Beyond God," *New York Times Magazine*, October 16, 1994, 50.

28 Quoted in introduction to May and Urofsky, *New Christian Right*, xvi.

29 Nearly 60 percent of successful congressional candidates in 1994 received backing from the Christian Coalition. See Coe and Domke, "Petitioners or Prophets?," 312.

30 Michael Weisskopf, "Energized by Pulpit or Passion, The Public is Calling," *Washington Post*, February 1, 1993, www.washingtonpost.com/archive/politics/1993/02/01/energized-by-pulpit-or-passion-the-public-is-calling/f747ded3-b7c5-4578-ad3b-2f500dbaeacf/. See also Howard Kurtz, "Evangelical Outrage," *Washington Post*, February 6, 1993, www.washingtonpost.com/archive/lifestyle/1993/02/06/evangelical-outrage/c6704db3-0f79-452d-bb5d-6da3bdc36202/;

and Miller, *Age of Evangelicalism*, 109. White evangelicals have long memories for this sort of thing—it came up again twenty-six years later in an op-ed. See Quin Hillyer, "*Washington Post* Smears Evangelicals, Again," *Washington Examiner*, February 7, 2019, www.washingtonexaminer.com/opinion/washington -post-smears-evangelicals-again.

31 Diamond, "Watch on the Right," 32.

32 Prothero, *Why Liberals Win the Culture Wars*, 229.

33 Among those who called for an exit was Rod Dreher, who in the late 1990s and again in 2017 called for American Christians to take the "Benedict option" and retreat from the corruption of public life into private communities of the faithful, as St. Benedict did in the sixth century C.E. See Dreher, *Benedict Option*; and Prothero, *Why Liberals Win the Culture Wars*, 229–30.

34 Moore, "Insiders and Outsiders in American Historical Narrative," 396–97.

35 Saberi, "From Moral Majority to Organized Minority." See also Green, Rozell, and Wilcox, *Prayers in the Precincts*.

36 Millard, *Rewriting of America's History*.

37 See, for example, Bob Unruh, "Ten Commandments Stunner: Feds Lying at Supreme Court," WND, November 14, 2006, www.wnd.com/2006/11/38823; Bob Unruh, "Ten Commandments 'Cover-up' Revealed at Supreme Court," WND, February 13, 2007, www.wnd.com/2007/02/40143; and Bob Unruh, "Now, God Banished from *Washington Monument*," WND, October 26, 2007, www.wnd.com /2007/10/44214/.

38 In his guidebook, Barton aims to "highlight many of the stories and artifacts within the Capitol that confirm the deep roots of religious faith throughout American public life" (*Spiritual Heritage Tour of the United States Capitol*, 5). He makes the case that the Founders were "strongly and openly religious" (19) and uses the paintings and statues found in the U.S. Capitol as an opportunity to teach his readers about the Founders' lives and faith. Other examples of Christian heritage guidebooks include McDowell and Beliles, *In God We Trust Tour Guide*; and Millard, *God's Signature over the Nation's Capital*.

39 Some mentioned seeing it on social media, and some may have seen WND's or related coverage.

40 The ominous implication of this comment is that the presence of God's name is tied to the survival of American democracy. Threats to Christian objects are ultimately threats to the nation.

41 In new materialist terms, the assemblage worked to make the objects invisible. See Hazard, "Material Turn in the Study of Religion," 64–69; and Kaell, "Seeing the Invisible," 142–45.

42 The inscription was added to the House Chamber in 1962 as a congressional protest of the Supreme Court's ruling against school prayer in *Engel v. Vitale*, 370 U.S. 421 (1962).

43 It is unlikely that Hatfield will be seen as an adequate replacement for Jason Lee by any Christian tourists; though he was both evangelical and Republican, he was fairly liberal with respect to both.

44 It is even more unlikely that Abigail Scott Duniway will be deemed acceptable

to replace Jason Lee, given her rejection of conservative gender roles that subordinate women. Oregon House Bill 2025 was not voted on during the 2017 legislative session. Jason Lee's statue remains in the Capitol at the time of writing, but efforts to replace it continue in Oregon. In Washington State, similar efforts began in 2019 to replace the statue of missionary Marcus Whitman, another favorite of Christian tourists, but proponents of the change have met resistance in the state legislature. See Tom Banse, "Proposal to Replace Marcus Whitman Statues Stokes Anger in Olympia," NW News Network, January 30, 2019, www.nwnewsnetwork.org/post/proposal-replace-marcus-whitman-statues-stokes-anger-olympia.

45 This approach especially undermines academic criticism by painting academics as uniquely biased against Christianity. Writers of Christian heritage history books, including Barton, make a similar move.

46 This is one of the functions of a public narrative. See Somers, "Narrative Constitution of Identity," 619; and Ammerman, "Religious Identities and Religious Institutions," 214.

47 Smith, *American Evangelicalism*, 89.

48 Smith, *American Evangelicalism*, 89.

49 They are wrong, however, in speaking of American Christianity as uniformly evangelical in these important historical moments, and they do exaggerate the role of Christianity to the exclusion of other contributing factors.

50 Tracy Fessenden calls this phenomenon "unmarked Protestantism." See Fessenden, *Culture and Redemption*, 3–12.

51 Gerber, *Seeking the Straight and Narrow*, 6–7.

52 Gerber, *Seeking the Straight and Narrow*, 6–7. See also Fessenden, *Culture and Redemption*, 3–12; and Brekus and Gilpin, *American Christianities*, 2. On the way that religion, particularly western Christianity, has created and shaped the content of "the secular" more broadly, see Jakobsen and Pellegrini, "World Secularisms at the Millennium"; and Mahmood, "Religious Reason and Secular Affect."

53 Fessenden, *Culture and Redemption*, 6.

54 Christian Smith's classic model of a (white) evangelical subculture neglects the dominance of Christianity in American history and the unmarked Protestantism that lingers in American norms and institutions. See Smith, *American Evangelicalism*, 89–119.

CHAPTER 3

1 Significantly, white evangelical Protestants believed that America was once a Christian nation but no longer is. See Jones et al., *Immigration and Concerns about Cultural Changes*, 17–19.

2 Jones et al., *Immigration and Concerns about Cultural Changes*, 15–18.

3 Robert P. Jones, "The Evangelicals and the Great Trump Hope," *New York Times*, July 11, 2016, www.nytimes.com/2016/07/11/opinion/campaign-stops/the-evangelicals-and-the-great-trump-hope.html. See also Jones, *End of White Christian America*.

4 Hochschild, *Strangers in Their Own Land*, 135–51.

5 This feeling echoes a broader feeling among white conservative Americans, who, as Arlie Russell Hochschild has documented, feel like they are strangers in their own land, which has been taken over by "line cutters" who have not played by the rules. See Hochschild, *Strangers in Their Own Land*, 135–51.

6 The swamp legend is untrue, though D.C.'s summer heat and humidity are oppressive enough to make it believable.

7 *Real Christian* was a phrase often used by guides and tourists to distinguish their white conservative evangelical Protestantism from other forms of Christianity, which they tended to see as "nominal" Christianity, or Christianity in name only. See discussion of terminology in the introduction.

8 According to Pew, 75 percent of "nones" voted for Barack Obama in the 2008 presidential election. See Pew Research Center, "Social and Political Views of the Unaffiliated," October 9, 2012, www.pew./2012/10/09/nones-on-the-rise-social-and-political-views/.

9 When asked for whom they would vote, tourists most often responded with something along the lines of "anyone but Hillary [Clinton]."

10 This was a position advocated most loudly during the 2016 election cycle by Russell Moore, president of the Southern Baptist Convention's Religious Liberty and Ethics Commission. See Moore, *Onward*, 6–9.

11 Franklin Roosevelt ordered the prayer to be inscribed in the State Dining Room in 1945. See "State Dining Room," White House Historical Association, www.whitehousehistory.org/white-house-tour/state-dining-room (accessed March 15, 2019).

12 *Obergefell v. Hodges*, 576 U.S. __, 2015.

13 White evangelicals have long accused the Supreme Court of being "anti-Christian" or "establishing secular humanism," ever since its rulings in *Engel v. Vitale* (1962) and *Abington School District v. Schempp* (1963) ended school prayer and devotional Bible reading, and its ruling in *Bob Jones University v. United States* (1983) allowed the Internal Revenue Service to revoke the tax-exempt status of religiously affiliated schools that discriminated on the basis of race. See Fraser, *Between Church and State*, 130–237; and Prothero, *Why Liberals Win the Culture Wars*, 191–206.

14 Miller, *Age of Evangelicalism*, 128.

15 Miller, *Age of Evangelicalism*, 121–24.

16 Quoted in Miller, *Age of Evangelicalism*, 128–29.

17 *Lawrence v. Texas*, 539 U.S. 558 (2003).

18 This later became known as the Marriage Protection Amendment. These efforts continued without success until 2015.

19 Quoted in Prothero, *Why Liberals Win the Culture Wars*, 237. Conservative evangelical leaders reacted similarly to the Court's ruling affirming same-sex marriage in *Obergefell v. Hodges* in 2015, calling it a "spiritual 9/11." See Peter Montgomery, "Religious Right Reax to SCOTUS: 'A Spiritual 9/11,'" *Religion Dispatches*, June 26, 2015, religiondispatches.org/religious-right-reax-to-scotus-a-spiritual-911/.

20 Prothero, *Why Liberals Win the Culture Wars*, 234–35.

21 Jenna Johnson, "Donald Trump Seems to Connect President Obama to Orlando Shooting," *Washington Post*, June 13, 2016, www.washingtonpost.com/news /post-politics/wp/2016/06/13/donald-trump-suggests-president-obama-was -involved-with-orlando-shooting/?utm_term=.ca4f10e9b60 f. The Trump campaign revoked the *Washington Post*'s press credentials after publication of this story.

22 Hochschild, *Strangers in Their Own Land*, 135–51. Robert A. Putnam and David E. Campbell found that the best indicator that someone would join the Tea Party was if they favored more involvement of religion in government. See Putnam and Campbell, "God and Caesar in America," 34.

23 Prothero, *Why Liberals Win the Culture Wars*, 235.

24 The Affordable Care Act became known in popular discourse as Obamacare.

25 Catholic institutions, including universities and hospitals, felt that they would be violating the Catholic Church's teachings if they in any way collaborated in the use of contraceptives, and many white evangelicals sided with Catholics on principle, standing by the pro-life alliance that had formed in the 1980s. In addition, many conservative Christians opposed the mandate because it included coverage for drugs that they believed caused an abortion.

26 See *Burwell v. Hobby Lobby*, 573 U.S. __ (2014). The next case on this issue to reach the Supreme Court, *Zubik v. Burwell*, 578 U.S. __ (2016), consolidated seven different challenges from various religious institutions, including Pittsburgh's Bishop David Zubik, Geneva College, and the Little Sisters of the Poor. In keeping with the Obama administration's compromise, these institutions were not required to pay for contraceptive coverage for their employees, but to be exempt they had to fill out a form indicating their conscientious objection. The insurance company would then provide direct coverage for contraceptives. The religious institutions objected to the form, since signing it, in their view, facilitated contraceptive usage, making them complicit in a practice that violated their religious beliefs. In May 2016 the Court vacated the decisions of the various Circuit Courts of Appeals and remanded the cases for further consideration of the ways in which contraceptive coverage might be provided by the insurance company without the religious institution's facilitation. The Court had requested supplemental briefings on this issue, an unusual move.

27 The national outrage over the law caused Indiana leaders to amend the law later to include protections for LGBTQ+ individuals, prohibiting the discrimination that its opponents feared.

28 Emma Green, "When Doctors Refuse to Treat LGBT Patients," *Atlantic*, April 19, 2016, www.theatlantic.com/health/archive/2016/04/medical-religious-exe mptions-doctors-therapists-mississippi-tennessee/478797/.

29 The bill, HB2, became known as the "bathroom bill" because it required all individuals to use the bathroom corresponding to their gender assigned at birth.

30 Project Blitz, led by the Congressional Prayer Caucus Foundation and Wall-Builders, provides templates for many of these efforts. See Congressional Prayer Caucus Foundation, *Report and Analysis on Religious Freedom Measures*, 35–101.

31 In Kentucky, marriage licenses are signed by the county clerk who issues them.

Davis felt that to perform this part of her job was to endorse same-sex marriage, which she could not in good conscience do. In July 2015 she began denying marriage licenses to same-sex couples. She then refused to issue marriage licenses to any couple, regardless of sexual orientation, to avoid issuing them to same-sex couples. Six of those denied couples sued her. In district court, Davis argued that requiring her to sign the marriage licenses in her capacity as county clerk violated her First Amendment right to free exercise of religion. See Mike Wynn, "KY County Clerk Invokes God in Denying Gay Marriages," *USA Today*, July 20, 2015, www.usatoday.com/story/news/politics/2015/07/21/ky-county-clerk -invokes-god-denying-gay-marriages/30493783/.

32 Quoted in Abby Olheiser, "Kentucky Clerk Kim Davis on Gay Marriage Licenses: 'It Was a Heaven or Hell Decision,'" *Washington Post*, September 1, 2015, www .washingtonpost.com/news/acts-of-faith/wp/2015/09/01/kentucky-clerk-kim -davis-on-gay-marriage-licenses-it-is-a-heaven-or-hell-decision/.

33 Quoted in "Huckabee: Jailing of KY Clerk Marks 'Criminalization of Christianity,'" *Fox News Insider*, September 4, 2015, insider.foxnews.com/2015/09/04 /mike-huckabee-jailing-kim-davis-marks-criminalization-christianity.

34 "Sen. Cruz Statement on the Arrest of Kentucky Clerk Kim Davis," U.S. Senator for Texas Ted Cruz, September 3, 2015, www.cruz.senate.gov/?p=press_release& id=2432.

35 American Family Association, "States Need to Make Religious Accommodations," September 10, 2015, www.afa.net/the-stand/culture/2015/09/states-need -to-make-religious-accommodations/.

36 Leading conservative voices that did not take Davis's side included Jeb Bush and Carly Fiorina, at the time both candidates in the Republican presidential primary, and Russell Moore, president of the Southern Baptist Convention's Ethics and Religious Liberty Commission.

37 *Masterpiece Cake Shop v. Colorado Civil Rights Commission*, 584 U.S. __ (2018), 12–13.

38 Falwell said the Christian Right learned strategies "from feminists and the other side." Quoted in Harding, *Book of Jerry Falwell*, 9.

39 Kennedy did not unequivocally call this statement hostility. He offered two options but suggested that one way of reading this statement is that the commissioner was being "dismissive" and not taking seriously Phillips' personal beliefs. See *Masterpiece Cake Shop*, 13.

40 *Masterpiece Cake Shop*, 13.

41 Notably, this understanding of hostility does not apply to other religious minorities, as the court made clear later in the same term in a ruling that affirmed Donald Trump's executive order banning travelers from majority-Muslim countries, despite Trump's inflammatory rhetoric about Muslims during and after his presidential campaign. See *Trump v. Hawaii*, 585 U.S. __ (2018).

42 Fea, *Believe Me*, 14. On the centrality of so-called family values in American evangelicalism, see Dowland, *Family Values and the Rise of the Christian Right*.

43 Bebbington, *Evangelicalism in Modern Britain*, 2–3.

44 Hunter, *Culture Wars*, 31–51. For more recent work on the ongoing American cul-

ture wars, see Prothero, *Why Liberals Win the Culture Wars*, 183–264; and Hartman, *War for the Soul of America*.

45 It is possible, of course, that the problem is the polling term. As some have argued, those who self-identify as "evangelical" in an exit poll may not be using the term in the way religion scholars use it. For an example of these arguments, see Thomas S. Kidd, "Polls Show Evangelicals Support Trump," *Washington Post*, July 22, 2016, www.washingtonpost.com/news/acts-of-faith/wp/2016/07/22/polls-show-evangelicals-support-trump-but-the-term-evangelical-has-become-meaningless/. I do not find this argument persuasive, given the support for Trump among white evangelical leaders and in public discourse among white evangelicals on social media, among other things. The statistics may not be precise, but the support is unmistakable.

46 John Fea offers a helpful discussion of the periods in American history that Trump seems to be referring to with *again*. See Fea, *Believe Me*, 165–78.

47 He made this promise both during the campaign and as president. See Sarah Pulliam Bailey, "We're All Going to Be Saying 'Merry Christmas,'" *Washington Post*, December 7, 2016, www.washingtonpost.com/news/acts-of-faith/wp/2016/12/07/all-going-to-be-saying-merry-christmas-here-are-donald-trumps-campaign-promises-on-religion/?utm_term=.ccd5607f98cc; and Amy B. Wang, "Trump Brings Up the War on Christmas—In July," *Washington Post*, July 2, 2017, www.washingtonpost.com/news/acts-of-faith/wp/2017/07/02/trump-brings-up-the-war-on-christmas-in-july/?utm_term=.1111795aae94.

48 Quoted in Lauren Markoe, "Trump Promises to Protect Christians at Liberty Commencement Speech," National Catholic Reporter/Religion News Service, May 15, 2017, www.ncronline.org/news/politics/trump-promises-protect-christians-liberty-commencement-speech. See also Reinbold, "'Honorable Religious Premises' and Other Affronts," 49–50.

49 Similar patterns emerged in white evangelicals' support for both Alabama senate candidate Roy Moore and Supreme Court nominee Brett Kavanaugh. Beyond a claim to shared conservative Christian morality, what both men had in common with white evangelicals was a sense of being persecuted for their efforts to restore America to an idealized past.

50 Hayley Miller, "One Hundred Anti-LGBTQ Bills Introduced in 2017," Human Rights Campaign, March 7, 2017, www.hrc.org/blog/100-anti-lgbtq-bills-introduced-in-2017.

51 Congressional Prayer Caucus Foundation, *Report and Analysis on Religious Freedom Measures*, 58–101.

52 For a sustained critique of current discourse about religious freedom and sexual freedom, see Jakobsen and Pellegrini, *Love the Sin*, 1–17, 45–73.

53 See, for instance, the description on the Supreme Court's website: Office of the Curator, "Courtroom Friezes: East and West Walls," Supreme Court of the United States, October 1, 2010, www.supremecourt.gov/about/eastandwestwalls.pdf; and Office of the Curator, "Symbols of Law," Supreme Court of the United States, May 23, 2002, www.supremecourt.gov/about/symbolsoflaw.pdf. A lengthy account of this controversy from the Christian heritage perspective can be found in

Catherine Millard, "The Ten Commandments above the Bench," Christian Heritage Ministries, www.christianheritagemins.org/articles/Ten_Commandments.htm (accessed May 9, 2016). According to several Christian heritage tour guides, the numerals were labeled the Ten Commandments in exhibits and publications until the building was designated as a national landmark and placed under the control of the National Park Service in 1988. The Office of the Curator relies on a letter from sculptor Adolf A. Weinman to architect Cass Gilbert, dated October 31, 1932, as evidence that the sculptor himself intended the numerals to represent the Bill of Rights ("Symbols of Law"). Millard argues that the letter is unsigned and potentially a forgery ("The Ten Commandments Above the Bench").

54 A minority of tourists did express satisfaction with their tour of the Capitol, but their positive reactions were expressed in contrast either to their own low expectations or to other tourists' negative experiences.

55 According to Capitol rules, members of Congress can offer private tours to their constituents, taking groups "behind the scenes" before or after the usual tour and business day. Some of the highlights include moments that are not possible on the public tour. Tourists can go on the House and Senate floors, see the Speaker's Lobby, stand on the Speaker's Balcony, and pray in the Congressional Prayer Room, all at their congressional guide's discretion. They also see the usual highlights of the public tour, including the Capitol crypt, Rotunda, and National Statuary Hall.

56 This number is an exaggeration. According to the Library of Congress, Jefferson owned only one Quran, a two-volume English translation by George Sale printed in London in 1764. The first Muslim member of Congress, Keith Ellison (D-Minn.), was sworn in on this Quran in January 2007. See Fineberg, "Solemn Oaths," 1–2.

57 Engelke, "Angels in Swindon," 158–59. See also Kaell, "Seeing the Invisible," 144, 160–62.

58 Morgan, "Soldier Statues and Empty Pedestals," 153–56. See also Kaell, "Seeing the Invisible," 144. In new materialist terms, the context within which the object is situated can be understood as the assemblage. See Hazard, "Material Turn in the Study of Religion," 64–69; and Bennett, *Vibrant Matter*, 4–5.

59 Tweed, "Mary's Rain and God's Umbrella"; Baker, "Robes, Fiery Crosses, and the American Flag"; Elias, "Truck Decoration and Religious Identity."

60 Mahmood, *Politics of Piety*, 118–52. See also Asad, *Genealogies of Religion*.

61 Morgan, *Visual Piety*, 9.

62 Morgan, *Visual Piety*, 207.

63 McDannell, *Material Christianity*, 52. See also Morgan and Promey, *Visual Culture of American Religions*, 10.

64 Morgan, *Religion and Material Culture*, 73; Meyer, *Aesthetic Formations*, 1–30; Meyer, "Mediation and the Genesis of Presence," 214–15; Hazard, "Material Turn in the Study of Religion," 62–64; Stolow, "Technology," 194–95.

65 Promey, "Public Displays of Religion," 39.

66 Such reactions are, of course, difficult to measure. See Engelke, "Angels in Swindon," 161–63.

67 Kaell, "Seeing the Invisible," 150–51.

68 Morgan discusses this function of ambient objects in the context of statues honoring Confederate soldiers, which became highly controversial in the United States in 2017. See Morgan, "Soldier Statues and Empty Pedestals," 155–56.

69 Mitchell, "Narrative," 125–33.

70 Carpenter, *Revive Us Again*, 116–19.

71 Ambient religious objects can still operate in the background, without the intense devotional "gaze" cultivated by Christian tourists in D.C. Kaell distinguishes between a "gaze" that takes place in devotional practice, a casual glance, and a "gaze-on-the-go" that is most viewers' interaction with roadside crosses. See Kaell, "Seeing the Invisible," 160-62. Morgan argues that some objects' power lies in the unconscious work they do while they are largely invisible. See Morgan, "Soldier Statues and Empty Pedestals," 155.

72 One important marker of this shift is that Christian prayer and devotional Bible reading are no longer standard features of public education in the United States, following the Supreme Court's decisions in *Engel v. Vitale*, 370 U.S. 421 (1962), and *Abington School District v. Schempp*, 374 U.S. 203 (1963). Equally important is that other religions have gained public recognition; for example, President Barack Obama's first inaugural address described the United States as "a nation of Christians and Muslims, Jews and Hindus, and nonbelievers" ("Barack Obama's Inaugural Address," *New York Times*, January 20, 2009, www.nytimes .com/2009/01/20/us/politics/20text-obama.html). Statistically, Christianity is also in decline as religious diversity increases, and more Americans identify as religiously nonaffiliated (see Pew Research Center, "America's Changing Religious Landscape," May 12, 2015, www.pewforum.org/2015/05/12/americas -changing-religious-landscape/). At the same time, the nation has been by no means completely de-Christianized, and to a large extent Christianity remains the de facto language of the nation.

73 In new materialist terms, the whole assemblage mattered, and the object's position in the assemblage made this easier or harder to do. See Hazard, "Material Turn in the Study of Religion," 64–69; Kaell, "Seeing the Invisible," 142–44; and Bennett, *Vibrant Matter*, 4–5.

CHAPTER 4

1 The rainstorm did not occur until the next day, as the fire was still burning. Parts of the Capitol did survive, but much of the building was destroyed. For a thorough account, see Pitch, *Burning of Washington*, 99–129.

2 George Washington Papers, Series 3, Varick Transcripts, 1775–1785, Subseries 3A, Continental and State Military Personnel, 1775–1783, Letterbook 7: Jan. 3, 1783– Dec. 23, 1783, Library of Congress, www.loc.gov/item/mgw3a.007/.

3 As far as I could tell, she asked this without prompting from her parents. The following day, the tour guide prompted her to ask the same question of another congressman, with a similar response.

4 Jones et al., *Immigration and Concerns about Cultural Changes*, 17–19.

5 Boym distinguishes between restorative and reflective nostalgia. See Boym, *Future of Nostalgia*, 42–43.

6 This quotation is accurate. Jay's words are from a private letter he wrote to Representative John Murray of Pennsylvania on October 12, 1816. See Jay, *Correspondence and Public Papers of John Jay*, 4:393.

7 Finney's original quotation, which Jonathan paraphrased, can be found in his *Lectures on Revivals of Religion*, 274.

8 Run, Ben, Run was a super-PAC created in 2013. See Leonardo Blair, "Run, Ben, Run," *Christian Post*, August 27, 2013, www.christianpost.com/news/run-ben -run-super-pac-formed-to-draft-gifted-hands-neurosurgeon-benjamin-carson -for-president.html.

9 2 Kings 5:1–2.

10 This story is almost certainly apocryphal, as the first mention of it is in a nineteenth-century biography by Peter's great-nephew.

11 Falwell said it was the devil's idea to keep Christians out of politics. See Harding, *Book of Jerry Falwell*, 22.

12 This argument echoes older trends among twentieth-century white Protestant fundamentalists as well as more recent responses from some leaders of the Christian Right following their attempt to impeach President Bill Clinton. See Dreher, *Benedict Option*; and Prothero, *Why Liberals Win the Culture Wars*, 229–30.

13 Putnam and Campbell, *American Grace*, 91–133; Jones and Cox, "America's Changing Religious Identity," 11, 21; Elizabeth Dias, "God Is Going to Have to Forgive Me," *New York Times*, November 1, 2018, www.nytimes.com/2018/11/01/us /young-evangelicals-politics-midterms.html; Eliza Griswold, "Millennial Evangelicals Diverge from Their Parents' Beliefs," *New Yorker*, August 27, 2018, www .newyorker.com/news/on-religion/millennial-evangelicals-diverge-from-their -parents-beliefs.

14 One could easily argue that Christianity remains a dominant feature of American life. As I describe in chapters 2 and 3, however, from tourists' perspectives it has been erased.

15 For details of this story, see chapter 2. See also Stephanie Condon, "Congress Wants 'God' in Capitol Visitors' Center," CBS News, July 22, 2009, www.cbsnews .com/news/congress-wants-god-in-capitol-visitor-center/.

16 This campaign continues at InGodWeTrust.com.

17 "PrayUSA: Government Leaders Calling the Nation to Prayer Initiative," PrayUSA, prayusa.com/about/ (accessed September 2, 2017).

18 Matthew 28:19.

19 Boym, *Future of Nostalgia*, xviii, 41–45.

20 Falwell, *Listen, America!*, 6.

21 Marshall and Manuel, *The Light and the Glory*, 1–2.

22 Marshall and Manuel, *The Light and the Glory*, 11–12.

23 D. James Kennedy, epilogue to DeMar, *America's Christian Heritage*, 85.

24 Barton names five academic trends he sees as attacking Christian history: "De-

constructionism, Modernism, Posts-Structuralism, Minimalism, and Academic Collectivism." He also objects to the peer-review process, which he says ensures that academics control what is accepted as "truth" or "fact" and grants undue authority to secondary sources. See Barton, *Jefferson Lies*, xvi.

25 Barton is alluding to Malachi 3:16, in which Malachi's book of remembrance is said to be "written before the Lord to record the names of those who fear the Lord and esteem his name."

26 Barton, *Myth of Separation*, 9.

27 Quoted in Chancey, "Rewriting History for a Christian America," 325.

28 Quoted in Chancey, "Rewriting History for a Christian America," 325. Here McLeroy, like many other Christian heritage makers, is inferring the existence of truth and a creator from the line, "We hold these truths to be self-evident, that all men are created equal."

29 Quoted in Chancey, "Rewriting History for a Christian America," 325.

30 For a longer discussion of this scene, see the introduction.

31 See chapter 1, note 10.

32 This is a common myth on D.C. tours. Tom Miller, a Marine Corps veteran who was at the Battle of Iwo Jima, wrote a booklet debunking this myth and others about the battle and the statue. The sculptor, Felix de Weldon, denies including an extra hand. See John Kelly, "One Marine's Moment," *Washington Post*, February 23, 2005, www.washingtonpost.com/wp-dyn/articles/A45559-2005Feb22.html.

33 Though the iconography may not be explicit, the Vietnam Veterans Memorial is certainly open to interpretation as a symbol of burial and resurrection, and the Vietnam Nurses Memorial includes a possible allusion to Michaelangelo's *Pietà* (the Virgin Mary holding the body of Jesus after the Crucifixion), which some groups mentioned in passing.

34 This is the same reason that Christian heritage activists want to rewrite school textbooks. See Chancey, "Rewriting History for a Christian America," 352.

35 Mordecai says, "Who knows but that you have come to your royal position for such a time as this?" Esther 4:14, New International Version.

36 Esther 4:16 (usually "if I perish, I perish," including in the King James and New International versions).

37 This story circulated widely on conservative Christian social media, and it was further amplified when Jim Daly, the president of Focus on the Family, wrote about it on his blog. Christian groups, including Focus on the Family, responded by holding vigils for the deceased and building houses for the bereaved families. The website 21Martyrs.com featured a video about their execution and the broader persecution of Christians around the world (as of March 2019 the video was unavailable because it had been removed by YouTube). See Jim Daly, "May the 21 Martyrs Cause Us to Remember, Unite and Pray," Focus on the Family, February 21, 2015, jimdaly.focusonthefamily.com/may-the-21-martyrs-cause-us-to-remember-unite-and-pray/.

CONCLUSION

1 This is how the museum's president, Cary Summers, described it in a 2017 interview. See Museum of the Bible, "The Gutenberg Bible 'Doors,'" www .museumofthebible.org/book/minutes/219 (accessed March 16, 2019).

2 *Burwell v. Hobby Lobby*, 573 U.S. __ (2014). See chap. 3, n. 26.

3 Quoted in Michelle Boorstein, "Hobby Lobby's Steve Green Has Big Plans," *Washington Post*, September 12, 2014, www.washingtonpost.com/lifestyle/maga zine/hobby-lobbys-steve-green-has-big-plans-for-his-bible-museum-in-wash ington/2014/09/11/52e20444-1410-11e4-8936-26932bcfd6ed_story.html?utm _term=.01230d64e57b. For more on the Museum of the Bible, its agenda, and the Green family backing it, see Baden and Moss, *Bible Nation*.

4 Interestingly, the Impact of the Bible on America exhibit concludes with the Civil Rights movement. Museum officials have stated that this is to avoid contro versy that would come from engaging more recent culture wars issues. See Nora Caplan-Bricker, "The Hobby Lobby President Is Also Building a Bible Museum," *New Republic*, March 25, 2014, newrepublic.com/article/117145/museum-bible -hobby-lobby-founders-other-religious-project. However, it also fits neatly with white evangelicals' outsider narrative, in which Christians and their Bible were banished from positions of influence in the mid-twentieth century.

5 *Laus Deo* in this ride appears on the western face of the Washington Monu ment's apex; in reality it appears on the eastern face.

6 The photo album and ride both include the Museum of the Bible itself as one of the main biblical attractions of the city.

7 "Museum of the Bible Celebrates First Anniversary," Museum of the Bible, November 17, 2018, www.museumofthebible.org/press/press-releases/museum -of-the-bible-celebrates-first-anniversary-with-festivities-prepares-to-wel come-millionth-visitor.

8 Non-Protestants and people of color are represented to some extent, but par ticularly in the sections on early America, they are on the periphery of the room, while white Protestants occupy the center.

9 Moore, "Insiders and Outsiders in American Historical Narrative," 397–98.

10 Fessenden, *Culture and Redemption*, 1–12; Jakobsen and Pellegrini, "World Secularisms at the Millennium," 7–8.

11 It is worth noting that the Christian tourists in this study talked about Christian objects in D.C. this way, but in other studies of ambient religion, subjects were content to let religious objects operate in the background. See Kaell, "Seeing the Invisible," 136–67; Engelke, "Angels in Swindon," 155–70.

12 Morgan discusses a similar potential in the context of Confederate soldier stat ues in the United States. See "Soldier Statues and Empty Pedestals," 156.

13 Parks and Reed, *Quiet Strength*, 16–18.

14 The Project Blitz guide to legislation offers several examples of this kind of strategy. See "*Report and Analysis on Religious Freedom Measures*," 23–35.

15 Wenger, *Religious Freedom*, 1–14.

16 Jakobsen and Pellegrini, *Love the Sin*, 9–14.

17 "Support for Same-Sex Marriage Grows," June 26, 2017, www.people-press.org

/2017/06/26/support-for-same-sex-marriage-grows-even-among-groups-that
-had-been-skeptical/.

18 An example of the conflation of these two binaries can be found in Pew Research
Center, "The Religious Typology," August 29, 2018, www.pewforum.org/2018/08
/29/the-religious-typology/. See also Winston, "Back to the Future," 977–86.

19 James Dobson, founder of Focus on the Family, called Trump a "baby Christian" in an offhand comment in June 2016, meaning that Trump was new to
faith. The comment was widely shared and debated. See Sarah Eekhoff Zylstra,
"Dobson Explains Why He Called Trump a 'Baby Christian,'" *Christianity Today*,
August 4, 2016, www.christianitytoday.com/news/2016/august/james-dobson
-explains-why-donald-trump-baby-christian.html. In January 2016, during an
address to students at evangelical Liberty University, Trump cited a verse from
"Two Corinthians" (as opposed to "Second Corinthians," the more common
usage among American Christians). See Jessica Taylor, "Citing 'Two Corinthians,' Trump Struggles to Make the Sale to Evangelicals," National Public Radio,
January 18, 2016, www.npr.org/2016/01/18/463528847/citing-two-corinthians
-trump-struggles-to-make-the-sale-to-evangelicals.

20 Fea, *Believe Me*, 7.

21 Barrett-Fox, "King Cyrus President." It is worth noting that a small subset of
Trump voters did find justification for their support in the Bible. As Barrett-Fox
discusses, they cast Trump as a figure analogous to King Cyrus of Persia, who
according to biblical tradition enabled the Israelites to return home from cap-
tivity and rebuild the temple. Several leading Trump supporters have made the
explicit comparison, and Liberty University supported the production of a film
called *The Trump Prophecy* (2018) that depicted Trump as a Cyrus figure. See
also Steve Rabey, "New Film Highlights Belief That Trump's Election Was God's
Plan," Religion News Service, September 26, 2018, religionnews.com/2018/09
/26/film-trump-prophecy-mark-taylor-gods-plan-liberty-university/; Katherine Stewart, "Why Trump Reigns as King Cyrus," *New York Times*, December
31, 2018, www.nytimes.com/2018/12/31/opinion/trump-evangelicals-cyrus-king
.html; and Joel Baden, "'The Trump Prophecy' Includes Troubling Parallels for
American Democracy," Religion News Service, October 4, 2018, religionnews
.com/2018/10/04/the-trump-prophecy-includes-troubling-parallels-for-ameri
can-democracy/.

22 The "lived religion" subfield has not often employed history as an explicit ana-
lytical category. Robert Orsi's 2016 work *History and Presence* is an exception,
and one that reveals the ways in which religious practices blur the boundaries
of past and present.

Bibliography

Ahlstrom, Sydney E. *A Religious History of the American People*. New Haven, Conn.: Yale University Press, 1972.

Albanese, Catherine. *America: Religions and Religion*. Belmont, Calif.: Wadsworth, 1981.

Allen, Brooke. *Moral Minority: Our Skeptical Founding Fathers*. Chicago: Ivan R. Dee, 2007.

Ammerman, Nancy T. "Religious Identities and Religious Institutions." In *Handbook of the Sociology of Religion*, edited by Michele Dillon, 207–24. Cambridge: Cambridge University Press, 2003.

Asad, Talal. *Genealogies of Religion: Discipline and Reasons of Power in Christianity and Islam*. Baltimore, Md.: Johns Hopkins University Press, 1993.

Baker, Kelly J. "Robes, Fiery Crosses, and the American Flag: The Materiality of the 1920's Klan's Patriotism and Intolerance." *Material Religion* 7, no. 3 (2011): 312–42.

Balmer, Randall. *Evangelicalism in America*. Waco, Tex.: Baylor University Press, 2016.

———. *God in the White House: A History*. New York: HarperOne, 2008.

———. *Thy Kingdom Come: How the Religious Right Distorts the Faith and Threatens America*. New York: Basic Books, 2006.

Barrett-Fox, Rebecca. "A King Cyrus President: How Donald Trump's Presidency Reasserts Conservative Christians' Right to Hegemony." *Humanity and Society* 42, no. 4 (2018): 502–22.

Barton, David. *America's Godly Heritage*. Aledo, Tex.: WallBuilders, 1993.

———. *The Jefferson Lies: Exposing the Myths You've Always Believed about Thomas Jefferson*. Nashville, Tenn.: Thomas Nelson, 2012.

———. *The Myth of Separation*. 3d ed. Aledo, Tex.: WallBuilders, 1992.

———. *Original Intent: The Courts, the Constitution, and Religion*. 5th ed. Aledo, Tex.: WallBuilders, 2008.

———. *A Spiritual Heritage Tour of the United States Capitol*. 2d ed. Aledo, Tex.: WallBuilders, 2000.

Bauman, Zygmunt. "From Pilgrim to Tourist—Or a Short History of Identity." In *Questions of Cultural Identity*, edited by Stuart Hall and Paul DuGay, 18–36. Thousand Oaks, Calif.: Sage, 1996.

Bean, Lydia. *The Politics of Evangelical Identity: Local Churches and Partisan Divides in the United States and Canada*. Princeton, N.J.: Princeton University Press, 2014.

Bebbington, David. *Evangelicalism in Modern Britain*. London: Routledge, 1989.

Bellah, Robert. "Civil Religion in America." *Daedelus* 96, no. 1 (1967): 1–21.

Bennett, Jane. *Vibrant Matter: A Political Ecology of Things*. Durham, N.C.: Duke University Press, 2010.

Bercovitch, Sacvan. *The American Jeremiad*. Madison: University of Wisconsin Press, 1978.

Berger, Peter. "The Desecularization of the World: A Global Overview." In *The Desecularization of the World: Resurgent Religion and World Politics*, edited by Peter Berger, 1–18. Grand Rapids, Mich.: Eerdmans, 1999.

———. *The Sacred Canopy*. New York: Anchor, 1967.

Boym, Svetlana. *The Future of Nostalgia*. New York: Basic Books, 2001.

Brekus, Catherine, and W. Clark Gilpin, eds. *American Christianities: A History of Dominance and Diversity*. Chapel Hill: University of North Carolina Press, 2011.

Brubaker, Rogers, and Frederick Cooper. "Beyond 'Identity.'" *Theory and Society* 29, no. 1 (2000): 1–47.

Buggeln, Gretchen. "Museum Space and the Experience of the Sacred." *Material Religion* 8, no. 1 (2012): 30–50.

———. "Religion in Museum Spaces and Places." In *Interpreting Religion at Museums and Historic Sites*, edited by Gretchen Buggeln and Barbara Franco, 159–68. New York: Rowman and Littlefield, 2018.

Buggeln, Gretchen, and Barbara Franco, eds. *Interpreting Religion at Museums and Historic Sites*. New York: Rowman and Littlefield, 2018.

Butler, Anthea. "African-American Religious Conservatives in the New Millennium." In *Faith in the New Millennium: The Future of Religion and American Politics*, edited by Matthew Avery Sutton and Darren Dochuk, 59–73. Oxford: Oxford University Press, 2016.

Butler, Judith. *Gender Trouble: Feminism and the Subversion of Identity*. New York: Routledge, 1990.

Casanova, José. *Public Religion in the Modern World*. Chicago: University of Chicago Press, 1994.

Carpenter, Joel. *Revive Us Again: The Reawakening of American Fundamentalism*. Oxford: Oxford University Press, 1999.

Cerulo, Karen A. *Identity Designs: The Sights and Sounds of a Nation*. New Brunswick, N.J.: Rutgers University Press, 1995.

Chancey, Mark A. "Rewriting History for a Christian America: Religion and the Texas Social Studies Standards Controversy of 2009–2010." *Journal of Religion* 94, no. 3 (2014): 325–53.

Chernow, Ron. *Washington: A Life*. New York: Penguin, 2011.

Chidester, David, and Edward T. Linenthal, eds. *American Sacred Space*. Indianapolis: Indiana University Press, 1995.

Coe, Kevin, and David Domke. "Petitioners or Prophets? Presidential Discourse, God, and the Ascendancy of Religious Conservatives." *Journal of Communication* 56 (2006): 309–30.

Cohen, Erik. "A Phenomenology of Tourist Experience," *Sociology* 13 (1979): 179–201.

———. "Pilgrimage and Tourism: Convergence and Divergence." In *Sacred Journeys: The Anthropology of Pilgrimage*, edited by Alan Morinis, 47–61. Westport, Conn.: Greenwood, 1992.

———. "The Tourist Guide: The Origins, Structure, and Dynamics of a Role."
　　Annals of Tourism Research 12, no. 1 (1985): 5–29.

Congressional Prayer Caucus Foundation. *Report and Analysis on Religious
　　Freedom Measures Impacting Prayer and Faith in America*. Chesapeake, Va.:
　　Congressional Prayer Caucus Foundation, National Legal Foundation, and
　　WallBuilders ProFamily Legislators Conference, 2017. https://www.au.org/sites
　　/default/files/2018-10/Project%20Blitz%20Playbook%202017.pdf .

DeMar, Gary. *America's Christian Heritage*. Nashville, Tenn.: Broadman and
　　Holman, 2003.

Demerath, N. J., III. "Cultural Victory and Organizational Defeat in the Paradoxical
　　Decline of Liberal Protestantism." *Journal for the Scientific Study of Religion* 34,
　　no. 4 (1995): 458–69.

Diamond, Sara. *Spiritual Warfare: The Politics of the Christian Right*. Boston: South
　　End Press, 1989.

———. "Watch on the Right: The Christian Right's Anti-Gay Agenda." *Humanist*
　　54, no. 4 (1994): 32–34.

Dings, Roy. "The Dynamic and Recursive Interplay of Embodiment and Narrative
　　Identity." *Philosophical Psychology* 32, no. 2 (2019): 186–210.

Dochuk, Darren. *Anointed with Oil: How Christianity and Crude Made Modern
　　America*. New York: Basic Books, 2019.

———. *From Bible Belt to Sunbelt: Plain-Folk Religion, Grassroots Politics, and the
　　Rise of Evangelical Conservatism*. New York: Norton, 2011.

Doss, Ericka. *Memorial Mania: Public Feeling in America*. Chicago: University of
　　Chicago Press, 2010.

Dowland, Seth. *Family Values and the Rise of the Christian Right*. Philadelphia:
　　University of Pennsylvania Press, 2015.

Dreher, Rod. *The Benedict Option: A Strategy for Christians in a Post-Christian
　　Nation*. New York: Sentinel, 2017.

Dreisbach, Daniel. "In Search of a Christian Commonwealth: An Examination
　　of Selected Nineteenth-Century Commentaries on References to God and the
　　Christian Religion in the United States Constitution." *Baylor Law Review* 48
　　(1996): 927–1000.

Eade, John, and Michael J. Sallnow, eds. *Contesting the Sacred: The Anthropology
　　of Christian Pilgrimage*. Eugene, Ore.: Wipf and Stock, 1991.

Elias, Jamal J. "Truck Decoration and Religious Identity: Material Culture and
　　Social Function in Pakistan." *Material Religion* 1, no. 1 (2005): 48–70.

Engelke, Matthew. "Angels in Swindon: Public Religion and Ambient Faith in
　　England." *American Ethnologist* 39, no. 1 (2012): 155–70.

Falwell, Jerry. *Listen, America!* New York: Bantam, 1980.

Fea, John. *Believe Me: The Evangelical Road to Donald Trump*. Grand Rapids,
　　Mich.: Eerdmans, 2018.

———. "Thirty Years of the Light and the Glory: The Perils of Providential History."
　　Touchstone 21, no. 6 (2008): 27–30.

———. "Using the Past to 'Save' Our Nation: The Debate over Christian America."
　　Magazine of History 27, no. 1 (2013): 7–11.

————. *Was America Founded as a Christian Nation? A Historical Introduction.*
Louisville, Ky.: Westminster John Knox Press, 2011.

Feldman, Noah. *Divided by God: America's Church State Problem—And What
We Should Do about It.* New York: Farrar, Straus, and Giroux, 2005.

Fessenden, Tracy. *Culture and Redemption: Religion, the Secular, and American
Literature.* Princeton, N.J.: Princeton University Press, 2006.

Fineberg, Gail. "Solemn Oaths: Members Borrow Historic Books from Library."
Library of Congress Information Bulletin 66, no. 1-2 (2007): 1-2.

Finke, Roger, and Rodney Starke. *The Churching of America, 1776-2005: Winners
and Losers in Our Religious Economy.* 2d ed. New Brunswick, N.J.: Rutgers
University Press, 2005.

Finney, Charles Grandison. *Lectures on Revivals of Religion.* 2d ed. New York:
Leavitt, Lord, 1835.

Fitzgerald, Frances. *America Revised: History Schoolbooks in the Twentieth Century.*
New York: Vintage Books, 1980.

————. *The Evangelicals: The Struggle to Shape America.* New York: Simon and
Schuster, 2017.

Flake, Kathleen. *The Politics of American Religious Identity: The Seating of Senator
Reed Smoot, Mormon Apostle.* Chapel Hill: University of North Carolina Press,
2004.

Fraser, James. *Between Church and State: Religion and Public Education in
Multicultural America.* 2d ed. Baltimore, Md.: Johns Hopkins University Press,
2016.

Friedman, Jonathan. "The Past in the Future: History and the Politics of Identity."
American Anthropologist 94, no. 4 (1992): 837-59.

Frykholm, Amy. *Rapture Culture: Left Behind in Evangelical America.* Oxford:
Oxford University Press, 2004.

Gell, Alfred. *Art and Agency: An Anthropological Theory.* Oxford: Oxford University
Press, 1998.

Gerber, Lynne. *Seeking the Straight and Narrow: Weight Loss and Sexual
Reorientation in Evangelical America.* Chicago: University of Chicago Press,
2011.

Giles, Thomas S. "Pick a Bible—Any Bible," *Christianity Today* 36, no. 12 (1992):
26-27.

Glaude, Eddie S. "The 'Trump Effect' and Evangelicals." *Harvard Divinity School
Bulletin* 45, no. 1 (2017): 61-63.

Gloege, Timothy E. W. *Guaranteed Pure: The Moody Bible Institute, Business, and
the Making of Modern Evangelicalism.* Chapel Hill: University of North Carolina
Press, 2015.

Gordon-Reed, Annette. *Thomas Jefferson and Sally Hemings: An American
Controversy.* Charlottesville: University Press of Virginia, 1997.

Graburn, Nelson H. H. "Secular Ritual: A General Theory of Tourism." In *Hosts and
Guests Revisited: Tourism Issues of the 21st Century*, edited by Valene Smith and
Maryann Brent, 42-50. Elmsford, N.Y.: Cognizant Communications, 2001.

Greeley, Andrew M., and Michael Hout. *The Truth about Conservative Christians:*

What They Think and What They Believe. Chicago: University of Chicago Press, 2006.

Green, John C., Mark J. Rozell, and Clyde Wilcox, eds. *Prayers in the Precincts: The Christian Right in the 1998 Elections*. Washington, D.C.: Georgetown University Press, 2000.

Green, Steven K. *Inventing Christian America: The Myth of the Religious Founding*. Oxford: Oxford University Press, 2015.

Griffith, R. Marie. *God's Daughters: Evangelical Women and the Power of Submission*. Berkeley: University of California Press, 2007.

Hale, Grace. *A Nation of Outsiders: How the White Middle Class Fell in Love with Rebellion in Postwar America*. Oxford: Oxford University Press, 2011.

Hall, David, ed. *Lived Religion in America: Toward a History of Practice*. Princeton, N.J.: Princeton University Press, 1997.

Handy, Robert. *A Christian America: Protestant Hopes and Historical Realities*. 2d ed. Oxford: Oxford University Press, 1986.

Harding, Susan Friend. *The Book of Jerry Falwell: Fundamentalist Language and Politics*. Princeton, N.J.: Princeton University Press, 2000.

Hart, D. G. *From Billy Graham to Sarah Palin: Evangelicals and the Betrayal of Conservatism*. Grand Rapids, Mich.: Eerdmans, 2011.

Hartman, Andrew. *A War for the Soul of America: A History of the Culture Wars*. Chicago: University of Chicago Press, 2015.

Haselby, Sam. *The Origins of American Religious Nationalism*. Oxford: Oxford University Press, 2015.

Hatch, Nathan O. *The Democratization of American Christianity*. New Haven, Conn.: Yale University Press, 1989.

Hazard, Sonia. "The Material Turn in the Study of Religion." *Religion and Society: Advances in Research* 4 (2013): 58–78.

Hedstrom, Matthew. *The Rise of Liberal Religion: Book Culture and American Spirituality in the Twentieth Century*. Oxford: Oxford University Press, 2013.

Helms, Jesse. *When Free Men Shall Stand*. Grand Rapids, Mich.: Zondervan, 1977.

Hendershot, Heather. *Shaking the World for Jesus: Media and Conservative Evangelical Culture*. Oxford: Oxford University Press, 2004.

Hochschild, Arlie Russell. *Strangers in Their Own Land: Anger and Mourning on the American Right*. New York: New Press, 2016.

Hofstadter, Richard. *The Paranoid Style in American Politics and Other Essays*. Cambridge, Mass.: Harvard University Press, 1963.

Hollinger, David A. "After Cloven Tongues of Fire." *Journal of American History* 98, no. 1 (2011): 21–48.

Houtman, Dick, and Birgit Meyer, eds. *Things: Religion and the Question of Materiality*. New York: Fordham University Press, 2012.

Hunter, James Davison. *Culture Wars: The Struggle to Define America*. New York: Basic Books, 1991.

Hutchison, William R., ed. *Between the Times: The Travail of the Protestant Establishment in America, 1900–1960*. Cambridge: Cambridge University Press, 1989.

Jakobsen, Janet R., and Ann Pellegrini. *Love the Sin: Sexual Regulation and the Limits of Religious Tolerance.* Boston: Beacon Press, 2004.

———. "World Secularisms at the Millennium: Introduction." *Social Text* 18, no. 3 (2000): 1–27.

Jay, John. *Correspondence and Public Papers of John Jay.* Vol. 4. Edited by Henry Phelps Johnston. New York: G.P. Putnam's Sons, 1890–93.

Jones, Robert P. *The End of White Christian America.* New York: Simon and Schuster, 2016.

Jones, Robert P., and Daniel Cox. *America's Changing Religious Identity: Findings from the 2018 American Values Atlas.* Washington, D.C.: Public Religion Research Institute, 2017.

Jones, Robert P., Daniel Cox, E. J. Dionne Jr., William A. Galston, Betsy Cooper, and Rachel Lienesch. *How Immigration and Concerns about Cultural Changes Are Shaping the 2016 Election: Findings from the 2016 PRRI/Brookings Immigration Survey.* Washington, D.C.: Public Religion Research Institute, 2016.

Jones, Robert P., Daniel Cox, Rob Griffin, Maxine Najle, Molly Fisch-Friedman, and Alex Vandermaas-Peeler. *Partisan Polarization Dominates Trump Era: Findings from the 2018 American Values Survey.* Washington, D.C.: Public Religion Research Institute, 2018.

Kaell, Hillary. "Seeing the Invisible: Ambient Catholicism at the Side of the Road." *Journal of the American Academy of Religion* 85, no. 1 (2017): 136–67.

———. *Walking Where Jesus Walked: American Christians and Holy Land Pilgrimage.* New York: New York University Press, 2014.

Kelner, Shaul. *Tours That Bind: Diaspora, Pilgrimage, and Israeli Birthright Tourism.* New York: New York University Press, 2010.

Kennedy, D. James. *What If America Were a Christian Nation Again?* Nashville, Tenn.: Thomas Nelson, 2003.

Kirshenblatt-Gimblett, Barbara. *Destination Culture: Tourism, Museums, and Heritage.* Berkeley: University of California Press, 1998.

Kramnick, Isaac, and R. Laurence Moore. *The Godless Constitution: A Moral Defense of the Secular State.* Rev. ed. New York: Norton, 2005.

Kruse, Kevin. *One Nation Under God: How Corporate America Invented Christian America.* New York: Basic Books, 2015.

Larson, Edward J. *Summer for the Gods: The Scopes Trial and America's Continuing Debate over Science and Religion.* 2d ed. New York: Basic Books, 2006.

Lewis, Jan, and Peter S. Onuf, eds. *Sally Hemings and Thomas Jefferson: History, Memory, and Civic Culture.* Charlottesville: University Press of Virginia, 1999.

Liebman, Robert C., and Robert Wuthnow, eds. *The New Christian Right: Mobilization and Legitimation.* New York: Aldine, 1983.

Lienesch, Michael. *Redeeming America: Piety and Politics in the New Christian Right.* Chapel Hill: University of North Carolina Press, 1993.

Lindsay, D. Michael. *Faith in the Halls of Power: How Evangelicals Joined the American Elite.* Oxford: Oxford University Press, 2008.

Linenthal, Edward T., and Tom Engelhardt, eds. *History Wars: The Enola Gay and Other Battles for the American Past.* New York: Metropolitan Books, 1996.

Lowenthal, David. *The Heritage Crusade and the Spoils of History*. Cambridge: Cambridge University Press, 1998.

MacCannell, Dean. *The Tourist: A New Theory of the Leisure Class*. New York: Schocken Books, 1989.

Mackenzie, Catriona. "Embodied Agents, Narrative Identities." *Philosophical Explorations* 17, no. 2 (2014): 154–71.

Mahmood, Saba. *The Politics of Piety: The Islamic Revival and the Feminist Subject*. Princeton, N.J.: Princeton University Press, 2005.

———. "Religious Reason and Secular Affect: An Incommensurable Divide?" *Critical Inquiry* 35, no. 4 (2009): 836–62.

Maier, Pauline. *American Scripture: Making the Declaration of Independence*. New York: Knopf, 1997.

Marsden, George M. *Fundamentalism in American Culture*. 2d ed. Oxford: Oxford University Press, 2006.

Marshall, Peter, and David Manuel. *The Light and the Glory*. Rev. ed. Grand Rapids, Mich.: Revell, 2009.

Marty, Martin E. *Righteous Empire: The Protestant Experience in America*. New York: Dial Press, 1970.

May, Martha, and Melvin I. Urofsky, eds. *The New Christian Right: Political and Social Issues*. New York: Routledge, 1996.

McDannell, Colleen. *Material Christianity: Religion and Popular Culture in America*. New Haven, Conn.: Yale University Press, 1995.

McDowell, Stephen. *America, a Christian Nation? Examining the Evidence of the Christian Foundation of America*. Charlottesville, Va.: Providence Foundation, 2004.

McDowell, Stephen, and Mark Beliles. *In God We Trust Tour Guide Featuring America's Landmarks of Liberty*. Charlottesville, Va.: Providence Foundation, 1998.

Menary, Richard. "Embodied Narratives." *Journal of Consciousness Studies* 15, no. 6 (2008): 63–84.

Meyer, Birgit, ed. *Aesthetic Formations: Media, Religion, and the Senses*. New York: Palgrave Macmillan. 2009.

———. "Mediation and the Genesis of Presence: Toward a Material Approach to Religion." *Religion and Society* 5, no. 1 (2014): 205–54.

Meyer, Birgit, and Marleen de Witte. "Heritage and the Sacred: Introduction." *Material Religion* 9, no. 3 (2013): 274–80.

Millard, Catherine. *God's Signature over the Nation's Capital*. New Wilmington, Penn.: SonRise, 1985.

———. *The Rewriting of America's History*. Camp Hill, Penn.: Horizon House, 1991.

Miller, Stephen P. *The Age of Evangelicalism: America's Born-Again Years*. Oxford: Oxford University Press, 2014.

Minkowitz, Donna. "The Christian Right's Antigay Campaign: Part Stealth, Part Muscle." *Christianity and Crisis*, April 12, 1993, 99–104. Reprinted in *The New Christian Right: Political and Social Issues*, edited by Martha May and Melvin I. Urofsky, 355–57. New York: Routledge, 1996.

Mitchell, Jolyon. "Narrative." In *Keywords in Religion, Media, and Culture*, edited by David Morgan, 123–35. New York: Routledge, 2008.

Moen, Matthew. "From Revolution to Evolution: The Changing Nature of the Christian Right." *Sociology of Religion* 55, no. 3 (1994): 345–57.

Moore, R. Laurence. "Insiders and Outsiders in American Historical Narrative and American History." *American Historical Review* 87, no. 2 (1982): 390–412.

———. *Religious Outsiders and the Making of Americans*. Oxford: Oxford University Press, 1986.

———. *Selling God: American Religion in the Marketplace of Culture*. Oxford: Oxford University Press, 1994.

Moore, Russell. *Onward: Engaging the Culture without Losing the Gospel*. Nashville, Tenn.: B&H Publishing, 2015.

Morgan, David, ed. *Keywords in Religion, Media, and Culture*. New York: Routledge, 2008.

———. *Religion and Material Culture: The Matter of Belief*. New York: Routledge, 2009.

———. "Soldier Statues and Empty Pedestals: Public Memory in the Wake of the Confederacy." *Material Religion* 14, no. 1 (2018): 153–57.

———. *Visual Piety: A History and Theory of Popular Religious Images*. Berkeley: University of California Press, 1999.

Morgan, David, and Sally M. Promey, eds. *The Visual Culture of American Religions*. Berkeley: University of California Press, 2001.

Morgan, Philip D. "'To Get Quit of Negroes': George Washington and Slavery." *Journal of American Studies* 39, no. 3 (2005): 403–29.

Murphy, Andrew R. *Prodigal Nation: Moral Decline and Divine Punishment from New England to 9/11*. Oxford: Oxford University Press, 2009.

Neuhaus, Richard John. *The Naked Public Square: Religion and Democracy in America*, 2d ed. Grand Rapids, Mich.: Eerdmans, 1984.

Noll, Mark. *America's God: From Jonathan Edwards to Abraham Lincoln*. Oxford: Oxford University Press, 2002.

———. *A History of Christianity in the United States and Canada*. Grand Rapids, Mich.: Eerdmans, 1992.

Noll, Mark A., Nathan O. Hatch, and George M. Marsden. *The Search for Christian America*. Westchester, Ill.: Crossway Books, 1983.

Orsi, Robert. *Between Heaven and Earth: The Religious Worlds People Make and the Scholars Who Study Them*. Princeton, N.J.: Princeton University Press, 2005.

———. *History and Presence*. Cambridge, Mass.: Harvard University Press, 2016.

———. *The Madonna of 115th Street: Faith and Community in Italian Harlem, 1880–1950*. New Haven, Conn.: Yale University Press, 1985.

Parks, Rosa, and Gregory J. Reed. *Quiet Strength: The Faith, the Hope and the Heart of a Woman Who Changed a Nation*. Grand Rapids, Mich.: Zondervan, 2000.

Persinos, John F. "Has the Christian Right Taken Over the Republican Party?" *Campaigns and Elections*, September 1994, 20–24.

Petrzela, Natalia. *Classroom Wars: Language, Sex, and the Making of Modern Political Culture*. Oxford: Oxford University Press, 2015.

Pitch, Anthony S. *The Burning of Washington: The British Invasion of 1814.* Annapolis, Md.: Naval Institute Press, 1998.

Porterfield, Amanda. *Conceived in Doubt: Religion and Politics in the New American Nation.* Chicago: University of Chicago Press, 2012.

Prothero, Stephen. *The American Bible: How Our Words Unite, Divide, and Define a Nation.* New York: HarperOne, 2012.

———. *American Jesus: How the Son of God Became a National Icon.* New York: Farrar, Straus, and Giroux, 2003.

———. *Why Liberals Win the Culture Wars (Even When They Lose Elections).* New York: HarperCollins, 2016.

Promey, Sally. "Public Displays of Religion." In *The Visual Culture of American Religions*, edited by David Morgan and Sally M. Promey, 27–48. Berkeley: University of California Press, 2001.

Putnam, Robert A., and David E. Campbell. *American Grace: How Religion Divides and Unites Us.* New York: Simon and Schuster, 2010.

———. "God and Caesar in America: Why Mixing Religion and Politics Is Bad for Both." *Foreign Affairs* 91 (2012): 34–43.

Reed, Ralph. *Active Faith: How Christians Are Changing the Face of American Politics.* New York: Free Press, 1996.

Reinbold, Jenna. "'Honorable Religious Premises' and Other Affronts: Disputing Free Exercise in the Era of Trump." *Studies in Law, Politics, and Society* 79 (2019): 31–54.

Saberi, Erin. "From Moral Majority to Organized Minority: Tactics of the Religious Right." *Christian Century*, August 11, 1993.

Savage, Kirk. *Monument Wars: Washington, D.C., the National Mall, and the Transformation of the Memorial Landscape.* Berkeley: University of California Press, 2009.

Schäfer, Axel R., ed. *American Evangelicals and the 1960s.* Madison: University of Wisconsin Press, 2013.

Schectman, Marya. *The Constitution of Selves.* Ithaca, N.Y.: Cornell University Press, 2007.

Scott, Joan. "The Evidence of Experience." *Critical Inquiry* 17, no. 4 (2004): 773–97.

Sedgwick, Eve Kosofsky. *Touching Feeling: Affect, Pedagogy, and Performativity.* Durham, N.C.: Duke University Press, 2003.

Sehat, David. *The Myth of American Religious Freedom.* Oxford: Oxford University Press, 2011.

Smith, Christian. *American Evangelicalism: Embattled and Thriving.* Chicago: University of Chicago Press, 1998.

———. *Christian America? What Evangelicals Really Want.* Berkeley: University of California Press, 2000.

Smith, Valene, ed. *Hosts and Guests: The Anthropology of Tourism.* 2d ed. Philadelphia: University of Pennsylvania Press, 1977.

Somers, Margaret R. "The Narrative Constitution of Identity: A Relational and Network Approach." *Theory and Society* 23 (1994): 605–49.

Stausberg, Michael. *Religion and Tourism: Crossroads, Destinations, and Encounters*. New York: Routledge, 2010.

Stolow, Jeremy. "Technology." In *Keywords in Religion, Media, and Culture*, edited by David Morgan, 187–97. New York: Routledge, 2008.

Sturken, Maria. *Tourists of History: Memory, Kitsch, and Consumerism from Oklahoma City to Ground Zero*. Durham, N.C.: Duke University Press, 2007.

Sutton, Matthew Avery. *American Apocalypse: A History of Modern Evangelicalism*. Cambridge, Mass.: Harvard University Press, 2014.

———. "New Trends in the Historiography of American Fundamentalism." *Journal of American Studies* 51, no. 1 (2017): 235–41.

Thomas, Cal, and Ed Dobson. *Blinded by Might: Why the Religious Right Can't Save America*. 2d ed. Grand Rapids, Mich.: Zondervan, 2000.

Throckmorten, Warren, and Michael Coulter. *Getting Jefferson Right: Fact-Checking Claims about Our Third President*. Grove City, Penn.: Salem Grove Press, 2012.

Turner, Victor, and Edith Turner. *Image and Pilgrimage in Christian Culture: Anthropological Perspectives*. New York: Columbia University Press, 1978.

Tweed, Thomas. "Mary's Rain and God's Umbrella: Religion, Identity, and Modernity in the Visionary Art of a Chicana Painter." *Material Religion* 6, no. 3 (2010): 274–303.

Urofsky, Melvin I., and Martha May, eds. *The New Christian Right: Political and Social Issues*. New York: Routledge, 1996.

Urry, John. *The Tourist Gaze*. 2d ed. New York: Sage, 2002.

Utter, Glenn H., and John W. Storey. *The Religious Right: A Reference Handbook*. Santa Barbara, Calif.: ABC-CLIO, 1995.

Viguerie, Richard A. *The New Right: We're Ready to Lead*. Falls Church, Va.: Viguerie Company, 1981.

Wenger, Tisa. *Religious Freedom: The Contested History of an American Ideal*. Chapel Hill: University of North Carolina, 2017.

Whitford, Kelly. "Activating Religious Objects in Public Spaces: Bernini's Angels on the Pont Sant'Angelo in Early Modern Rome." *Material Religion* 14, no. 3 (2018): 339–67.

Williams, Daniel K. *God's Own Party: The Making of the Christian Right*. Oxford: Oxford University Press, 2012.

Winston, Diane. "Back to the Future: Religion, Politics, and the Media." *American Quarterly* 59, no. 3 (2007): 969–89.

Wong, Janelle. *Immigrants, Evangelicals, and Politics in an Era of Demographic Change*. New York: Russell Sage, 2018.

Wuthnow, Robert. "The Political Rebirth of American Evangelicals." In *The New Christian Right: Mobilization and Legitimation*, edited by Robert C. Liebman and Robert Wuthnow, 168–87. New York: Aldine, 1983.

———. *The Restructuring of American Religion: Society and Faith since World War II*. Princeton, N.J.: Princeton University Press, 1988.

Index

Bacon, Francis, 37
Barbary States, 3, 119, 147n2
Barrett-Fox, Rebecca, 145, 170n21
Barton, David: as leader of Christian
heritage tours, 40; on Thomas Jefferson, 40, 44, 45, 154n33; as public
speaker, 40, 154n35; on Christian
heritage story, 40–42, 45, 147n5,
159n38, 160n45; private tours of U.S.
Capitol for members of Congress,
41; and Kirk Cameron, 42; and Texas
textbooks, 42; on school prayer, 62;
on American history, 118, 167–68n24;
on Malachi's book of remembrance,
118, 168n25; and quotations of Founding Fathers as proof-texts, 152n8; on
use of proof-texts, 156n54; and Ted
Cruz, 157n62
Bebbington, David, 9, 91, 145, 148n11
belonging, sense of, 14, 22, 134
Benedict, Saint, 114, 159n33
Bible: Christian heritage tour guides'
quoting of, 1, 23, 112, 126, 150n44,
168n35; America-themed Bibles, 4,
34, 41; as ultimate moral authority,
9; U.S. Supreme Court's ruling on
devotional Bible reading in public schools, 13; and insider and outsider narratives, 16; Jefferson Bible,
32, 100, 153n14; Abraham Lincoln's
use of, 33; and Library of Congress,
36–37, 100; Gutenberg Bible, 36–37,
100, 130, 153n20, 154n22; Geneva
Bible, 41, 47, 155n40; specialty Bibles,
41, 154–55n37; proof-text approach to,
44; and outsider narrative, 63; presidential Bibles, 69; biblical stories
depicted in Washington National
Cathedral, 77; influence on United
States, 132, 169n4; as inspiration for
American music, 144–45. *See also*
Museum of the Bible
Bible studies: and Christian heritage
story, 4, 25, 42; in Washington, D.C.,
82

Bible wars, 12
biblical inscriptions: on monuments
and buildings, 16, 22, 23, 46, 102; at
Union Station, 23, 151n60; on Wash-
ington Monument, 30, 59, 70, 152n6;
on Lincoln Memorial, 33; at Library
of Congress, 37; at U.S. Capitol, 48,
49
biblicism, 9, 145
Bill of Rights, 35, 39, 98, 148n22, 165n53
Bob Jones University Press, 42
Bob Jones University v. United States
(1983), 161n13
Braddock, Edward, 31
Brewster, William, 47
Buggeln, Gretchen, 153n21, 157n65
Burwell v. Hobby Lobby (2014), 87
Bush, George H. W., 86
Bush, George W., 15, 86–87
Bush, Jeb, 163n36
business leaders, and white conserva-
tive Protestants' political activity, 13,
149n30

Cameron, Kirk, 42, 110, 147n5, 155n40
Campbell, David E., 162n22
capitalism, 18, 39, 148n24
Capitol Hill: and Christian heritage
tours, 5, 28, 95, 105, 115, 116; and supporters of Christian Right, 68
Carroll, Charles, 26
Carson, Ben, 111–12
Carter, Jimmy, 149n33
Catholics: white evangelical Christians'
omission of, 11, 142; and Protestant
hegemony in public schools, 12; and
IRS challenge to private segregated
schools, 13; as part of Christian Right,
147n4; and outsider narrative, 157n9;
and contraceptives, 162n25
Chancey, Mark, 149n37, 155n46
Chapman, John Gadsby, 47
charismatics, as part of Christian Right,
147n4
Cheney, Dick, 108

Chester, Daniel, 38

Christian Coalition, 66–67, 158n29

Christian heritage: Christian Right on, 4, 5, 39–40, 43; Jerry Falwell on, 4, 40, 156n47; and films, 4, 25, 39, 41–42, 45, 110, 117, 155n38; and textbooks, 4, 39–40, 42–43, 118, 149n37, 155nn44–46, 168n34; reclaiming of, 4–5, 22, 115, 116; threats to, 5, 23, 24, 81, 103, 104, 118, 129, 138; on Christian God as historical actor, 29; academic historians on, 29–30, 31, 33, 44, 45, 157n5; and material culture, 29–30, 55, 115; on sincerity of Founding Fathers, 29–34, 39, 42, 46, 48, 51, 55, 61, 62, 107, 109–10, 112, 113, 152n4, 159n38; and proof-text approach, 31, 44, 152n8, 156n54; and devotional literature, 39, 41, 44; and accounts of founding, 39, 154n27; market for, 39–43, 45, 51, 56–59; and Israel, 41, 42, 107; John Fea on, 43–44, 45, 154n27; resistance to "Christian nation myth," 43–45; credibility of genre, 44; and separation of church and state, 51; and nostalgia, 51–52, 75, 92, 108, 117–18, 119, 128–29, 134, 137, 145, 167n5; guidebooks advocating, 69, 159n38; challenges to, 74; and Museum of the Bible, 133; as secret history, 154n32

Christian heritage tour guides: celebrity status of, 1; monologues of, 1, 21, 28, 32, 47–49, 108, 110–11, 119, 135, 151n60; Bible quoted by, 1, 23, 112, 126, 150n44, 168n35; Founding Fathers quoted by, 1–2; on outdoor monuments, 3; on Islam, 3, 100, 119; on Christian features of memorials or buildings, 5, 30, 36–37, 47–48, 62, 71; and traditions of Christian Right, 6; qualitative interviews with, 8; conservative social values of, 9; as whites, 9; and outsider narrative, 16, 54–55, 60–62, 74; and insider narrative, 16, 55; and Washington Monument, 19–20,

53–54; "secrets" imparted by, 22; tourists hurried by, 22, 26; on statues of Christian leaders, 23, 29, 47, 113, 157n64; on prayers of Founding Fathers, 28; narratives of Founding Fathers, 28, 30–34, 51, 62, 85, 107, 113; on founding documents as sacred texts, 34–37, 136; on Library of Congress, 36–37, 100; David Barton's trainings for, 40–41; on U.S. Capitol, 47–49, 60, 98; on public schools, 60–61; on separation of church and state, 61–62, 113, 114, 140; on erased evidence of Christianity, 70, 71, 100–101; and Washington National Cathedral, 77, 79, 80; and victim role, 81; definition of Christianity, 82, 161n7; on biblical allegories, 83; on White House, 83–84; on U.S. Supreme Court, 85, 93, 98, 165n53; on security guards, 95–96; political action encouraged by, 110–16, 125–29; on American military service, 119–22, 124–25, 168n32; and Museum of the Bible, 133

Christian heritage tourists: characteristics of, 1, 7, 8–9; as white, 1, 9, 10; ambivalent relationship to nation, 2; responses to tour guides, 2, 7, 37, 47, 49–50, 53–54, 60, 62, 71, 85, 98, 107, 110–11, 140; and outdoor monuments, 2–4; Christian heritage experienced by, 4–5, 19–24, 45–50, 135; embodied experiences of, 5, 19–24, 45–50; photographs taken by, 5, 20, 26, 28, 37, 49, 53, 54, 77, 84, 95, 102, 130, 138–39, 140, 142, 151n60; activities of, 5, 152n61; qualitative interviews with, 8, 148n18; conservative social values of, 9, 81; class status of, 11–12; and outsider narrative, 16, 24, 54–55, 56, 58–59, 71, 72, 95, 103, 135; and insider narrative, 16, 24, 56, 71, 72, 135; on Founding Fathers, 16, 25, 29, 34, 80, 109–10; and metanarratives, 18–19;

and security guards, 21, 22, 35, 81, 85, 92–96, 105, 130, 140; access and knowledge granted to, 22; interaction with disruptive objects, 24, 55, 71, 72, 81, 96, 100, 102, 103, 104, 138, 142; and exile role, 55–56, 59–62, 71, 72, 104; on public schools, 61; on separation of church and state, 61–62; on Christian features erased from D.C. sites, 69–72, 96, 99–101, 159n40, 159n43, 160n44, 167n14; and Washington National Cathedral, 77, 79, 80, 102; and victim role, 81, 82–83, 96, 104, 127; definition of Christianity, 82, 83, 161n7; and Barack Obama, 82, 83–84, 115–16; on same-sex marriage, 84; and U.S. Supreme Court, 92–96, 98; and U.S. Capitol, 98–100, 105–7, 165n54; and Library of Congress, 100; and savior role, 108; and sense of crisis for nation, 108–10, 125; on American veterans, 122, 124–25; sharing experiences of Christian heritage tours, 138–41; gaze of, 151n60; rhythms of, 151n60

Christian heritage tours: characteristics of, 1, 8, 95; prayers said during, 1–2, 7, 9; outdoor monuments visited by, 2–4; and songs, 4, 7, 9; Christian heritage experienced on, 4–5, 19–24, 45–50; market for, 5, 56–57; and white evangelical Christians' dissonant relationship with United States, 5, 6; and savior role, 5–6, 108, 114, 116, 146; Christian Right's role in, 6–7, 39; white evangelical Christians as primary audience of, 6–12, 146; norms of, 7; participant observation of, 7–8, 147–48n9; duration of, 8; size of, 8; and devotions, 9; private tours for Christian school groups, 9, 147n6; and narrow definition of Christianity, 10–11; cost of, 11, 19–20; income level of, 11, 148n18; and United States as Christian nation, 12, 39, 43–45, 48, 51,

55, 58, 74, 112, 137, 156n58, 156–57n59; advertisements of, 16–17, 45–46, 56–58, 59, 133, 137, 157n63; narratives of, 16–19, 25, 28, 135; physical discomfort of, 20–22, 26–28, 92–95, 96, 105–6, 124, 137, 140; alienating aspects of, 22, 75, 81, 85, 95–96, 134; activation of ambient religious objects, 23, 48, 55, 81, 85, 101, 138, 151n60, 151–52n61; and insider narratives, 24; and outsider narrative, 24, 54–59, 75; lived history of, 34, 55, 71; David Barton as leader of, 40; films promoted by, 42; and exile role, 69; and victim role, 80–81, 95; guest speakers for, 82–83; on American soldiers as exemplary saviors, 108, 119–22, 124–25; as initiation ritual into secret knowledge, 108, 154n32; and Christian leisure industry, 147n3

Christian homeschool movement, 39–42

Christianity: role in American history, 4–5, 14, 23, 24, 25, 29–30, 34, 36–37, 41, 43, 46–50, 51, 71, 74, 75, 98, 100, 108–10, 118, 141, 160n49; internal diversity of American Christianity, 10, 11, 144–45; white evangelical Christians' definition of, 10–11, 14, 34, 79, 80, 82, 83, 100, 137, 160n49, 161n7; "real Christians" opposed to "nominal Christians," 11, 82, 137, 161n7; percentage of Americans self-identifying as, 15; national identity linked with, 39, 103, 136, 166n72, 167n14; and erased evidence from D.C. sites, 69–72, 75, 96, 99–101, 159n40, 159n43, 160n44, 167n14; as influence on American mainstream culture, 74–75, 76, 103, 160n50, 160n54; tradition of persecution and martyrdom, 81; visibility of, 141–42, 144–45; insincere public expressions of, 152n4; academics portrayed as biased against, 160n45. *See also* Catholics; Protestantism

Christian heritage genre, 43–45; and proof-text approach to Bible, 44; and conservative Christian groups, 68, 69, 86, 91; and victim role, 81, 86
custodial attitude, of white evangelicals toward United States, 51–52, 102
Cyrus, King of Persia, 170n21

Dalai Lama, 79
Daly, Jim, 168n37
Darrow, Clarence, 12
Davis, Kim, 88–89, 162–63n31, 163n36
Dead Sea Scrolls, 36
Declaration of Independence: Signers Island as memorial to signers of, 26, 28; Thomas Jefferson as signer of, 26, 32; Christian heritage tour guides on, 35; as founding document, 35; as derived from biblical tradition, 39, 118, 168n28; mythology around, 153n19
deism, 30, 57
DeMar, Gary, 40
Democratic Party, 15, 71–72, 82
desegregation, 13
De Soto, Hernando, 47
deviance, rhetoric of, 63, 68
devotional literature, and Christian heritage story, 39, 41, 44
Diamond, Sara, 68
displacement, sense of, and Christian heritage tours, 22
Dobson, James, 86, 170n19
Don't Ask, Don't Tell, 68
Dreher, Rod, 114, 159n33
Dreisbach, Daniel, 153n17
Du Mez, Kristin Kobes, 9
Dunbar, Cynthia, 155n44
Duniway, Abigail Scott, 72, 159–60n44

ecumenism, 149n27
Ellison, Keith, 165n56
embodied experiences: of Christian heritage tourists, 5, 19–24, 45–50, 92–95; and identity narratives, 21, 101; and insider narrative, 22, 23, 51

Engelke, Matthew, 23, 101–2
Engel v. Vitale (1962), 159n42, 161n13, 166n72
Episcopal Church, 33, 79–80
Esther, Queen, 16, 112, 126–27, 150n44
evangelicalism: definitions of, 9–10, 91, 148n11, 164n45; racial divide in, 10, 11; and revivals of nineteenth century, 12; and church membership, 12, 148n21; Founding Fathers as proto-evangelicals, 28–29; evolution of, 146. *See also* White evangelical Christians
exile role: and white evangelical Christians, 5, 6, 14, 16, 19, 23, 25, 52, 55–56, 59–62, 65, 66, 67, 71, 72, 75, 76, 80, 81, 86, 87, 92, 104, 108, 135, 136–37, 146; and ancient Israelites, 55, 63, 65; and founder role, 56; and Christian Right, 63, 64–66, 67, 68, 69; and fundamentalists, 63–64

Falwell, Jerry: on Christian heritage, 4, 40, 156n47; political strategy of, 64–65, 66, 67, 90, 113, 158n22, 158n23, 163n38, 167n11; on biblical stories, 65, 158n16; on victim role, 80–81; on savior role, 117
Farris, Mike, 67
Fea, John: on Christian heritage story, 43–44, 45, 154n27; on Donald Trump, 145, 164n46; on Christian Right's political agenda, 149n37; on historical writing principles, 156n52
federal government: role of evangelical Christianity in, 12; conservative attitudes toward, 22; secularizing forces in, 82, 98; Christian heritage tourists' attitudes toward, 83; disestablishment of religion in, 148n22
Federal Marriage Amendment, 86
feminism, 13, 66
Fessenden, Tracy, 160n50
films: and Christian heritage story, 4, 25, 39, 41–42, 45, 110, 117, 155n38; and

insider and outsider narratives, 16; and WallBuilders, 155n38

Finney, Charles, 111, 167n7

Fiorina, Carly, 163n36

Focus on the Family, 86, 168n37, 170n19

Forbes, Randy, 71–72, 115

Foster, Marshall, 42

founder role: of white evangelical Christians, 19, 25, 34, 51–52, 76, 135, 136, 146; and exile role, 56

Founding Fathers: Christian heritage tour guides' quoting of, 1–2; and Christian Right's myth of origin, 5, 6, 14, 28–29; Christian heritage tourists' narratives of, 16, 25, 29, 34, 80, 109–10; Christian heritage tour guides' narratives of, 28, 30–34, 51, 62, 85, 107, 113; as proto-evangelicals, 28–29, 33, 39, 51, 154n33; assumption of sincerity of faith, 29–34, 39, 42, 46, 48, 51, 55, 61, 62, 107, 109–10, 112, 113, 152n4, 159n38; and public displays of religion, 30; quotations as proof-text, 31, 44, 46, 57–58, 61, 152n8; and specialty Bibles, 41

Franklin, Benjamin, 26, 41, 153n18

Frazer, Greg, 44

French and Indian War, 16, 31, 119

fundamentalists: and outsider narrative, 12, 14, 63–64, 167n12; as part of Christian Right, 147n4

Gallup, George, Jr., 66

gay rights, 66, 67. See also LGBTQ+ rights

gender, 6, 15, 146

gender identity, 88, 92, 162n29

Gerber, Lynne, 75

Gerson, Michael, 86

Giant Bible of Mainz, 36

Gilbert, Cass, 165n53

Giles, Thomas S., 154–55n37

Gingrich, Newt, 105

Green, Steve, 132

Gutenberg, Johannes, 36

Gutenberg Bible, 36–37, 100, 130, 153n20, 154n22

Gwinnett, Button, 26

Hale, Grace, 64

Hamilton, Alexander, 153n18

Hammurabi, 48

Hancock, John, 26

Hatch, Nathan O., 44, 156n58, 156–57n59

Hatfield, Mark, 72, 159n43

HB2 ("bathroom bill"), 162n29

Hemings, Sally, 154n33

heritage: history distinguished from, 29, 44, 156n56; and canonization of cultural forms, 152n3; rewriting past as function of heritage making, 154n23; as secret history, 154n32. See also Christian heritage

higher education, 13

hippies, 64

Hispanics, 9

Hobby Lobby Stores, Inc., 132, 162n26

Hochschild, Arlie Russell, 161n5

Holy Land, and Christian leisure industry, 45, 147n3

Home School Legal Defense Association, 67

Honor Flight Network, 122

Huckabee, Mike, 89

identity: of white evangelical Christians, 16–19, 145, 146, 150n39; and metanarratives, 17, 18; narratives of, 17–19, 21, 24–25, 101, 135, 145; religious identities, 17, 24, 101, 152n62; dynamic nature of, 17, 24–25, 135, 138, 146, 150n45; religious objects participating in identity formation, 24, 81, 101, 102–3, 104, 152n62; Christian Right's narrative of communal identity of inheritance of nation, 29, 30; national identity linked with Christianity, 39, 103, 136, 166n72, 167n14; subculture's identity, 74, 75, 160n54; contestations over, 101–2

Indiana, 88, 162n27

In God We Trust campaign, 115, 116

insider narrative: and role of white evangelical Christians in American history, 14, 17, 19, 51, 134; major plot arcs of, 16, 17–18; and Christian heritage tourists, 16, 24, 56, 71, 72, 135; and founder role, 19, 136; and embodied experiences of Washington, D.C., 22, 23, 51; Christian heritage tourists moving between narratives, 23–24, 51–52, 54–55, 56, 71–72, 75–76, 80, 81, 85–90, 96, 100, 103, 104; historical development of, 24; on Founding Fathers' Christian faith, 32, 55; outsider narrative's tension with, 55, 65, 72, 135; outsider narrative compared to, 63, 134; and Washington National Cathedral, 80; and religious objects, 102

Internal Revenue Service, tax-exempt status of all-white Christian private schools, 13, 161n13

Islam, 3, 100, 119

Islamic State (ISIS), 127, 168n37

Israel (ancient): and Christian heritage story, 41, 42, 107; and exile role, 55, 63, 65

Iwo Jima Memorial (Marine Corps War Memorial), 2–4, 119, 168n32

Jackson, Andrew, 37

Jay, John, 111, 167n6

Jefferson, Thomas: and Barbary States, 3, 119; as signer of Declaration of Independence, 26, 32; Christian faith of, 30, 31–33, 34, 154n33; accusations of atheism, 31–32, 33, 62; on separation of church and state, 32, 61, 62, 107; and U.S. Capitol church services, 32, 107, 153n13; David Barton on, 40, 44, 45, 154n33; "creationist" position of, 41; writings as proof-text for

Christian heritage story, 44, 62; engraved relief portrait of, 48; Quran of, 100, 165n56

Jefferson Bible, 32, 100, 153n14

Jefferson Memorial, 30, 32, 62, 128, 132

jeremiads: of Christian Right, 14, 15, 34, 40, 51–52, 65, 92, 117, 134; of Donald Trump, 15, 91; of Christian heritage authors, 40; of white evangelical Christians, 91, 107, 125–26, 140; metanarratives of, 134–35, 141

Jesus Christ: and outsider narrative, 63; popular devotional images of, 101; Great Commission of, 116; sacrifice of, 120, 121, 125

Jesus People, 64

Jews, and outsider narrative, 157n9

Jones, Robert P., 80

Joseph, Chief, 72

Justinian I, 48

Kaell, Hillary, 102, 151n61, 166n71

Kavanaugh, Brett, 164n49

Keep the Promise Political Action Committee, 157n62

Kennedy, Anthony, 89–90, 163n39

Kennedy, D. James, 4, 40, 117–18

Kentucky, 88–89, 162–63n31

King, Martin Luther, Jr., 64, 77, 84

Korean War Veterans Memorial, 121

LaHaye, Tim, 40

Latinx voters, 10

Lawrence v. Texas (2003), 86

Lee, Jason, 72, 73, 100, 103, 159n43, 160n44

Lewinsky, Monica, 68

LGBTQ+ rights, 86, 89, 90, 92, 162n27

liberals: American history endangered by, 6, 25, 57; caricatures of, 62; Christian Coalition's characterization of, 67; and Episcopal Church, 79; and political activity of white evangelical Christians, 92; on separation of church and state, 114

24, 81, 101, 102–3, 104, 152n62; and separation of church and state, 49; and contestations over identity, 101–2

Oregon, and statue of Jason Lee in U.S. Capitol, 72, 84, 159–60n44

Orsi, Robert, 170n22

outsider narrative: and white evangelical Christians, 6, 10, 13, 59, 63–64, 66–68, 80, 81, 88, 91, 135, 158n22, 169n4; and fundamentalists, 12, 14, 63–64, 167n12; and Christian Right, 13, 63, 66–68, 92, 135; and role of white evangelical Christians in American history, 14, 15, 17, 19; and Donald Trump, 15; major plot arcs of, 16, 17–18; and Christian heritage tourists, 16, 24, 54–55, 56, 58–59, 71, 72, 95, 103, 135; and Christian heritage tour guides, 16, 54–55, 60–62, 74; and War on Christmas, 18; and school prayer, 18, 60, 166n72; and embodied experiences of Washington, D.C., 22, 92–94; Christian heritage tourists moving between narratives, 23–24, 51–52, 54–55, 56, 71–72, 75–76, 80, 81, 85–90, 96, 100, 103, 104, 136–37; historical development of, 24; and Christian heritage tours, 24, 54–59, 75; disruption of, 24, 55, 71, 72, 81, 96, 100, 102, 103, 104, 138, 142; and public schools, 55, 56, 60–61, 74; insider narrative's tension with, 55, 65, 72, 135; function of, 56, 68, 74; and separation of church and state, 57, 61–62, 137; insider narrative compared to, 63, 134; and moral authority, 64, 65, 74, 81, 88, 92, 138; and experience of African Americans, 74, 157n9; and exile role, 137; and victim role, 137

Paine, Thomas, 41
Palin, Sarah, 41
Parks, Rosa, 99, 142
Pence, Mike, 88

Pennsylvania, and Muhlenberg brothers, 47, 113

persecution, of Christians, 18, 81, 83, 89–90, 91, 127–28, 168n37; Christian heritage tourists' expectation of, 128–29

Pew Research Center, 161n8

Philadelphia tours, 100

Phillips, Jack, 89, 128, 163n39

Pilgrims, 63

pluralism, 150n50

Pocahontas, 47–48

Powell, William Henry, 47

prayer journals, 4

prayers: during Christian heritage tours, 1–2, 7, 9, 83, 115–16; of Founding Fathers at Constitutional Convention, 16, 28; in paintings in U.S. Capitol Rotunda, 47–48; Founding Fathers' support for, 61; in Washington National Cathedral, 79; Congressional Prayer Room, 83; in White House, 83–84; and George W. Bush, 86; Donald Trump's support for, 91; and George Washington, 107; of Christian heritage tourists, 115–16; and Barack Obama, 115–16; and savior role, 115–16; of Franklin Delano Roosevelt, 124. *See also* school prayer

PrayUSA, 116

Presbyterian Church, 33

progressives: progressive evangelicalism, 11; white evangelical Christians being pushed to margins by, 61, 91; and political activity of white evangelical Christians, 92; on separation of church and state, 114; public narratives of, 150n50

Project Blitz, 43, 92, 162n30, 169n14

pro-life alliance, 162n25

Promey, Sally, 101, 151n60

Protestantism: white Protestants' role in American history, 4; white evangelical Christians' ignoring of mainline Protestants, 11, 51, 79, 80, 144; unofficial establishment of, 12; white Protestants as American insiders, 12; dominance of liberal and mainline Protestants, 12, 149n27; and white conservative Protestants' political activity, 12–14; Christian heritage tour guides on, 33–34, 37; and religious experience, 45; role in New World, 63; fundamentalists' divergence from mainline Protestants, 63–64; unmarked Protestantism, 74–76, 160n50, 160n54; and Museum of the Bible, 169n8

public narratives, 17–19, 51, 59, 135, 150n50, 160n46

public schools: Protestant hegemony in, 12; teaching of evolution in, 12; desegregation of, 13; removal of prayer and Bible reading in, 13; and outsider narrative, 55, 56, 60–61, 74; and sex education, 60; white evangelicals' distrust of, 60–61; and religious freedom, 68; and Common Core education standards, 69, 81, 103. *See also* school prayer

publishing industry: and Christian heritage story, 4, 25, 39, 40–44, 45, 46, 51, 59, 117, 160n45; and insider and outsider narratives, 16

Puritans, 18, 63, 151n53

Putnam, Robert A., 162n22

Quakers, 28

Quran, 100

race: and Christian heritage tourists as white, 1, 9, 10; and white evangelical Christians' political activity, 6, 10, 146; racial divide in evangelicalism, 10, 11. *See also* African Americans; white Americans

Reagan, Ronald, 14, 66, 77, 151n53

Reed, Ralph, 66–67, 87

Regent University, 67

relativism, 85

religion: disestablishment of, 12, 148n22; lived religion, 24, 152n52, 170n22; civil religion, 29, 31; public displays of, 30. *See also* Christianity; Islam

religious conscience, 88

religious freedom: desegregation as attack on, 13; and Project Blitz, 43; and same-sex marriage, 43, 81, 82, 88, 90, 144; arguments for, 43, 81, 82, 144; and public schools, 68; and contraceptives, 87–88; interpreted to privilege white evangelicals, 144

Religious Freedom Restoration Act, 87, 88

religious hostility, 89, 90, 163n41

religious minorities, and outsider narrative, 74

Religious Right. *See* Christian Right

Republican Party: political discourse of, 4, 6; Christian heritage tourists' allegiance to, 9, 71–72, 82; white evangelical Christians as essential base for, 14–15, 66, 67–68, 114, 150n39, 159n30

rhetoric: and role of white evangelical Christians, 6, 75, 92; of deviance, 63, 68; of Christian Coalition, 67; insider and outsider rhetoric, 136

Rice, Condoleezza, 86

Robertson, Pat, 66–67

Roe v. Wade (1973), 13

Rolfe, John, 48

Roosevelt, Franklin Delano, 124, 161n11

Rush, Benjamin, 28

Rutledge, Edward, 26

Sale, George, 165n56

Sallman, Warner, 101

same-sex marriage: and presidential election of 2016, 15; and religious freedom arguments, 43, 81, 82, 88, 90, 144; and Washington National Cathedral, 79; U.S. Supreme Court on, 84–85, 88, 89, 161n19; at state

supernaturalism, 29, 157n5

Svetlana, Boym, 167n5

Tea Party, 41, 87, 118, 162n22

Ten Commandments: in National Archives Museum, 35–36, 102; in U.S. Supreme Court, 84, 96, 102, 164–65n53

Tennessee, 88

Tennyson , Alfred, Lord, 37, 38

Texas, Christian heritage story in textbooks of, 42–43, 118, 149n37, 155nn44–46

textbooks: and Christian heritage story, 4, 39–40, 42–43, 118, 149n37, 155nn44–46, 168n34; and outsider narrative, 56

Thomas Nelson (publisher), 154n33

Throckmorten, Warren, 154n33

transgender rights, 43, 92

Treaty of Tripoli, Article 11 of, 147n2

Tripoli, 3, 119, 147n2

Trump, Donald: white evangelical Christians' support for, 6, 10, 15, 90–92, 145–46, 147n8, 164n45, 170n21; as outsider, 15; on Barack Obama, 87, 162n21; as savior, 91; as victim, 91; "Make American Great Again" slogan, 91, 164n46; on holiday greetings, 91, 164n47; and press credentials of news media, 162n21; ban on travelers from majority-Muslim countries, 163n41; James Dobson on, 170n19

Truth, Sojourner, 99, 142

Twain, Mark: students opting out of reading, 67

Union Station, biblical inscriptions at, 23, 151n60

Unitarianism, 32, 152n12

United States: dissonant relationship of white evangelical Christians to, 5, 6; disestablishment of religion in, 12, 148n22; and covenant with God, 18, 35, 39–40, 42, 51, 133, 134, 151n53; founding documents of, 21–22; white evangelical Christians' dynamic relationship with, 24, 146; and Christian heritage tourists' sense of crisis, 108–10, 125. *See also* American history; Christian heritage

U.S. Capitol: private tours of, 22, 41, 47, 98, 99, 105, 157n64, 165n55; Thomas Jefferson's attendance of church services in, 32, 107, 153n13; National Statuary Hall Collection, 47, 72, 99–100, 105, 142, 159n38; and Rotunda paintings, 47–48, 60, 99, 159n38; House of Representatives Chamber, 48, 71, 105, 115, 159n42; Christian iconography in, 48–49; Visitor Center of, 71, 72, 115; Congressional Prayer Room, 83, 102, 165n55; "redcoat tour," 98–99, 105; Speaker's Lobby, 105; and War of 1812, 106, 166n1; James Madison's attendance of church services in, 153n13

U.S. Constitution: as founding document, 35; Christian heritage tour guides on Christianity in, 35, 153n17; as derived from biblical tradition, 39; Christian heritage authors on, 40. *See also* Constitutional Convention

U.S. Holocaust Memorial Museum, 127

U.S. Supreme Court: on abortion, 13; on school prayer, 13, 159n42, 161n13, 166n72; and erasing evidence of Christianity, 69; on same-sex marriage, 84–85, 88, 89, 161n19; Christian heritage tour guides on, 85, 93, 98, 165n53; on antisodomy laws, 86; on Affordable Care Act provisions, 87, 132; and white evangelical Christians' support for Donald Trump, 90; and Christian heritage tourists, 92–96, 98; Great Hall, 93–94; visitor center of, 95; South Wall Frieze, 96; Office of the Curator, 96, 98; East Pediment, 96, 132; East Wall Frieze, 98,

164–65n53; and tax-exempt status of segregated private religious schools, 161n13

University of Virginia, 62

Vermont, and recognition of same-sex civil unions, 86

victim role: and white evangelical Christians, 5, 6, 16, 19, 23, 25, 55, 67, 75, 76, 80–81, 87–90, 91, 92, 95, 127–28, 135, 137, 146; and demands for equal protection, 6; and Christian Right, 63, 67, 68; and Christian heritage tours, 80–81, 95; and Christian heritage tourists, 81, 82–83, 96, 104, 127; and Donald Trump, 91; and savior role, 127, 168n37; and outsider narrative, 137

Vietnam War, 13

Vietnam Nurses Memorial, 168n33

Vietnam Veterans Memorial, 19, 26, 121, 122, 168n33

Viguerie, Richard A., 65

WallBuilders, 41, 43, 92, 152n8, 154n36, 155n38, 162n30

war memorials, and Christian heritage tours, 5, 28, 108, 119–22, 124–25, 129

War of 1812, 106, 166n1

War on Christmas, 18, 103

Washington, D.C.: tourism industry of, 4; Christian heritage tourists sense of ownership of, 22; Christian iconography of, 22; monumental architecture of, 22; embodied experiences of, 22–23, 92–94; ambient Christian objects of, 23, 26, 29, 48, 55, 75, 81, 85, 100–101, 133, 136, 141, 142, 151n60, 151–52n61, 169n11; officially licensed tour guides, 69; Christian evidence erased from sites of, 69–72, 75, 96, 99–101, 159n40, 159n43, 160n44; swamp as metaphor for, 82–85, 161n6. *See also* Christian heritage tours

Washington, George: miraculous victory in French and Indian War, 16, 31, 119; Christian heritage tour guides on, 30–31; Christian faith of, 30–31, 33, 34, 61–62, 107, 152n5; as divinely chosen as president, 31; Farewell Address of, 31, 152n8; Thanksgiving Proclamation of, 31, 61–62, 113, 152n8; and slavery, 34, 153n16; writings as proof-text for Christian heritage story, 44; depictions of military victories, 48; letter of resignation from Continental Army, 107. *See also* Mount Vernon

Washington, Martha Custis, 34, 153n16

Washington Monument: observation deck of, 19–21; as sacred center of Christian heritage tours, 19–21, 53; views from Signers Island, 26, 28; and Christian faith of George Washington, 30; *Laus Deo* ("Praise Be to God") inscription, 30, 53–54, 55, 70, 71, 96, 132, 169n5; Christian inscriptions on interior of, 30, 70, 71, 152n6; aluminum pyramid at apex of, 53; construction of, 53, 157n1; and earthquake of 2011, 70

Washington National Cathedral: Darth Vader gargoyle of, 77; and Christian heritage tourists, 77, 79, 80, 102; celebration of same-sex marriage, 79; and earthquake of 2011, 79; interfaith services at, 79; and insider narrative, 80

Washington State: effort to replace state's statues in U.S. Capitol, 160n44

Webster, Daniel, 41

wedding vendors, 43

Weinman, Adolf A., 165n53

Weir, Robert W., 47

Weldon, Felix de, 168n32

Whitaker, Alexander, 47

white Americans: and Christian heritage tourists as white, 1, 9, 10; Chris-